Peter Gomez, Mark Lambertz
Leading by Weak Signals

De Gruyter Transformative Thinking and Practice of Leadership and Its Development

———

Edited by
Bernd Vogel

Volume 5

Peter Gomez, Mark Lambertz

Leading by Weak Signals

Using Small Data to Master Complexity

DE GRUYTER

ISBN 978-3-11-079698-8
e-ISBN (PDF) 978-3-11-079788-6
e-ISBN (EPUB) 978-3-11-079792-3
ISSN 2701-4002

Library of Congress Control Number: 2023910199

Bibliographic information published by the Deutsche Nationalbibliothek
The Deutsche Nationalbibliothek lists this publication in the Deutsche Nationalbibliografie;
detailed bibliographic data are available on the internet at http://dnb.dnb.de.

© 2023 Walter de Gruyter GmbH, Berlin/Boston
Cover image: Anna Bliokh/iStock/Getty Images Plus
Typesetting: Integra Software Services Pvt. Ltd.
Printing and binding: CPI books GmbH, Leck

www.degruyter.com

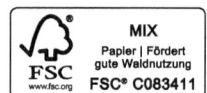

MIX
Papier | Fördert
gute Waldnutzung
FSC
www.fsc.org   FSC® C083411

Advance Praise for *Leading by Weak Signals*

"In today's VUCA world, transforming a company requires observation of 'weak signals' to uncover early signs of change or disruption. This insightful book provides readers with practical examples and tools to navigate complexity and stay ahead of the competition, as I have personally witnessed in my own company's journey."

– Torsten Leue, CEO of Talanx AG

"'Leading by weak signals' would be seen as 'the art of leading' if there were not a science behind it. Peter and Mark are excellent at making its principles and tricks useful for practitioners. In a world of increasing complexity, *Leading by Weak Signals* is not only part of every leader's toolkit, but also part of their survival kit."

– Dr. Martin Pfiffner, author of *The Neurology of Business*

https://doi.org/10.1515/9783110797886-202

To Jannik, Noel, Timon, Annica, and Elina
–Peter Gomez

To Carl
–Mark Lambertz

Foreword

"A key concern of leading by weak signals is to generate impact by intervening with minimal invasion . . ."
  – Peter Gomez and Mark Lambertz, *Leading by Weak Signals: Using Small Data to Master Complexity* (2023, p. 18).

I received an email one day . . .

. . . from Peter Gomez and Mark Lambertz, with a few breadcrumbs about the core idea for this book and I knew immediately, in the language of the book, that it was curious, felt a bit out of place, and yet was hugely noteworthy, so all in all, it was a weak signal to adhere to most definitely. Knowing Peter for quite some time, I was also aware that this work will be routed in deep and demanding thinking and at the same time matched by deep practice, otherwise why spend the time!

However, are you like me, inherently an intellectually lazy person or an early-stage learner in this area of leadership thinking practice? Then you might start reading and ponder on the following: This all looks a bit complicated! In that case, I give you one advice: Trust these two authors!

Leading by Weak Signals: Using Small Data to Master Complexity is rich and demanding. And it has to be that way, so we can start to catch up with businesses and our economic, ecological, and social spheres, that are in fact rich, demanding, dynamic and complex, instead of the illusion of leading easy, linear, and predictable organizational challenges.

As quoted above, this book is about the hard leadership task of minimal invasion, given that such an approach may be the only way that will actually work to co-create change. However, the learning and doing of minimal invasion is hard work. This book will enable you to become an expert.

This is a book that opens many doors to a seemingly different world . . .

. . . however, you realize very soon: This is our world of organizations, society, leading and influencing. This book helps to look at these areas differently. Once you start reading and working with it, your lens on the institutions you are involved with and your engagement in leading as an executive, manager or co-worker will change, first a little and then ever more.

Leading by Weak Signals equips you with both, a strong understanding of looking at organizations from a perspective of small data in dealing with complexity and a myriad tools, instruments, and frameworks which allow you to practically lead organizations as open or closed systems.

The eight steps for leading with small data offer a powerful, multi-layered, circular and recursive journey for managers and co-workers. Each of these steps open nu-

https://doi.org/10.1515/9783110797886-204

merous anchors to think *and* practice differently, and in doing so, enables the reader to engage more successfully with their organizations, teams or communities.

In line with the principle of "The Purpose of a System Is What It Does", this book will be a strong element of the doing and co-creation of purpose of this book series. It therefore continuously assists the process of reproducing the identity of this book series: to ultimately impact the readers' networks and organizations and to create positive change in key areas of society.

Rephrasing a quote by one of Peter and Mark's favorite authors, Stafford Beer (1972, 69) – "Instead of trying to organize [an author group] in full detail, you organize [them] only somewhat; you then ride on the dynamics of the [author] system in the direction you [hope for]" – I could not have hoped for more. Peter and Mark, a huge thank you for trusting us with your ideas and practices. A privilege to have your work in this book series.

Bernd Vogel
Henley-on-Thames, UK
July 2023

Contents

Prologue

"The world is full of obvious things which nobody by any chance ever observes."
Sherlock Holmes (Conan Doyle 2019, 34)

In 2008, Philip Morris, one of the world's leading tobacco companies, started their research in tobacco heating systems, replacing cigarettes with smoke-free products. Although the new technology would not reduce addiction to nicotine, it promised to eliminate the majority of diseases caused by burning tobacco. In 2016 Philip Morris announced its new purpose to end cigarette sales within 10 to 15 years in many countries. Since then, the company has fully aligned its employees with this purpose and shifted its organizational focus and resources to smoke-free alternatives. What has caused such an unprecedented disruption of a commercially successful company with a global workforce of 70,000? Was it pressure from civil society, prohibitions from regulatory authorities, declining sales due to increased competition or directives from a new CEO? Was Philip Morris forced to change by strong impact from the outside world, or were they lead by "weak signals" originating from reflections about the future of their ecosystem? We will never know, as Philip Morris' beliefs and decision-making processes are not accessible to the outside world due to the autopoietic nature of the company – a concept to be discussed later the book. Nevertheless, the direction and the speed of the change process leads to the conclusion that weak signals have certainly played a decisive role.

What are the characteristics of **"weak signals"** in a leadership context? The term was first introduced in the context of strategic management by Igor Ansoff (1975), but the underlying concept barely received the attention it deserved in the scientific community and in managerial practice. Therefore, in view of the lack of a generally accepted definition and body of knowledge, it proves to be appropriate to start the investigation by conveying concrete examples from Philip Morris. At the turn of the century, the company environment (its "ecosystem") started to change fundamentally, and still existing trends were dramatically reinforced. Philip Morris had to shift its modus operandi from running the business to changing the business, provoked by

- a degenerating image of smoking in society
- smoking bans in hotels, sport arenas, and public transportation
- an increasing speed of legislation on smoking
- rising health consciousness of the population
- a growing aversion towards Philip Morris as large and harmful company
- a progressively poor image of Philip Morris as employer
- new technologies for inhaling purposes
- new marketing approaches ("Apple stores")
- new opportunities for diversification

https://doi.org/10.1515/9783110797886-206

At the time, the emergence of these developments and their sequence of entry was not immediately apparent. The first indications of change – or "weak signals" – were small, subtle shifts in areas such as Philip Morris' hiring process, which suggested a decline in its reputation as an employer, as well as changes in the focus of scientific research towards new inhalation technologies, and new marketing approaches aimed at replacing traditional advertising methods. In order to become a pioneer in the tobacco industry, Philip Morris needed to interpret the underlying patterns behind these changes early on. Despite the uncertainties, the company had to develop new strategies based on "small data" as there was no time to wait for more evidence.

At Philip Morris, just as in most other companies, a primary task of executives is to detect fundamental change at an early stage and to cope with it proactively. In times of complexity and uncertainty, three basic concepts could lead the way to meet the challenge: Serendipity, Big Data and Weak Signals. **Serendipity** is the art of gaining crucial insights by chance while searching for other topics. Even though significant discoveries are often made this way, leadership cannot rely on this approach, as it is too arbitrary to initiate proactive moves. **Big Data** on the other hand is emerging as a prominent managerial concept. Executives have always trusted in numbers and data: the more comprehensive and accurate they are, the better. It is therefore not surprising that Big Data is highly welcome as a promising way to cope with the complexity of managerial practice. By sophisticated computation of enormous data sets, Big Data claims to identify patterns of human behavior that have a major influence on the corporate growth path. This pledge opens completely new horizons, but caution is still advised when applying the "magic of advanced statistics." Big Data provides excellent results when exploiting business processes or improving their efficiency – it is perfectly suited for "running the business." The current state of technological progress in the operational domain is astonishing, there is no doubt that new algorithms will become more sophisticated to enhance these processes.

In the realm of strategic management and innovation operations, a greater focus on Small Data – or more accurately, Weak Signals – is becoming increasingly necessary. When organizations dismiss such data as "not big enough," they risk missing out on potential business opportunities or innovative ideas, as well as overlooking potential dangers. While Deep Learning Networks and Large Language Models are making significant progress, the concept of Leading by Weak Signals remains important. Identifying weak signals and their underlying patterns is not solely dependent on human ingenuity or machine intelligence, but on the ability to distinguish them from noise and take proactive measures to stay ahead of the competition.

The purpose of this book is to provide leaders with a framework to master the emerging shift to small data. Based on a novel understanding of corporate intelligence, Leading by Weak Signals strives for a holistic interpretation of **"what is going on here"** – the only meaningful question in the face of radical uncertainty (Kay and King 2020). As shown in Figure P..1, it amplifies weak signals to become strong insights which lead the way to proactive measures. The resulting intervention aims at maximum impact with minimal invasion, and it develops solutions to tackle future surprises proactively.

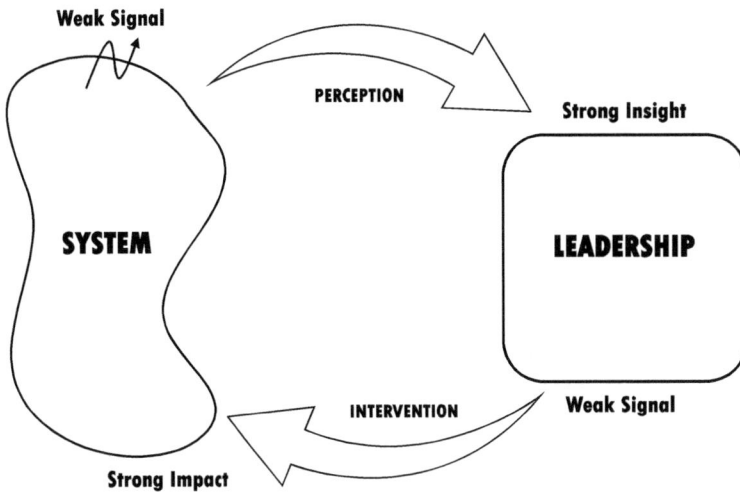

Figure 1: Leading by Weak Signals – a closed loop.

This book presents a framework and a step-by-step methodology to unleash the power of weak signals for leadership in times of complexity and uncertainty:

- In the perception phase, **weak signals** are the tiniest and earliest indications of change, when there is no evidence yet about its origin and its background pattern. They can be data or stories that are just surprising or inconsistent with the present state of knowledge, whereas after the fact the context often seems obvious (Smith 2020, 71) During the intervention phase, leadership activities should be guided by the principle of weak signals, focusing on exploiting the self-organizational forces of the system rather than direct intervention.
- **Leadership** has many connotations, in academic circles as well as in managerial practice. For the authors, the purpose of leadership is to ensure the viability of enterprises, by co-evolving sustainably with the demands of their stakeholders and ecosystems. Leadership is interpreted in an inclusive way, as a dynamic constellation between people, but it can also be attributed to individual executives.
- *Leading by Weak Signals* aims to discover and interpret change at the earliest stage, proactively and inclusively managing its complexity with the goal of ensuring and evolving an enterprise's viability.

The methodology of *Leading by Weak Signals* comprises eight steps, each characterized by a keyword and dedicated to answering a question of fundamental importance for managerial practice:

1. **"System"** How to identify an enterprise in its overarching ecosystem?

2.	**"Edges"**	How to look for weak signals at the system's periphery?
3.	**"Patterns"**	How to detect regularities and their generating forces ("power laws") behind the weak signals?
4.	**"Evolution"**	How to develop scenarios of pattern dynamics to explore potential paths into the future?
5.	**"Indicators"**	How to develop performance measures and supporting narratives to enhance and monitor the evolutionary path?
6.	**"Framing"**	How to create self-organizing viable systems to support proactive intervention?
7.	**"Tipping points"**	How to intervene with minimal invasion?
8.	**"Alertness"**	How to organize for future surprise?

The methodology is composed of three main components. First, the theoretical background is presented to establish a well-structured design process. Next, methodological procedures and tools are introduced and illustrated through practical use. Finally, two integrated case studies document the application of the methodology in managerial practice. The two cases, one in the strategic and one in the operational domain, run in parallel to emphasize the importance of understanding the operational "engine room" for successful strategizing. Additionally, infoboxes provide supplementary information that is not directly related to the procedural logic. This coherent structure enables a comprehensive understanding of Leading by Weak Signals, while allowing for the flexibility to focus on specific issues or immediately apply practical insights.

In the process of developing this framework, many friends and colleagues from the research community and from managerial practice provided invaluable insight, advice, and support – we owe them our sincere thanks. For Peter Gomez, the University of St. Gallen in Switzerland was a lifelong breeding ground for developing new insights and innovative frameworks in the spirit of viable organizations. To test their impact in managerial practice, SIX Swiss Exchange served as an ideal platform for learning about change. Philip Mosimann provided invaluable support in the development of the Bucher Industries case, Markus Schwaninger was the loyal guardian of the cybernetic knowledge base, and Dominique Fässler illustrated the concept of weak signals in communication technology. Mark Lambertz is indebted to his former colleagues at anyMOTION; together they gained practical experience about starting and developing a business. Special thanks are due to all clients which shared learnings about digitalization, agile practices, and dealing with complexity; elsewhere, thanks go to the corporate peers who enabled the integration of the concept into a worldwide organization.

Finally, both our heartfelt thanks belong to our families for continuously supporting our journey of discovery leading to his book. We dedicate it to Peter's grandchildren Jannik, Noel, Timon, Annica, and Elina and to Mark's son Carl.

1 Mastering complexity: The emerging shift to Small Data

In times of complexity and radical uncertainty, with its permanently changing contexts and structures, it is impossible to predict the future based on past and present data. The algorithms of Big Data and the computing power of "the cloud" are well suited to handle constellations which remain structurally invariant most of the time; with enough data and processing time they find a proper solution or detect relevant patterns. But decision-makers are increasingly challenged by situations which dynamically change over time and therefore remain inaccessible to a complete understanding:

> Complex problems cannot be solved,
> radical uncertainty cannot be resolved.

Still, there are ways to gain valuable insight into this complexity and to influence its dynamics by proactive moves. This is achieved by focusing on weak signals, a special kind of Small Data, and by initiating a leadership approach that ensures viability.

First, basic distinctions must be drawn for a thorough understanding of Leading by Weak Signals. Famous quotes, some based on insights gained decades ago, shall prepare the path to this endeavor.

1.1 Basic distinctions

Complicated and complex

> Turbulence, by definition, is irregular, non-linear, erratic. But its underlying causes can be analyzed, predicted, managed. Peter Drucker (1980, 2)

The Netflix movie *Don't Look Up* gained widespread attention at the end of 2021. It tells the story of the discovery of a meteorite that would destroy the earth within six months, yet nobody cares as their daily routines take priority. While the story may be compelling, it reveals a fundamental misunderstanding of the laws of nature. The impact of a meteorite on earth can be predicted in detail and is therefore a complicated problem that humankind can attempt to deal with in a timely manner, such as by deflecting the meteorite's orbit. However, Covid-19 and climate change are complex problems with evolving structures and behaviors that cannot be predicted in their entirety. This complexity can be overwhelming, leading people to retreat to their daily routines and exhibit a phenomenon of not caring.

Complicated systems are characterized by a multitude of parts and relations whose structural coupling remains relatively invariant over time. It takes time to understand such a system (a perpetual calendar watch or a logistical infrastructure), but

https://doi.org/10.1515/9783110797886-001

once known, it is forever. **Complex systems** also consist of a high number of parts and linkages, but their composition changes over time, as do their structural couplings. Societal shifts due to a pandemic are an actual example. Complex systems escape complete human analysis and understanding. It becomes even more confusing as the ideas of complexity and complicatedness are never disjunct. They are often intertwined, so parts of a system might be highly complex, while others are "just" complicated. This means that we can understand parts of the system, but never the complete system as such in every detail. Accepting that complexity exists is most challenging. One can sometimes work with it – but never against it. And complaining about complexity is as useless as if one would rally against gravity.

Sharon Varney summarizes the challenges of complexity for leadership:

- Entanglement: We can never be fully in control
- Uncertainty: We can never know how actions will play out
- Patterning: We are easily lulled into a false sense of familiarity by pretending that the world is more stable than it is
- Emergence: Surprises are common

Varney (2021, 27)

In *Simply Complexity*, Neil Johnson explains the reasons why this is the case:

- The system contains a collection of many interacting objects or "agents"
- These objects' behavior is affected by memory or "feedback"
- The objects can adapt their strategies according to their history
- The system is typically "open"
- The system appears to be "alive"
- The system exhibits emergent phenomena which are generally surprising and may be extreme
- The emergent phenomena typically arise in the absence of any sort of "invisible hand" or central controller
- The system shows a complicated mix of ordered and disordered behavior

(Johnson 2011, Chapter 1, 1.4)

How can complex systems be accessed? As they can move freely between disorder and order, **pockets of order** will arise which can be used to predict and influence the system. Furthermore, emergent phenomena have some universal properties, called **"power laws,"** which will be discussed extensively later. And if small complex systems cannot be accessed, their behavior might be better understood by adding new members and feedbacks. These aspects will be explained and illustrated in the following chapters.

Risk and uncertainty

> To identify a probability of inventing the wheel is to invent the wheel. To ask, either before or after the event, 'What was the probability of such an event?' is not an intelligible question. John Kay/Mervyn King (2020, Chapter 3, paragraph 3)

In **situations involving risk**, probabilities can be assigned to upcoming events, such as in a game of roulette where the possible outcomes and their frequencies are known. However, in **situations of uncertainty**, the future is not known, as structural couplings change dynamically over time – it becomes a complex system. Kay and King (2020, chapter 2) use the terms "puzzle" for risk and "mystery" for uncertainty: Puzzles have well-defined rules and a single solution, while mysteries offer no clear definition and have no "correct" answer. Instead, mysteries require an approach that involves asking "What is going on here?" to unravel their complexity.

Dealing with complexity and uncertainty requires a different approach from dealing with complicated problems and risks. It is not enough to apply traditional analytical methods or assign probabilities, as these do not adequately capture the dynamic interactions and emergent phenomena of complex systems. Instead, it is necessary to comply with the **"law of requisite variety,"** which means that to deal with complexity and uncertainty, one must have a variety of responses that match the variety of situations that can arise. In other words, one must have a diverse set of tools, strategies, and perspectives to address complex and uncertain situations. Additionally, it is important to adopt a mindset of continuous learning and adaptation, as complex systems are constantly evolving and changing.

In *Radical Uncertainty*, John Kay and Mervyn King identify the following characteristics:
- Dealing with "mysteries" means changing the focus: "What is going on here?"
- Vagueness cannot be reduced or eliminated by exact definition because such definition is itself arbitrary
- Probabilities cannot meaningfully be attached to alternative futures
- "Black swans" are examples of, but not identical with, radical uncertainty
- "Big data" is about correlation, not causation
- "Nudging" is an unjustified claim to know an uncertain world

(Kay and King 2020, chapter 1, pg. 6)

How can **radical uncertainty** be accessed? The focus lies on narratives and incremental decision-making, by assessing situations as familiar and not by comparing options. This approach could be characterized as evolutionary or ecological rationality.

"The effective use of narrative is in sharp contrast to the idea that narratives are a recourse of ill-informed and "biased" agents who prefer storytelling to computation . . . The mark of the first-rate decision-maker confronted with radical uncertainty is to organize action around a reference narrative while still being open to the possibility that his narrative is false and that alternative narratives might be relevant" (Kay and King 2020, chapter 12, paragraph 1, and chapter 16, paragraph 2). The difference between storytelling and narratives cannot be overemphasized. Whereas both are built upon plausibility and therefore can be a door-opener, a storyteller will not care if the story fits to the given circumstances and often just wants to pursue her or his personal goal (e.g., convince a crowd). The developer of a narrative wants to deal with uncertainty and is open to new narratives because relevance is the gradient to determine if the narrative is appropriate – or not.

The accessibility of complexity and radical uncertainty requires a specialized approach and corresponding tools, which will be developed in the following discussion. To lay the necessary scientific foundations, we will begin by using a cube to illustrate the fundamental concepts behind the application of Ashby's law in complex and uncertain problem situations.

Exploration and exploitation

> Instead of trying to organize a system in full detail, you organize it only somewhat; you then ride on the dynamics of the system in the direction you want to go. Stafford Beer (1972, 69)

Any enterprise needs to balance two basic operational modes, the **exploration** of new customer needs and business opportunities driven by technological progress or new insights (weak signals!), and the **exploitation** of the current business focused on improving process efficiency to generate value for customers. The exploitation usually finances exploration activities, which often causes friction in an organization. While "some" are busy keeping the production alive, "others" are allowed to think about the future course. However, if well balanced, it allows leadership to differentiate between **running the business** (exploitation) and **changing the business** (exploration). This is closely related to the pairings of complicate and complex as well as of risk and uncertainty, as it allows a better understanding of the concept of "value in use" (Vargo and Lusch 2014, 23).

At the beginning of the discovery phase for a new feature, one does not know much about the optimal configuration of a product. Over time, more insights are generated to streamline the production process, as illustrated (in line with the above quote) in Figure 1.1.

The focus shifts from an initial understanding of the "real" problem of a customer toward the optimization of the value-generating chain or network. This pair is also present in the language of the "Agile world," where it is known as the complementary couple of "**Product Discovery**" and "**Product Delivery**."

Variety reduction and variety generation

> A wealth of information creates poverty of attention. Herbert A. Simon (1971, 40)

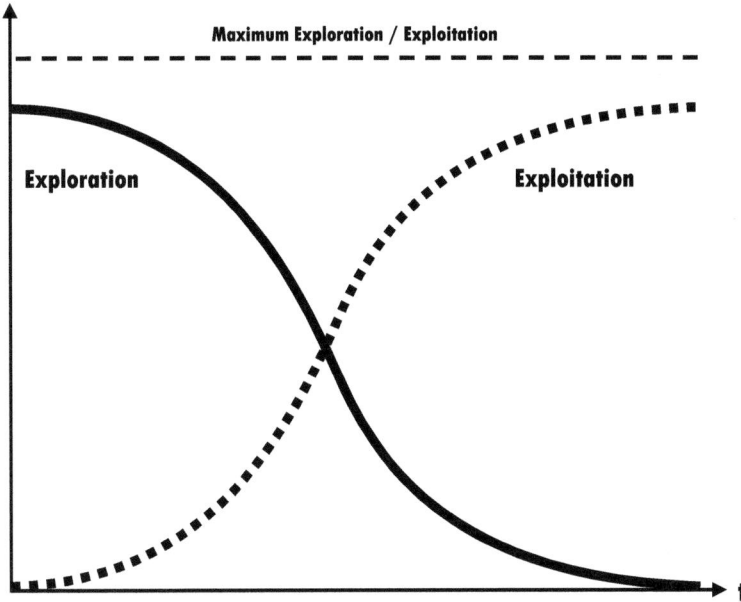

Figure 1.1: Exploitation and exploration as S-shaped functions over time.

"Only variety can destroy variety" – Ashby's law was introduced above as prerequisite to deal with complexity and uncertainty. The following drawing by Stafford Beer in Figure 1.2 makes this law easily accessible:

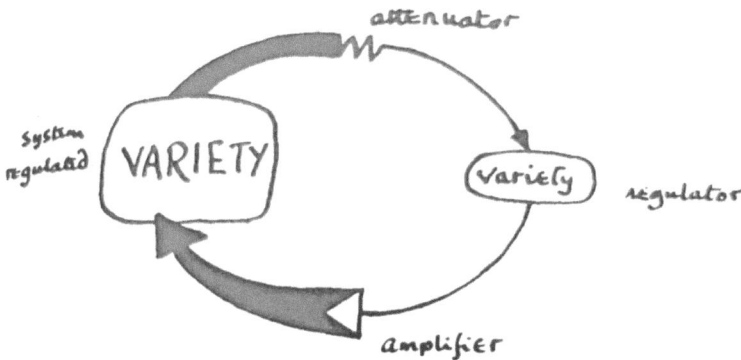

Figure 1.2: Ashby's Law in circular perspective (Beer 1974, 30).

On the left, the variety of a problem situation (the "system regulated") is shown in proportion to the variety of the "regulator" on the righthand side. To balance the equation, the variety of the problem situation has to be attenuated and the variety of the regulator to be amplified.

Stafford Beer (1974, 30) states that "examination of institutional systems often reveals that the attenuators and the amplifiers have been installed in the wrong loops – on the wrong side of the equation." Or to paraphrase Herbert Simon's quote, the wealth of information provided by Big Data often leads to a lack of attention for the development of promising options to intervene in the system.

A closer look at the arrows leads to four steps to achieve this balance which provide the essential structure of the proposed framework of this book:

Variety reduction:
    1. Variety attenuation
    2. Variety consolidation

Variety generation:
    3. Variety proliferation
    4. Variety amplification

In a first step, an **attenuation** of the meandering variety is achieved by detecting patterns and regularities in the flow of seemingly unordered events and processes. Redefining the regulated systems' boundaries will bring first results, which are reinforced by identifying basic causal (feedback) loops and emergent phenomena of self-organization. In a second step, the results of this inquiry are **consolidated** in the form of "leading indicators" which are further refined as objectives and performance measures for managerial variety engineering.

To generate requisite variety on the regulator side, a process of **proliferation** of variety will be initiated in the third step. The focus will not be on singular interventions, but on the options to influence the balance of the system's cohesion and the autonomy of its parts. The concept of loose coupling will provide deep insights. In a fourth and final step, the **amplification** of planned interventions should be based on identifying "tipping points" and by making use of the "entropic drift" of the system. This stepwise procedure will be illustrated and documented in detail in the context of introducing the concept of "weak signals."

Detecting regularities and patterns in the flow of events in a complex and uncertain environment provides management with the necessary **insight** to think about their options. But only translating this knowledge into **"leading indicators"** in form of objectives and performance metrics will enable proactive behavior. To achieve the desired **impact**, managerial activities must be designed based on minimal invasive intervention, but with the goal of maximum **empowerment**.

Autopoietic systems and input-output systems

> When I kick a stone, I give energy to the stone, and it moves with that energy; when I kick a dog,
> . . . it responds with energy got from metabolism. Gregory Bateson (1979, 101)

The distinction between autopoietic and input-output systems is fundamental for understanding and aligning leadership activities in complex and uncertain environments. **Autopoietic systems** are the predominant form of natural life to ensure organismic viability. They are also characteristic for various socio-economical institutions like political parties, family-owned businesses, or associations of conspiracy theorists (Gomez and Probst 1989). "Autopoiesis" denotes the modus vivendi of organizationally closed viable systems: they produce their own boundaries and autonomously reproduce their own organization (Maturana and Varela 1972). They are "closed" with respect to their beliefs, decisions, knowledge, and communication. There is no direct access from the outside, be they stakeholders, consultants, or other interest groups. But they are "open" to people, energy, material, and information, which means that there are ways to influence such systems through "structural coupling," a concept that will be illustrated later.

Input-output systems on the other hand can deliberately be designed and organized from the outside. They are part of an overarching ecosystem, and leadership from the outside can guide the system in its process of adaptation to a changing environment. In this context, leadership means setting and changing system boundaries, specifying the purpose, and designing structures and processes. Input-output systems are common in the business areas of production, logistics, finance, and informatics. They are designed for optimal functioning, but in an increasingly interconnected world, this gets ever more demanding, as unexpected breakdowns require complicated bridging solutions.

Autopoietic systems dominate in the context of enhancing the viability of the enterprise when normative and strategic aspects are in the focus of decision-making. Here the design process comes to its limits; a self-referential evolution from within takes its place (von Krogh and Roos 1995). This leads to **a new understanding of leadership**: "The idea of a firm as goal-setting system based on normative models should be abandoned. We should work with empirical descriptions of how firms operate their production and reproduction" (Koskinen, 2013, 146). It also gives a new meaning to the concept of "purpose": "**POSIWID**: The purpose of a system is what is does!" (Beer 1985, 99). According to one of the "fathers" of the autopoiesis concept (Varela 1984, 26), a central prerequisite of good leadership is the "clean epistemological accounting" between autopoietic and input-output systems.

The terms "autopoietic" and "input-output" might sound strange for management; "closed" and "open" are more accessible. But a precise understanding of their meaning is essential for good leadership. **"Closed"** means that beliefs, decisions, knowledge, and communication are only accessible to insiders, they cannot be directly managed from outside. But these systems are open to people, energy, material, and information, and in this respect not isolated from their environment. **"Open"** systems can be designed and managed from outside. There are powerful concepts and instruments available to meet this challenge, especially the Viable System Model (Beer 1972).

Participant role and observer role

> We are standing on a 'burning platform', and we must decide how we are going to change our behaviour. Stephen Elop, Former Nokia CEO (2011)

The distinction between observer and participant is crucial, especially for autopoietic systems. Acting as a **participant** means having direct access to beliefs, decisions, knowledge, and communication. Outside **observers** can access the system only indirectly by "structural coupling," as shown above. In 2007, Nokia had 50% of global market share for smartphones, and they were admired as a worldwide leading company. But they became complacent and didn't react to Apple's iPhone – pathological autopoiesis was setting in. In 2010, this became clear even to outside analysts, before Stephen Elop finally gave insight into the interna of Nokia.

Input-output systems are not prone to this kind of limitation, they can be designed from the inside and the outside. Especially in management consulting, this distinction is often overlooked. Proposals for purpose-driven leadership or cultural change fall short of recognizing that beliefs are autonomously reproduced in autopoietic systems – a process which they have no access to, even with intensive interviews and conversations.

Integrating these basic, science-driven concepts in form of a cube, and reinterpreting them for managerial practice in Figure 1.3, provides the framework for our upcoming discussions.

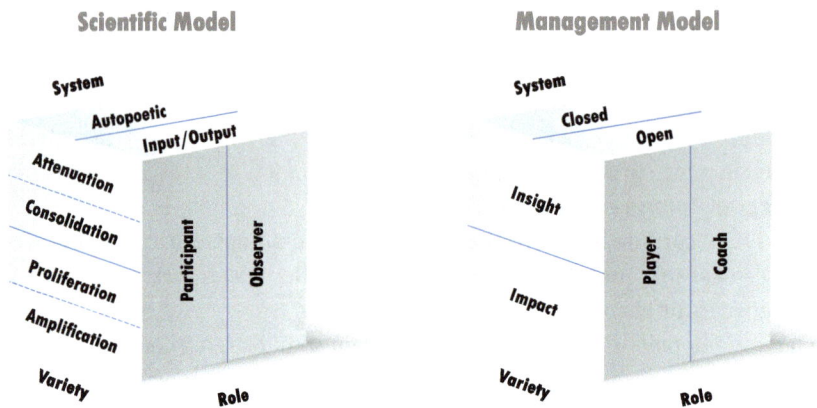

Figure 1.3: Scientific and managerial framework of Leadership by Weak Signals.

In the management model, the parts of the scientific model are relabeled to provide a better access to managerial practice: the course of closed systems can only be influenced by **participating leaders**, whereas **coaches** can deliberately design and manage open systems. It is therefore essential to first identify the degrees of freedom of management and coaching before in-depth analysis starts.

The two cubes provide a **reference frame** to explore and cope with complexity and radical uncertainty in compliance with the law of requisite variety. To start such a process and to gain first insights, regularities and patterns of a problem situation must be identified and interpreted. Here the weak signals come into play.

1.2 Weak signals – Initiating the process to cope with complexity and uncertainty

"Complex problems cannot be solved, and radical uncertainty cannot be resolved" – this insight has shaped our discussion of Ashby's law of requisite variety so far. The concept of "Big Data" claims to offer a way out of this dilemma – but as argued above, the computation of huge past and present data sets will not serve the purpose to predict a complex and uncertain future. "Big Data" is well suited for complicated problems, and the resulting correlations provide valuable insights. But understanding complexity is all about detecting multiple causal loops of dynamically evolving systems, and here the classic statistical modelling comes to its limits (even though Deep Learning techniques like "Unsupervised Learning" look very promising).

The concept of weak signals

To overcome this challenging situation, the attention is directed to the other end of the spectrum by focusing on "weak signals." The concept of weak signals is intuitively appealing, but not easily definable. Scott Smith suggests the following:

> Weak signals are generally described as the earliest, smallest signals of change, particularly where the overall pattern they point to isn't readily evident. Weak signals are the items, data, or stories that catch your eyes as curious, out of place, and potentially noteworthy, based on your experience and knowledge. The idea of a weak signal is that it feels as if it points to a meaningful change in direction, a forking of possible developments or a significant evolution of a pattern already observed. They're often easy to rationalize or define retrospectively because the examples seem obvious after the fact. (Smith 2020, 71)

Figure 1.4 illustrates how weak signals are hidden in the omnipresent, data-induced noise of complex environments. To trigger timely and proactive measures, they must be discovered way ahead of turning into strong signals.

Figure 1.4 is an ideal visualization for quantitative contexts – it is an input-output-driven type of explanation. One could even object that it is a mechanistic "down-grading" of the context. Because next to quantitative phenomena, there are areas with qualitative properties, mainly in the environment of autopoietic systems. Here, weak signals appear in the form of the rarities and anecdotes. Quantitative data, often represented as timeseries, are associated with input-output-systems, but it is not as simple as it sounds. As will be shown later, it is important to be able to work with quantitative

Signal Strength

Time to react

**Strong
Signal**

Level of Noise

**Weak
Signal**

t

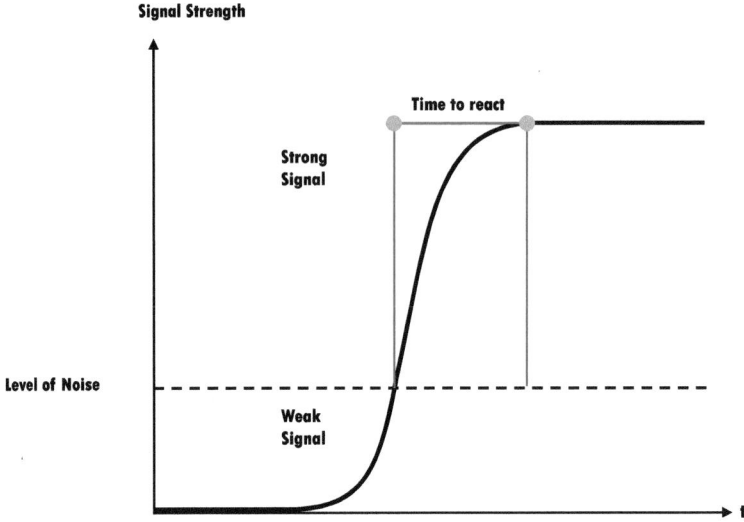

Figure 1.4: Weak signals, hidden in the noise (Coffmann, 1997).

and qualitative data to extract weak signals. It is the combination of both types shown in Figure 1.5 which allows the user of this framework to get the best of both worlds.

Data point type	Examples	System type
Quantitative	Outliers in datasets, surprising peaks, unusual seasonality, strange patterns	Input-Output
Qualitative	Anecdotes, rumors, weird stories, crazy ideas, spontaneous insights	Autopoietic

Figure 1.5: Weak Signals derived from quantitative and qualitative data points.

The examples in Figure 1.5 do not automatically imply the existence of a "real" weak signal with a power law acting in the background. It is always possible to over-interpret data points and to underestimate the fact that human being's sensors are simply too sensitive. Therefore, leading with weak signals means continuously going through a loop of "inspect and adapt" – it is inevitable to review weak signals and evaluate their epistemological value. Bluntly asked: are we now smarter and able to anticipate the future, or have we created cognitive waste that increased the confusion in the organization?

To illustrate the nature of **quantitative weak signals**, we are moving back in time to the beginning of the COVID-19 pandemic. Researchers in Europe were studying fecal wastewater in major cities for pathogenic agents. They found indications of a new type of virus which was spreading slowly, but at an exponential rate. They treated their discovery according to the scientific principle of "what if" and tested several laws of contagion as to the virus's origin. They were among the first to find a weak signal of the pandemic rising, but they didn't have the means to communicate these findings to a broader public, not least because of the simultaneously emerging proliferation of false information. In our days, their approach has become the standard procedure for detecting mutations of the virus in advance. It is no longer a weak signal, but an early warning signal initiating proactive action in the context of a well-understood pandemic.

Weak Signals in communication technology

Weak signals are measured in relation to ambient noise whose origin is random or man-made. Whatever the sources of noise might be, it delimits information readability when the signal-to-noise ratio *SNR* is marginal. Very small signals might be registered but not read due to poor *SNR*. **Filtering** incoming signals can increase readability; it reduces the resolution bandwidth of the receiver or, in over-the-air systems, sharpens the **directivity** of the antenna. Smaller bandwidth is reducing the quantity of successfully processed information. A typical example of reduced bandwidth is the audio resolution of the telephone. As a HIFI enthusiast you expect your music system to allow audio signals up to 44,000 Hz, which means that you cannot listen your favorite symphony via telephone. The limited bandwidth of the telephone cuts out audio frequencies below 200 Hz and above 2 KHz. Very small signals from satellites far out in space require all of the above, especially big parabolic antennas with signal directivity of e.g., 0.0001 degree and a resolution bandwidth of just several Hz. The amount of information exchanged is drastically reduced to maybe several bites/hour. The SNR is at an extremely low level. In order to still exchange the ultimately required information continuously repeating the very small amount of information and modeling the sum of received fragments of data allows to read the content. This is called **averaging** or **compounding**. With these highly technical measures smallest signals even below the noise-floor can be leveraged. Obviously analog times are over. They have been substituted in these fields by the computer. Our ears and brain cannot compete in such a mathematical challenge.

A **qualitative weak signal** initiated a strategy process at the University of St. Gallen (HSG), one of Europe's leading business schools. By proactively initiating a process of reorganization of its teaching system, it became one of the first universities to implement the so-called Bologna Reform. In 1998, Education Ministers signed the Sorbonne-declaration to establish a common higher education area in Europe. This memorandum of understanding was an expression of political intent, but it was neither coordinated with nor communicated to the universities. But a handful of them interpreted it as a weak signal of emerging change. HSG immediately established an interdisciplinary group to develop a new framework for all teaching activities, in anticipation of the forthcoming Bachelor/Master System which then was unfamiliar to most universities in Central Europe. When in 1999 the Bologna Reform was officially launched by political instances, HSG was already way ahead with its planning activities. In autumn 2001, the Bachelor program started, and the first students got their degree in autumn 2004, followed by the first Master graduates in 2006. Only then, most other universities in Europe started the change process – after debating at length the benefits and the threats of this new framework. In the meantime, HSG strengthened its edge as an leading institution in research and teaching.

Another example of a qualitative weak signal in the corporate context deals with changing expectations of Generation Z regarding jobs offerings. Typically, Human Resources were focused on promoting the secure environment of a multinational enterprise, such as possibilities to grow on a personal and professional level. But this was no longer enough to attract the best talents. By sharing anecdotes from different job interviews, the department learned that many applicants were asking about the corporate purpose and the contribution to public value. This was discovered during a coffee break when two colleagues were chatting about the issues. Instinctively, they realized the potential to change their argumentation. By developing a credible storyline, the talent scouts were able to proactively promote the societal contributions of the company, to get better applications and have better conversations with the candidates.

Weak signals in managerial practice

Simon Wardley provides a hands-on set of practical examples of how weak signals can be discovered and interpretated – and where and how to anticipate the future:

– Tracking tail numbers of private jets registered to relevant companies to see when executives are meeting prior to an important deal.
– Watching job listings to see what type of key employees are being hired, or which departments seem to be rapidly growing.
– Watching for significant commitments or investments in a supply chain. E.g., Apple making investments in flash memory; manufacturers signaled that they expected to consume large quantities of this component. An analyst could look at Apple's current or likely business to see which areas were likely to need this component and were therefore probably growing.
– AWS (Amazon Web Serves) can withhold information about their costs, but since they may lease space in buildings, you may be able to find out about the power budget in that building and estimate the number of servers that can provide support. From that, you may be able to estimate AWS' actual physical capacity and thus part of their costs.

(wardleypedia.org, accessed June 30, 22)

Leading by weak signals – from insight to impact

Weak signals will lead the way in the process of developing our methodology to cope with complexity and radical uncertainty, in the process of gaining **insight** as well as with the aim to achieve **impact,** as the extended form of Ashby's law in Figure 1.6 illustrates:

Weak signals appear at the boundaries of the system in focus. In the **perception** phase, they are converted into "leading indicators" for managerial decision-making, based on strong insights about power laws governing the dynamics of the system. In the **intervention** phase, the process starts again with weak signals in the form of minimally invasive measures to enhance self-organization in the system. Contrary to traditional concepts of planning and controlling, leading by weak signals gives priority to discovery and empowerment, rather than to analysis and prescription; it acts according to the **jiu-jitsu principle**.

To provide a first intuitive grasp, the eight steps of our methodology will now be introduced and illustrated in annotative form.

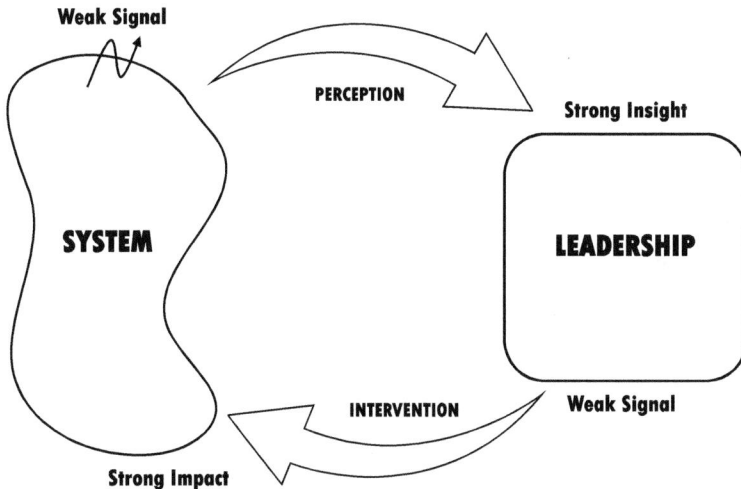

Figure 1.6: Leading by Weak Signals – from insight to impact.

1.3 Leading by weak signals – The methodology in a nutshell

Step 1: "System": Setting the stage and identifying its boundaries

Systems are not given "objects"; they must be identified by drawing a distinction – a boundary – with respect to their environment. Hereby, autopoietic ("closed") systems and input-output ("open") systems must be approached differently. **Autopoietic systems** reproduce their boundaries autonomously, so they can only be understood from within. Participative leadership is the prerequisite to identify the "arena," and it can be achieved by adding outside members to their internal management team. Family businesses could serve as examples or political parties – they are mainly "closed" to external influence.

When dealing with **input-output systems**, another approach applies: "A system is a way of looking at the world" (Weinberg 1975, 51). A product is a different system when taking the view of marketing success, of benefits to the customer, or of potential environmental hazards. This leaves the observer with many options to define the arena to detect weak signals. Drawing boundaries of input-output systems by identifying their role in an ecosystem is very demanding, whereas bringing new team members into autopoietic systems requires a delicate touch. But both decide on the success of the following methodological steps.

Step 2: "Edges": Searching the periphery for weak signals

"The balance point – 'edge of chaos' – is where the components never entirely lock into place, and never quite dissolve into turbulence either . . . ." Cleveland et al. (2020, 17) illustrate their definition of "edges" by pointing to vibrant democracies, healthy markets, or flexible networks. In their terms, **autopoietic systems** get access to the environment by "sensors" at their periphery. They consist of a swarm of autonomous agents, operating by simple rules and in loosely coupled networks. These agents experiment in short cycles and produce tiny shifts – which might influence the internal sense-making process. The Disney Company installed experimental teams at the leading Swiss Technical University ETH to enter promising new fields; the pharmaceutical giant Roche acquired Genentech for specific research projects. In the long term, those ventures influence their companies' cultures – and they are a rich source of weak signals.

The edges of **input-output systems** are more easily identified by applying the concepts of "High Reliability Organizations" (Weick and Sutcliffe 2015) and "Early-Warning Systems," as illustrated in "Predictable Surprises" (Bazerman and Watkins, 2004) and in "Normal Accidents" (Perrow 1985). They share a common focus on highly complicated systems like atomic power plants, aircraft carriers, or intensive care units, which are rather stable over time although extremely difficult to understand in all their details. But for their early-warning signals they can rely on given standards of security, and for any deviation there exist clear options for problem-solving.

In managerial practice, most of the time there is no either-or, but a combination of aspects of closed and open systems. This means that procedures for both cases must be deployed to establish a rich source for weak signals.

Finally, what do we mean by **"weak signals"** at the edges? To search for a definition would prove to be futile. It would be as meaningless as if trying to explain in detail how to ride a bike. It is inevitable that this way of "looking at the world" needs to be practiced. Therefore, the first paraphrase given above serves well as a first intuitive idea of the concept. We deliberately do not want to dive any further here. By developing a framework to embed "weak signals" its meaning will become clear step by step in the sense that when you see weak signals, you know them.

Step 3: "Patterns": Detecting regularities and power laws

Patterns are regularities in a flow of events which enable insights into the driving forces of a systemic context. These patterns are the result of universal forces (in the following referred to as **"power laws"**), and they trigger activities which finally find their expression in weak signals. These patterns provide indications about possible future developments by unleashing their evolutionary path.

The search for regularities or patterns behind weak signals is quite demanding. There are universal laws which apply to natural phenomena as well as to the socio-economic sphere – and therefore convey the learning from each other. But these laws are not easily accessible without serious guidance, as an unprofessional approach opens the door for biases, guessing, and trial-and-error, which does not live up to the seriousness of today's problems. Therefore, the presentation and application of "power laws" in the book will be challenging. A first glance is given by the following list of potential laws to be discussed:

- Inflection points
- Scaling and universal proportions
- Critical transitions
- Power curve of economic profit
- Punctuated equilibrium
- Rules of contagion
- Network principles
- Cybernetic management rules
- Technology laws and heuristics

Just to give a few examples, "inflection points" (McGrath, 2019) arise in the context of growth processes when an upward trend suddenly tips over. Such growth curves abound in nature as well in the socio-economic context; they are the result of universal laws to be discussed later. "Scaling" (West 2017) refers to how the system responds when its size changes. What happens when the size of a corporation doubles in a short time, be it by organic growth or by acquisitions? And which weak signals give indication that danger looms? Finally, "power curves of economic profit" (Bradley, Hirt, and Smit 2018) show, based on empirical research of a worldwide data set of leading companies, how value creation is optimized by combining 10 basic variables which drive success.

The starting point for the search of "power laws" are weak signals detected by our procedure so far. Here the distinction between complicated and complex systems comes again into play. Complicated systems are driven by the type of universal laws governing physical systems, like Newton's laws of motion and gravity. But of greater importance are empirical findings in business contexts, to be discussed in the form of the concepts of "high reliability organizations" (Weick and Sutcliffe 2015), "predictable surprises" (Bazerman and Watkins 2004) or "normal accidents" (Perrow 1985).

In complex systems, the allocation of "power laws" proves to be significantly more demanding. Although weak signals give some indication which patterns should be searched for, it turns out to become an "educated guess." In the next chapter, a "deck of cards" representing a variety of such "power laws" will be presented together with their potential fields of application. Examples from managerial practice will illustrate the process and give executives confidence in their own abilities to handle this challenging approach.

Step 4: "Evolution": Developing scenarios of pattern dynamics

The patterns revealed by weak signals are not stable; they change over time, driven by their underlying laws. The better the knowledge about the law and its influence on the dynamics of a system, the better the quality of scenarios about its future development. Scenarios are "meaningful memories of the future" (Ramirez and Wilkinson 2018, 44). As argued in our introductory remarks, in complex and uncertain environments, predictions are virtually impossible. Only by inventing narratives that paint pictures of possible futures in each environment, potentially, some light can be brought into the dark. Scenarios can be extensions of recent paths of development; they can combine present knowledge about the business with expectations in the light of technical progress, or they can just present phantasies about the world to be. But all these scenarios are somehow arbitrary. There is no conclusive evidence to prefer one to the other.

In contrast, scenarios based on pattern dynamics ("power scenarios") follow the evolutionary curves determined by universal laws or empirical business laws. In his ground-breaking book ***Scale – The universal laws of life and death in organisms, cities and companies***, Geoffrey West (2017, 391) shows how the universal laws of scale can be translated into scenarios for the business world: ". . . companies are more like organisms than cities and are dominated by a version of economic scale rather than by increasing returns and innovation . . . Their metabolic rate is neither sub- nor super-linear but falls right in the middle by being linear . . . consequently, the difference between sales and expenses, which is the driver of growth, also eventually scales approximately linearly . . . Scaling leads to exponential growth and this is what companies strive for." From this follows that company growth must be higher than market growth, driven by short innovation circles and linear development of sales and expenses. With respect to **weak signals,** this means that special attention should be given on the dynamics of size changes, market growth, innovation cycles, and linearity of sales and cost. When compared to the empirical laws of **"power curves of economic profit,"** there are many parallels, as will be shown in Chapter 3.

Based on the observation of weak signals, **scenarios** can now be developed using the insights of the above two laws. These scenarios are of a different quality than traditional approaches, as they refer to scientific research and empirical evidence. The practice of **scenario development** is supported best by Wardley maps (Wardley, 2020), as they take a narrative yet systemic approach.

Step 5: "Indicators": Shaping metrics and their narratives

Weak signals and their scenarios are the "raw material" for developing **"leading indicators."** A change of managerial behavior in the perception of and the reaction to fundamental developments requires a metric that is easily understood and motivates the user. The number of warning signals should be limited to allow a first broad assessment by simply looking at the control panel.

There are three types of indicators to be distinguished: lagging, current and leading indicators. Examples of **lagging** indicators are margins, EBITDA, RONA; **current** indicators are operating cash flows or production costs. **Leading** indicators "represent things that are not facts yet in your business. They have the potential to lead to facts later, but at the moment . . . they are only suppositions, conjectures, and assumptions . . . they are often told as narratives and stories rather than in metrics . . . " (McGrath 2019, 66). An example would be Microsoft's move from "profit" to "customer love" as leading indicators. Nowadays, the methodology of Objectives and Key Results (OKR, see Doerr 2018) is quite popular to develop leading indicators which support the organization in staying on track towards the desired future. The idea of OKRs is interesting, as they strive to combine qualitative goals (objectives) and measurable metrics (key results). Even though the theory is quite simple, the practice is not easy because it requires a change in the behavior of the management: from output to outcome.

For **input-output systems**, their **resilience** would be good starting point for developing leading indicators. Weick and Sutcliffe (2015) present five principles which characterize resilient companies: preoccupation with failure, reluctance to simplify, sensitivity to operations, commitment to resilience, and deference to expertise.

In the case of **autopoietic systems**, it is more challenging to specify metrics or principles as leading indicators. Hence, **narratives** play the most important role. This is highlighted by the research topic of "Narrative Economics" (Shiller 2020) which gains attention not only in the scientific community. Contrary to mainstream economics which focuses on allocating probabilities to future trends, narratives aim to familiarize decision-makers with complexity and uncertainty. In the management context this means associating weak signals with the background, the language, and the interests of the people in charge. Good leadership has been often characterized with the ability to use metaphors to unify different skills in a company, e.g., the designers, engineers, or blue collar workers.

Step 6: "Framing": Creating self-organizing viable systems

With this step, the phase of generating **impact** is being launched. When leading indicators point to change, be it by surprise or by deviations from expected behavior, proactive measures must be initiated. Prerequisite is a carefully crafted portfolio of options to avoid improvisation. This, in turn, requires an integrated framework with a clear purpose. Coping with change just by launching singular activities to solve local problems is doomed to failure. All proactive moves must be anchored in this framework which serves to ensure the **viability** of the enterprise.

Here, the **Viable System Model** (Beer 1972) comes into play. It provides the necessary and sufficient organizational prerequisites to achieve viability in a complex world, and it locates a system in its nurturing environment. For managerial practice, the model presents a metaframe to identify and design the essential subsystems of any viable corporation: Operations, Tactical Planning, Strategy and Innovation, Norms and Policies. Furthermore, it provides two functions which are responsible for the handling of weak signals. For internal purposes, the VSM offers the so-called "audit channel," which allows to detect anomalies within the organization. It also makes use of an "external sensor" which continuously observes strategically relevant changes in the environment. The VSM offers managerial practice an elegant way to combine the "here and now" with the "outside and then" (Beer 1985). For the field of education, Markus Schwaninger (2019) illustrates its application in teaching at the University of St. Gallen. It so provides the basic logic to focus interventions on the optimal place and to achieve the best leverage. In the case of **input-output systems**, this means designing and navigating the system to meet the preconditions of viability. For **autopoietic systems**, it provides propositions for "structural coupling," with the ultimate goal to gain access to an otherwise closed system.

A key concern of leading by weak signals is to generate impact by intervening with minimal invasion. In managerial practice, this can only be achieved if the corporation and its parts are characterized by a high degree of self-organization. Therefore, the Viable System model must be complemented by additional frameworks which provide organizational blueprints for this alignment. In this context, corporate structures must be distinguished from organizational forms of teams, and self-organization must be customized to the goals to be achieved: technological leadership, customer-orientation, agility, and performance. Four types of self-organizing structures will be presented with their basic characteristics: web-centered ecosystems, market-oriented ecosystems, classical agile structures, and performance-oriented team structures.

Step 7: "Tipping Points": Intervening with minimal invasion

The term "tipping point" was coined by Malcolm Gladwell (2000, 12): ". . . the moment of critical mass, the threshold, the boiling point." The subtitle of his book gives some further information: "How little things can make a big difference." This concept serves as an entry door to influence a system's self-organizing forces by experimenting with structural changes. As shown above, **input-output systems** can be approached in a straightforward way by implementing the logic of the Viable System Model. **Autopoietic systems** require a fundamentally different approach. They dispose of sensors at their boundaries to enable co-evolution with their environment. Interventions from outside use this environmental drift to influence the self-organizing processes of the system. A consumer product company could be influenced by digitization as a trigger to move their beliefs towards Microsoft's "customer love"; a financial company might occupy central management positions with executives open to digital innovation to meet the expectations of younger customers. Tipping points of autopoietic systems must not be confused with the concept of **nudge** (Thaler and Sunstein 2012). "Nudging" means using fine control to move a system in a certain direction. This concept claims to know promising paths into a complex and uncertain future, which proves to be futile in a complex and uncertain future. The only way to initiate change in autopoietic systems is by experimentation at the system's boundaries.

After having specified in the previous step the options to access and navigate the system, the way to influence the **balance between autonomy and cohesion** comes now into focus. Cohesion is often triggered by market pressure, new technologies, and common enemies. Autonomy is mainly achieved by trust. **Swarm intelligence** often serves as a metaphor for self-organization by answering the question: how to achieve autonomy and cohesion without a leader? Essential is the "relevant information." Everybody who possesses this information can become a leader. Tiny impulses can initiate a change process. The relevant information is either local outside information or knowledge of a few scattered participants. "Intervention" here means to influence the swarm of agents at the system's boundaries according to the rules of swarm intelligence. In a swarm of 100 people, there should be at least five people with relevant information (Fladerer and Kurzmann 2019, Chapter 6, pg. 11).

To complement these insights about intervention for self-organization, **four additional approaches** will be presented: value streams, theory of constraints, ergodicity, and living composition. They serve as a guide to enhance managerial practice.

Step 8: "Alertness": Organizing for future surprise

The last step of the methodology anchors leading by weak signals in managerial practice as the core framework to deal with complexity and uncertainty. It is institutionalized as a corporate function of the same importance as human resources, controlling, and marketing and establishes a "corporate look out or radar system" that continuously collects information about the environment and internal issues. This function commonly bears the name of **"Corporate Intelligence" (CI)**, which differs from the traditional market and competitor analyses, as it goes beyond desk research and the creation of data dashboards.

Anchoring the weak signal spirit in managerial practice has two directions of thrust: enabling – on a permanent basis – profound insights on relevant futures and setting up monitoring devices to sustainably secure the impact of interventions. The institutionalization of Leading by Weak Signals requires a different approach for input-output systems and autopoietic systems. To gain insights on critical changes in input-output systems, perception must be perfected by establishing and calibrating state-of-the-art early warning systems. To secure lasting impact of interventions and to enable sustainable evolution, **the principle of subsidiarity** must be consistently updated organizationally. In autopoietic systems, the focus on change lies at their boundaries, as this allows access by using **peripheral sensing** to detect weak signals. The monitoring of impact finally is achieved by **permanent experimentation** and optimization of interventional activities

This concludes the overview of the book's basic ideas and contents. The steps of the methodology are now presented in detail, following the logic of

- detecting weak signals and their underlying patterns (Chapter 2),
- crafting leading indicators of change and their narratives (Chapter 3),
- navigating for impact by weak signal leadership (Chapter 4),
- anchoring the weak signal spirit (Chapter 5).

2 Detecting weak signals and their underlying patterns

2.1 Starting the exploration

Quite a few organizational charts of corporations and in consequence also of business school curricula reveal a perspective of management that seemed to have lost relevance in our fast-moving times: The "thinking in silos." In their first years at the university, students are taught all the details in the fields of purchasing, production, logistics, marketing, sales, finance, personnel, and nowadays also in the areas of ethics, sustainability, and diversity. This is under the assumption that the acquired knowledge will later, like pieces of a jigsaw puzzle, fit together to form a picture of what is called "Management." Charts of corporate organizations also provide such a view, as below the hierarchical level of the CEO and his or her staff functions, similar "silos" are assembled in a horizontal line. Surprisingly, this so-called "functional organization" is still fashionable, especially in small- or midsize companies. It is the expression of a reductionist view, which still governs the thought patterns of many corporate executives and business schoolteachers used to operate in hierarchical structures and in complicated environments.

This approach is also common in the field of natural sciences, especially in public school education. The distinction between physics, chemistry, and biology leads to a siloed way to perceive phenomena in nature. But to understand photosynthesis, one needs all three disciplines to get the full picture of this fascinating process. This illustrates the dilemma of reductionism quite well, since it also explains why STEM subjects are not liked by many students: instead of learning how aspects are connected, they are taught as separate entities.

Back to management; it is not to be equated with the "the sum of the parts," by just adding the detailed knowledge on marketing, logistics, finance, and other functional areas to run a corporation. Nor is it "more than the sum of its parts," as the popular saying goes. It is "something different than the sum of its parts." Here the **system's approach to management** comes into play. The way the University of St. Gallen in Switzerland introduces students into the topic of "management" may serve to illustrate this approach in first approximation. They take a **"helicopter view."** On the proper ground of a corporation the students board a helicopter and rise high above the territory. From there they have a perfect overview of the corporation in its natural environment. In analogy the students also reflect on its embeddedness in social, societal, economic, and political ecosystems. They learn that corporations are not given "objects," but systems defined by observers from different perspectives, considering their role in an ecosystem. Based on these insights, the students develop a first model of the corporation. In a next step, the helicopter lands on a spot called "marketing" or "finance," where the students drill a deep hole and take a sample of the soil.

https://doi.org/10.1515/9783110797886-002

The helicopter again takes off again and the students interpret their sample high above the ground in relation to their first modelling. With this procedure, "marketing" or "finance" no longer remain a body of knowledge separated from the rest but are perceived as interrelated to many other aspects of the corporation. The students have **diagnosed the system of the corporation** (Beer, 1985), and they are no longer caught in the silos of traditional business approaches.

The process of discovering or identifying the system in each context will be guided by the logic of the scientific model and its application in the management context, as presented in Figure 1.2 and shown again in Figure 2.1. First, a distinction must be drawn between autopoietic (closed) systems and input-output (open) systems. This also requires a differentiation of the roles of participant (player) and (observer). As to variety engineering, the scientific focus is on variety attenuation, in managerial practice, gaining insights is in the foreground.

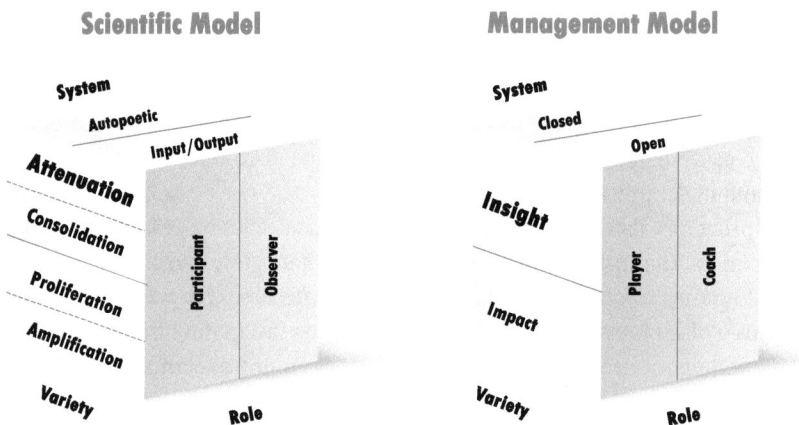

Figure 2.1: Scientific and managerial framework of Leading by Weak Signals.

This leads us to the first step when Leading by Weak Signals: Setting the stage.

2.2 Step 1: "System": Setting the stage and identifying its boundaries

Conceptual foundations

In the classical natural sciences, the **input-output modelling of systems** prevails: organisms adapt to their environment by a process of optimizing given inputs. Social sciences, economics and business studies also follow this research trail, denoted as "contingency theory" (Lawrence and Lorsch 1969), until these days. This is justified when dealing with

complicated problems where the "mechanisms" of interacting parts within a system and connecting it to its environment are known in all their details.

But in the case of **complex problems**, these attempts to explain the world fail. Here the **autopoietic modelling of systems** comes into play. In managerial practice one often finds businesses which fail to react to environmental change at all or at least not in an – in terms of input-output modelling – explainable way. The rise and fall of Eastman Kodak serve as a classic example. Even though they invented the "next big thing" called digital photography, they missed out on operationalizing it in a profitable way. The reason for this failure is quite simple: management in those days could not imagine that the discovery of digital photography would change an entire industry. They believed that the quality of analog pictures could never be beaten by a digital apparatus. An input-output perspective cannot explain such behavior. But **what if** Eastman Kodak's strategy was shaped by the "Eigenbehavior" of an autopoietic system, which treats environmental changes as just perturbations to its autonomously set beliefs and decisions?

The same kind of question was asked by the two Chilean scientists Humberto Maturana and Francisco Varela (1972) in the context of biological systems. And they came up with the **concept of autopoiesis** which also applies to social systems and to the business context. Autopoiesis is a special case of **autonomy.** The concept of autonomy is well-established in the business context when dealing with the degree of freedom of organizational subunits of a corporation. But here the focus lies on the positioning of the entire organization in its environment. Varela (1984, 25) uses the term "operationally closed" to define autopoietic systems: "Every operationally closed system has Eigenbehavior . . . and changes by natural drift." "Eigenbehavior" is characterized by a process of constant reproduction to achieve coherence and internal regularities, and that in a broad range of environments. "Natural drift" means to successfully cope with those without losing the identity. Just look at one of the most fascinating species in the world: ants. They can live in almost all sorts of ecosystems, from arctic regions to deserts, yet they are able to keep their identity (building colonies, work force differentiation, etc.).

At first sight, this concept seems somehow farfetched to gain insights in a business context. It has a perfect fit with processes in the human brain and the nervous and immune systems. And whereas biological autopoiesis takes place within clear boundaries of cells or physiological systems, the boundaries of social systems and business situations are not evident; they must be discovered and identified. All the same, the concept of autopoiesis allows access to knowledge not available for leadership before.

Four concepts are at the center when dealing with autopoiesis in a business context:

- Operational closure
- Organization versus structure
- Boundaries of the system
- Participant versus observer

Operational closure: autopoietic systems are closed with respect to beliefs, decisions, communication, and knowledge. But they are open to people, energy, material, and information.

Organization versus structure: the organization of an autopoietic system is characterized by a permanently self-reproduced network of beliefs, decisions, and communications, whereas the structure provides people, energy, and information to enable a smooth functioning of the system. The organization remains invariant over time, the physical and informational structure changes in dependence of environmental changes.

Boundaries of the system: they are not physically or topologically given (as the membrane of a cell), but are the result of functional and behavioral processes and patterns to maintain the identity. Typical examples from the business world are "love brands" where the traditional difference between employee and customer gets quite fuzzy. The emotional connection to companies like Apple is outstanding. Customers sleep in front of a store to get the newest gadget or wait for hours in lines to pay for a product. The same applies to Tesla – even though here the admiration for a charismatic personality is more important than the products as such. But both examples show that the boundaries of companies are not clearly defined.

Participant versus observer: organizationally closed systems perceive inputs to their organization as perturbations or noise. The only way to exert direct influence on the organization is by active participation within the system. External observers or coaches can get (some) access to the system, by initiating a process called structural coupling. This means operating via agents (people, energy, material, information) at the boundaries of the system. In managerial practice, this structural coupling often takes the form of working contracts, which define the scope of external coaching and limit the variety of interventions. Most of the time, activities of external coaches are of temporary nature. This has a tricky consequence for the hired coach as well as for the people within the organization: The structural coupling has a deadline; therefore, internals know that it will be anyhow over soon. They know by experience, that nothing will change . . . and that the autopoietic forces of the organization will take over again.

In complex and uncertain environments, autopoietic systems abound. Therefore, knowing how to deal with such systems becomes of great importance. On the other hand, there are many situations when an input-output modelling makes perfect sense. But as Varela (1984, 26) states, it is important to have a **"clean epistemological accounting,"** to know (and to explicitly state) when to deal with input-output situations and such of autopoiesis.

The design of manufacturing processes is typical for **input-output modelling**. Any kind of sequence of working steps, which produces "something," is based on input-output thinking. The whole process can be broken down into steps, which are inherently logical, since one first needs raw material before it is possible to perform the following production steps. The activities and tools for these steps are measurable, the whole process can be defined, specified, and structurally modified. The same logic applies to the production of a more abstract item like a piece of programming code. Instead of raw material, typically the needs for certain results flow into the work system, also known as user requirements or specifications. Such a need is often phrased (in agile environments) as a user story – a good way to describe a task from the user perspective. After this input has been analyzed, the production process continues, and the typical steps of the "waterfall process" are conducted: concept and design, coding and testing, and delivery and maintenance. In the end the output of a piece of software runs on a hardware. Again, most of the steps and process aspects can be specified and measured, like the lead time (cycle time) of a user story, or typical performance measures like code deployment frequency and number of errors. Even though the cognitive demands for so-called knowledge work are higher than those of a simple production line in a factory, both working systems are usually modelled as input-output systems. There is an identifiable external input, which is "internally" processed, and at the end the output is delivered towards the environment.

To illustrate **autopoietic modelling,** one first must go back to some roots in the context of management. In the second half of last century, the topic of **"corporate culture"** received a lot of attention. The eminent management thinker Peter Drucker is credited with the quotation: "Culture eats strategy for breakfast." One of the best characterizations of corporate culture was given by Thomas Watson from IBM already in the sixties (Watson 1963, 4): "I firmly believe that any organization, in order to survive and achieve success, must have a sound set of beliefs on which it premises all its policies and actions . . . to meet the challenges of a changing world, it must be prepared to change everything about itself except those beliefs . . . as it moves through corporate life." This statement reflected the fundamental issue of operational closure: the system maintains its identity in a changing environment by holding invariant its beliefs (organization) while changing everything else about itself (structure). Under the leadership of Watson and up until today IBM has lived this conviction, although the environment has changed dramatically.

In our days, the concept of **"purpose"** has superseded that of corporate culture. It aims at answering the question about the "why" and the "what for" of a business, the "license to operate." Answering these questions is of great importance, but the "purpose movement" has developed into a kind of hype, led by the big consulting companies of this world. As will be shown later, autopoiesis impedes importing a purpose from the outside; it can only evolve in the process of strengthening the internal coherence. Or, in the words of Stafford Beer (1985, 99): "POSIWID – The purpose of a system is what it does!"

Another example of an autopoietic system is the Roman Catholic Church. The secret of its sustained existence over centuries lies in a strong set of beliefs – the catholic faith – and in an institution to protect these beliefs from environmental disturbances – the curia. In the second Vatican Council of the 1960s, new possibilities for participation of the lay movement in the discussion of themes like birth-control, integration of women, and redefinition of authority had been initiated. From a perspective of input-output modelling, this meant opening the church to influences of a radically changing environment – as happened to many other religions. But the curia blocked the process and allowed only minor cosmetic changes like new forms of the holy mess. It seemingly demonstrated adaptiveness to external demands but did not want to break up the operationally closed system. And this course is being followed to this day.

With Covid-19 and Climate Change, a new level of uncertainty has reached our societies. The autopoietic concepts of "organization" and "structure" give important insights into the complexities of the situation. Armin Nassehi (2021, 115) describes two mutually interacting dimensions shaping society, the social and the factual dimension. The social dimension comprises common values, semantical ciphers, and figures, an established "ideal" order, it is the "organization" of a society. The factual society is formed by interest groups or "identities," each with its own perspective and goal on how to approach the problem. The ideal state for Covid-19 in the social dimension would be solidarity for the aging population and maintenance of the health care infrastructure, for Climate Change it would mean leaving behind a healthy and functioning world to our descendants. In our society, there is a basic agreement about these values. But when it comes to acting in the factual world, competition of interests and goals takes over. In normal times, autopoiesis is achieved in the social dimension in the form of common values and narratives. But in times of crisis, a multitude of structures take over, each with its own goals . . . and autopoiesis! This all leads to a new phenomenon open for discussion: pathological autopoiesis – a concept to be discussed later.

Methodology and tools

The process of Leading by Weak Signals is initiated by identifying the **system in focus**. Systems are not given in nature, nor are they in societal or business environments. They must be **discovered** or **identified**. This distinction is crucial in the light of our discussions about input-output systems versus autopoietic systems as well as on the roles of participants versus observers.

To repeat our findings in a nutshell:

Input-output systems are mainly embedded in complicated settings, they are part of natural ecosystems and/or human-made infrastructures. They can be **identified** by taking specific perspectives and by determining the main driving elements and relationships. After drawing the system's boundaries, the ground for the search for weak signals is prepared.

Autopoietic systems are typical for complex environments. They must be *discovered*, as their autonomously reproduced boundaries are not directly observable and not accessible from the outside. To influence the evolution of such systems requires internal participation, or – in special cases – structural coupling with its environment.

Whereas input-output modelling is perfectly suited for complicated problem situations, complex settings require a more differentiated approach. Due to the distinction of an autopoietic system's "organization" and "structure," both autopoietic and input-output modelling come into play. Whereas the first deals with topics of beliefs, decision-making, communication, and knowledge, the second focuses on people, energy, material, and information. Varela's above quote on "clear epistemological accounting" is of greatest importance when applying the two approaches.

Under these preconditions, the process of defining the system can now be set up to suit managerial practice. Figure 2.2 gives an overview of required **activities** and appropriate **tools**.

	Observer/Coach	Participant/Player
Input-Output Systems	Defining a system's driving forces from different views	Evaluating the system's role in a changing environment
	Circular Networks	**Ecosystems Modelling**
Autopoietic Systems	Discovering the system as an autonomous entity	Interpreting the system as a network of reproductive processes
	Structural Coupling	**Living Composition**

Figure 2.2: Activities and tools for systems definition.

For an **observer** (a coach, a problem-solver), "setting the stage" starts with gaining initial insights about the situation at hand. First comes an assessment of the situation as being **complicated or complex.** In the introductory chapter we gave some guidance on how to draw this distinction. In a complicated situation, we can dive directly into the process of identifying the system. In a complex situation, we must run a search procedure to discover autonomous entities with "Eigenbehavior."

Observers/coaches facing input-output systems: Circular networks
"A system is a way of looking at the world" (Weinberg 1975, 51). This insight forces the problem-solver to observe mainly **complicated situations** from different perspectives or viewpoints, as shown in an example from daily life. A chair is not a given "object," but a system with specific characteristics, depending on the viewpoint taken. Defining a chair from the perspectives of aesthetics, material, stability, comfort, price, and many more leads to different systems. The next step localizes the entity in the broader context of its ecosystem. The chair could be exhibited in a museum or placed in a restaurant. Or its wood could be used to maintain a fire. This leads to the following guidelines for an observer/coach in a complicated situation:

- Take different perspectives or viewpoints
- Identify the driving forces and relationships of the system
- Locate these forces in their wider environment
- Determine the boundaries of the system

In practice, taking **different perspectives** starts with setting up a workshop with people representing relevant stakeholder interests. To take as an example the problem of forest maintenance in times of climate change, these representatives would take the perspectives of forest ownership, recreational offerings, surrounding communities, wildlife protection, rangers' empowerment, wood processing, and more. An experienced facilitator will successfully navigate the workshop group, as is shown in the infobox below.

To achieve the next goal – to understand the **basic drivers** of the system – a round of individual idea generation and result sharing will help to identify the central forces and their relationships. In a business context, one always starts with the customer and identifies major influencing factors. It is helpful to identify three major types of factors: value creating elements, usually close to the boundary of the system to shorten the delivery of goods and the service to the market; supporting elements which take care of the infrastructure like internal IT or accounting; management elements enhancing the overarching decision-making and the long-term development of the organization.

The first result of the workshop is shown in Figure 2.3: a network of circular causal relationships which represents the "engine" of the business. A plus in the circle is read as "the more . . . the more," but also "the less . . . the less." Higher customer

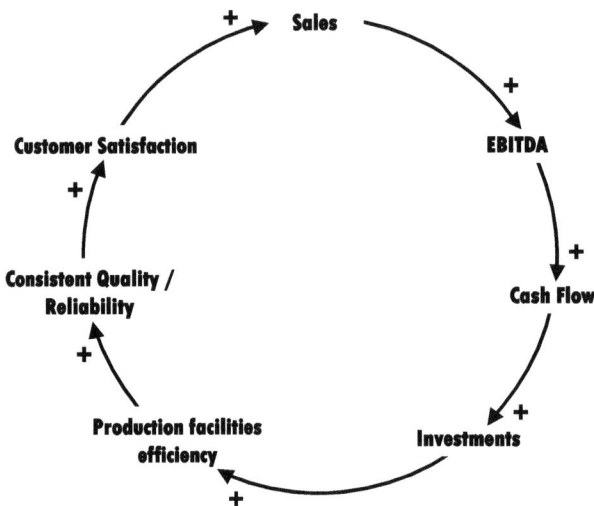

Figure 2.3: A basic circle or "engine" driving the business.

satisfaction leads to higher sales, to an improvement of the profits (EBITDA), to higher cash flows, to new investment opportunities, to higher efficiency of the production facilities, to higher quality and reliability . . . and again to an improvement of customer satisfaction. But as soon as one of the parts develops negatively, the circle becomes vicious, as the + reinforces the downward trend.

Simpson's Paradox – the importance of a confounding variable
Correlations must not be mixed up with causal relations. Figure 2.4 illustrates the danger of interpreting a linear relationship by looking at the data without further abstraction.

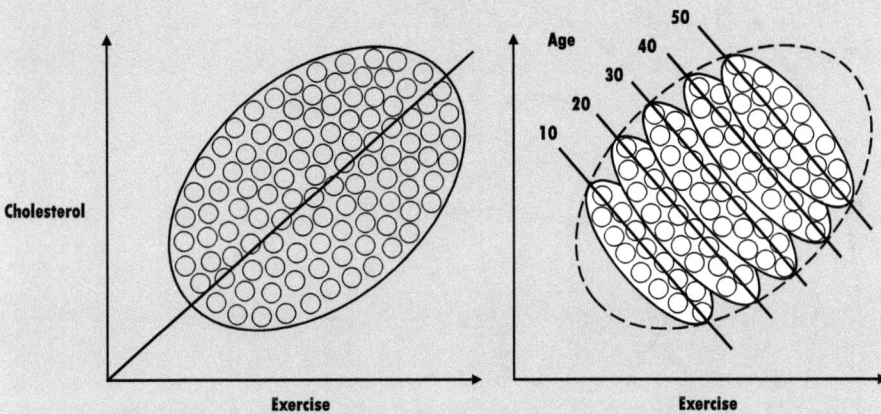

Figure 2.4: One can be easily fooled without a confounding variable (Pearl and Mackenzie, 2016, 211).

The example suggests that the more you exercise, the higher the levels of cholesterol – which is obviously nonsense. What is missing is a confounding variable (age) to understand that exactly the opposite relationship is "logical," a lot of exercise leads to lower cholesterol levels.

In the next step, the driving elements of Figure 2.3 are **connected to their wider environment**, here illustrated by the strategic map of a company in cement manufacturing. As shown in Figure 2.5, some forces have an inverse effect (-), e.g., competitive rivalry on prices or higher efficiency on production costs. This is read as "the more . . . the less" or "the less . . . the more." Negative influences (-) stabilize the system, whereas positive influences (+) reinforce a development.

The **boundaries of the system** are given by all the elements and relationships which constitute the system. The circular network will be the basis for the next step in the process of identifying weak signals – in the following context they are named early-warning indicators because we are dealing with an input-output system.

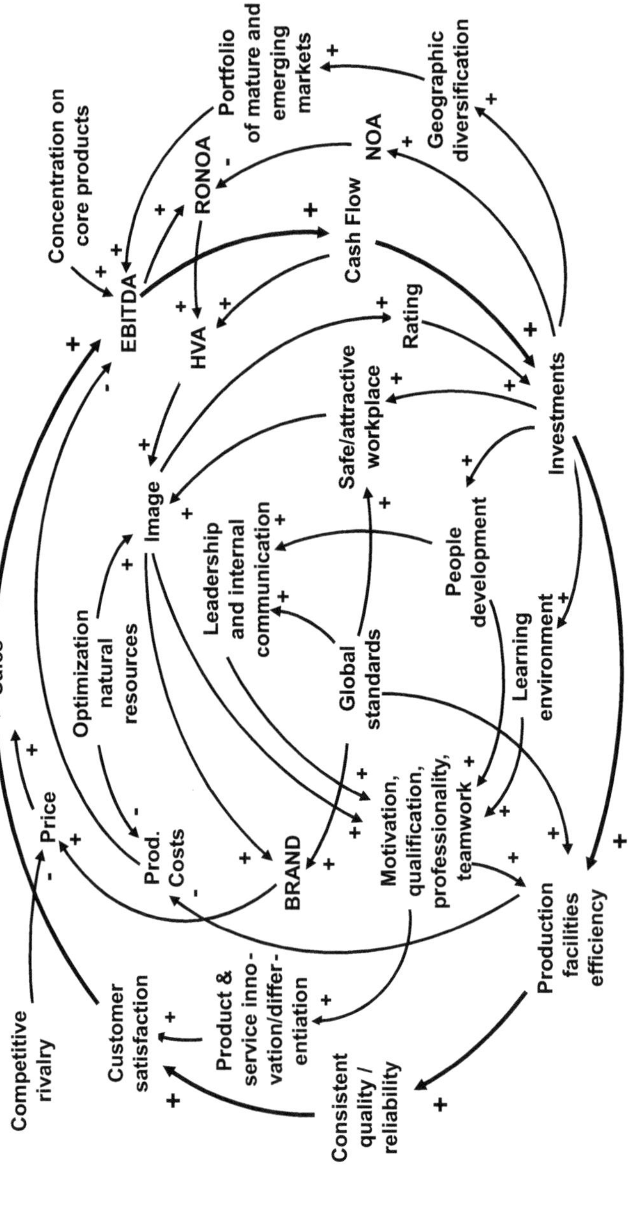

Figure 2.5: Embedding an enterprise in cement manufacturing in its ecosystem (EBITDA, HVA, NOA and RONOA are financial indicators).

How to trigger a collaborative atmosphere in the workshop?
Different perspectives provide a lot of value – once they are incorporated. But how could this be achieved? It starts with the people that may contribute to a holistic picture of the system. Obviously, the right mix of characters is crucial for such an endeavor, but what does that mean in detail? At first, it makes sense to include colleagues from core functions like production, sales, or customer services, because they are usually well connected to the environment, and know operational topics the best. The functional diversity can be increased by incorporating typical support functions like HR, IT, or controlling. These colleagues usually know about internal operational matters the best – including the internal bottlenecks in the organization. As a complementary function, it makes sense to integrate people who work typically on strategic topics like innovation, customer, or market research. Next to this differentiation, it is helpful to have the right mix of characters on board, which means that it is a group of people who can switch contexts, as described in the "St. Gallen helicopter" metaphor.

Traditionally, workshops start like this: setting the context, asking participants about their expectations, launching the process of model building. This procedure lacks sufficient time to accommodate the people with the situation – and it is even worse when people with contradicting perspectives meet for the first time. They don't even know each other, and then they are expected to come up with innovative ideas or solutions. But creative thinking needs a relaxed atmosphere, a safe place for failure and experimenting. A simple way to ignite a sparking conversation is the use of the TRIZ technique of the US Army (RTHB 2015, 210). Instead of doing the usual expectation management, you start with the second point of the agenda, asking the following question: "What could be the most disastrous outcome of the workshop? What would be the biggest failure? And please dare to be creative and think about wild ideas!" For this purpose, the moderator sets a timebox of a few minutes, so that the participants can write their ideas on stickies. When people start to share their ideas, e.g., 50% of the colleagues quit after the workshop, the absurdity of the ideas helps participants to calm down and discover that nobody wants such an outcome. After exchanging about the "what" it is time to ideate on the how: "How should we behave to make sure that the worst outcome will 100% happen?" Again, a timebox is set and again the generated ideas regarding the behavior are shared, "we laugh about bad ideas," "only perfect thoughts allowed," or "always yell at each other when having a different opinion."

It is most important to have serious fun because it will lead to better results. A creative atmosphere demands communication on eye level. This kind of introduction helps the group to switch perspectives and be aware of the power of subjective perception. It encourages openness and critical thinking, and subsequently it allows to create new ways to look at the given problem.

Participants/players in input-output systems: Ecosystems modelling

Moving from an observer/coach to a **participant/player in complicated systems**, the role changes slightly. It makes perfect sense to start the process of system definition anew, especially in a situation of environmental change. But the most important task is to locate the system in its ecosystem. This process is illustrated by developing a circular network based on insights about its contribution to societal well-being, the "public value" (Meynhardt 2009). Hereby, the central circle of an enterprise's driving forces (see Figure 2.3 above) is supplemented by considering moral-ethical, hedonistic-aesthetic, utilitarian-instrumental, and political-social values. This process aims at answering the following questions which leads to the representation in Figure 2.6.

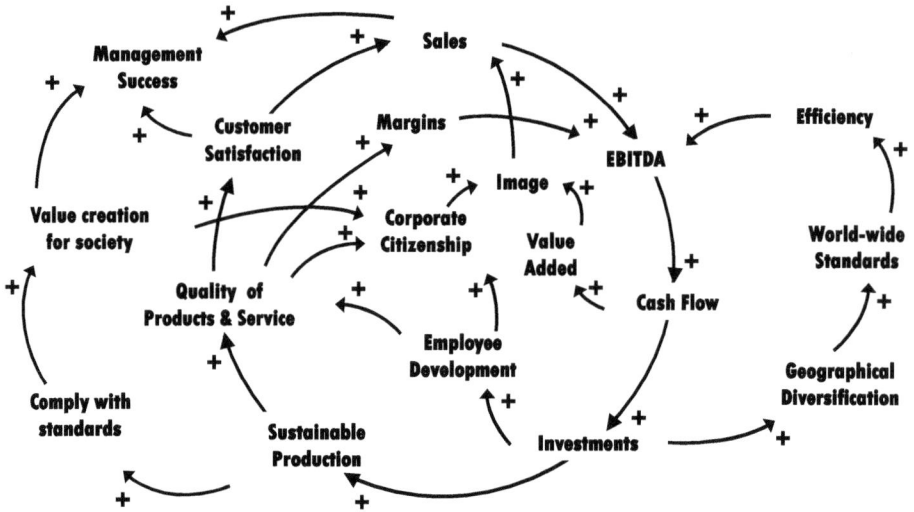

Figure 2.6: A firm's contribution to public value (Gomez, Lambertz, and Meynhardt 2019, 155).

- Is it useful?
- Is it profitable?
- Is it politically acceptable?
- Is it a positive experience?
- Is it decent?

Whereas the questions about the contribution to "public value" refer to the parts of the system, the circular network integrates the answers in a dynamic way. It is interesting to note that all relationships are positive (+) and reinforcing. But this also means, that if only one or a few of the parts fail, the system as such might move into a downward spiral.

Observers/coaches facing autopoietic systems: Structural coupling
In the case of **complex situations**, the process of discovering and identifying the system becomes more demanding. From **the point of view of the observer**, this means detecting autonomous entities with "Eigenbehavior." Koskinen (2013, 33) proposes the following procedure:
- Determine, through interaction, if an entity has identifiable boundaries and is capable of continually reproducing them. These boundaries differ fundamentally from "atomistic" notions of traditional business theory. They can be knowledge pools, behavioral patterns of specific professions or groups of top-notch researchers.
- Investigate environmental inputs to the system and note if they are neglected or treated as perturbations (autopoietic system) or as triggers for adaptation (input-output system).

– Identify the different roles of the systems' organization and structure. Whereas the organization (consisting of beliefs, decisions, knowledge, and communication) reproduces according to its own internal rules, the structure (in form of people, energy, material, and information) enables a link to the environment.

Discovering autopoietic systems requires a great sensitivity for the context. There is no checkup list available, but: "When you see it, you know it." Language patterns can also indicate that autopoiesis comes into play.

If language drives complexity, let's use it!
"When you see it, you know it" could be also rephrased as when you hear it, you know it. The statement points towards the typical language that one finds in organizations (or in parts of it). For an observer it is relatively easy to detect patterns in the usage of language, be it phrases, proverbs, or just words that signal to the insiders: they speak the same corporate lingo and share certain meanings – it indicates membership. This phenomenon also creates a great deal of organizational cohesion. But corporate dialects are not limited to companies, but also exist in sectors like the consulting or an IT-specific industry. Buzzwords are always flying around, therefore one needs the ability of active listening to detect the language patterns. A perfect example is the word "alignment," which seems to be extensively used in every international company. But you could go even a step further and examine the occurrence of English terms in a foreign language. As a simple example, Figure 2.7 shows how the popularity of the word "alignment" in German books developed over time (according to Google's Ngram Viewer, measured in %):

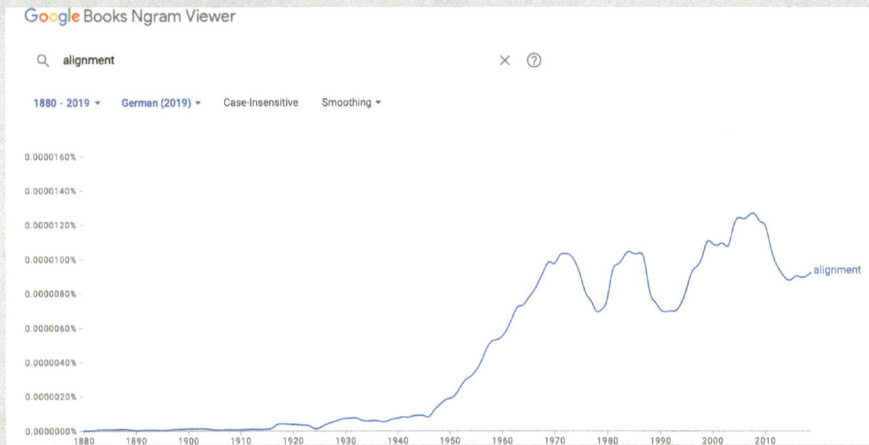

Figure 2.7: The different waves of using the word "alignment" in German.

Once detected, a specific term is useful to "align" the meaning of the word "alignment"! It starts with the simple question: What does one intend to express when the word is used? One is consciously avoiding defining the meaning, because there is a very high likelihood that one will never be able to finish such an exercise, simply because one gets into a never-ending loop of discussions. Therefore, it is sufficient to share the meaning – in short:

> Intention beats definition
>
> The usage of corporate lingo reveals another important property. The enterprise-specific language is helpful to reduce complexity. Since the enterprise as an autopoietic system depends on its self-reproducing identity, each member knows by intuition what is meant, even though an official clarification never happened.
>
> To initiate structural coupling (see below) as a coach, the creation of a glossary is a simple yet powerful step, not only to connect as an external observer, but also to enable an internal coupling, since also within the organization the "players" might use certain terminology, but the interpretation and inherent practices are totally different.
>
> If a mutual glossary has been built, it will be much easier to create a shared reality that enables better decision making and, in the very end, creates the desired impact.

Access to an autopoietic system might be gained through structural coupling. Here an input-output view comes into play. Autopoietic systems are organizationally closed to inputs and outputs, but all the same they have to co-evolute with their environment. Without such co-evolution, they cannot sustain their viability and they reach the state of pathological autopoiesis. Structural coupling provides them a way to survival, as shown in Figure 2.8.

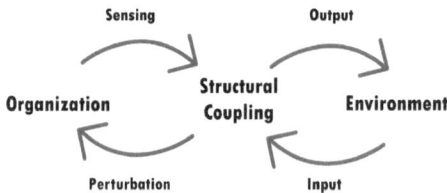

Figure 2.8: Structural coupling to get access to an autopoietic system.

Perturbations directly hitting the system's organization are either ignored or "translated" into its own logic so that they fail to reach the desired effect. But structural coupling could serve the purpose of bypassing this defense. It focusses on the **open** elements – the structure – of the system, mainly on people, energy, material flows, information, and language. It aims at influencing the system indirectly, with the goal to change these elements to impact the system's beliefs, decisions, and communications. But where should these inputs be docking? Mainly at the boundaries of the system, where the autopoietic system has placed its own co-evolutionary sensors.

A practical example to illustrate this approach features an observer (a competitor, an activist shareholder, a state agency) in the pharmaceutical industry. The leading companies are guarding the secrets of their innovation processes until the patents are granted by the authorities. Decision-making processes and patterns of communication are shielded from the outside world. To get some access to this hidden world, observers focus on **"swarms"** of researchers at the system's boundaries which are testing new areas of innovation. As they are in contact with other researchers outside the system, product or process innovations will come to the surface which in the future could shape the organization of system, its beliefs, decisions, and communications. In this context, observing means detecting weak signals at the boundaries of the system to learn about the potential course of the corporation.

Participants/players in autopoietic systems: Living composition

As autopoietic systems cannot be accessed directly from the outside, **active participation** often becomes inevitable, guided by the insight already quoted above: "The idea of a firm as a goal-setting system based on normative models should be abandoned. We should work with empirical descriptions of how firms operate their production and reproduction." (Koskinen, 2013, 146).

Being part of autopoietic systems means being integrated into the network of beliefs, decisions, knowledge, and communication. This network is not identical to the classical hierarchical structure of the past – and is still present in many corporations in our days. The case of specifying the purpose of an institution will serve as an illustration. Consulting companies abound offering their services to develop such a "purpose" for all different kinds of firms. But as learned above, this is doomed to failure, because basic beliefs define a system's organization which is not accessible from the outside. At the same time, the organization's internal mode of operation is not set up in a top-down fashion; the purpose is the result of a multitude of interactions in the network. Or as Beer (1985, 99) paraphrases this fact: "POSIWID – The purpose of a system is what it does!" This view is not in line with mainstream business thinking and practice of our days. And it means that finding a purpose is not the result of a finely grained strategic process, but the outcome of a **game of (soft) power**. And here basic knowledge about the organization's network processes is decisive for success.

Maula (2006, 75) introduces the concept of **living composition** to characterize the network of activities determining leadership within autopoietic systems. She discusses her findings in the context of leading consulting firms (2006, 109). This concept will be one of the cornerstones of the integrated case study on the practice of strategic management to be launched in the following paragraph.

Managerial practice

The methodology and the tools presented so far will now be illustrated in their practical application by two integrated case studies which will accompany our methodology in all its steps. Their focus lies on two main areas of managerial practice, operations and strategy.

Case study: "Mobile App development in the wholesale industry"

In the realm of **operations**, the case study of a worldwide active wholesaler discusses the development of a mobile app. As the company is archetypical for the wholesale industry, it need not be introduced in detail, and because the project is still in progress, the case bears the name of "mobile app development in wholesale." The company has no global competitor – except for its own organizational complexity. The **perspective** taken is the one of a stakeholder within the business itself, with the qualities of **an observer (or coach)**, and not someone being integrated into reporting lines. The task is to standardize and harmonize the digital touchpoints (web and app) and to present the varying business models in a coherent way that allows to scale the solution and to leverage the potential of such an approach. Obviously, the direct influence is quite limited, and it needs a lot of coaching and consulting to move the system into a desired direction. The "system" consists of the country organizations responsible for profit and loss, the tech organization of the group ("corporate IT") and the corporate function which shall standardize the digital touchpoints.

The App case models an input-output-system in the sense of the left upper quadrant in Figure 2.2, characterized by a simple, transactional logic. The app is designed to support customers before, during, and after a purchase in the physical store. For instance, it contains a digital version of the customer card, which is needed before one can enter a store. This is a core feature for customers, besides other basic functionalities like promotions, offers, or coupons. Additionally, the app allows to place online orders for food delivery. The business aspects of the app, however, are more on the autopoietic side of the spectrum. Many different belief systems collide when questions about the strategic importance and direction of the app need to be answered.

To start the case of **mobile App development in wholesaling**, the application of Circular Networks is presented in line with the upper left quadrant of Figure 2.2. First, some fundamental premises need to be clarified – which is a rather autopoietic exercise. Even in relatively operational topics, one can discover many undecided issues of the organization and can learn about the autopoietic nature of the system.

A great deal of organizational confusion results from a misunderstanding of what the app shall achieve, and how the mobile application is different from the web-based touchpoints. There are people who believe that the app is just the "website in your pocket" – so to speak a mirrored version of the customer-facing website. But this interpretation leads to incoherent signals regarding the direction of the app, and thus creates frustration on the tech and the business side. To solve this problem, a simple distinction was introduced, based on Peter Drucker's famous quote (1954, 37): "The purpose of a business is to create and keep customers." By having this general idea at hand, it is easy to derive in Figure 2.9 a basic marketing and sales funnel.

With this initial insight, it was possible to strengthen the original positioning of the app and set the strategic focus for the overall purpose of the mobile application: serve **existing** customers and enrich their lives with useful functions for wholesale customers (with B2B needs).

Having this general clarification at hand, it was clear what is needed: stable customers in terms of shopping frequency and average basket size. Therefore, customer

Create Customers

Search Engines

Website

Become a
Customer

App

Keep & Grow Customers

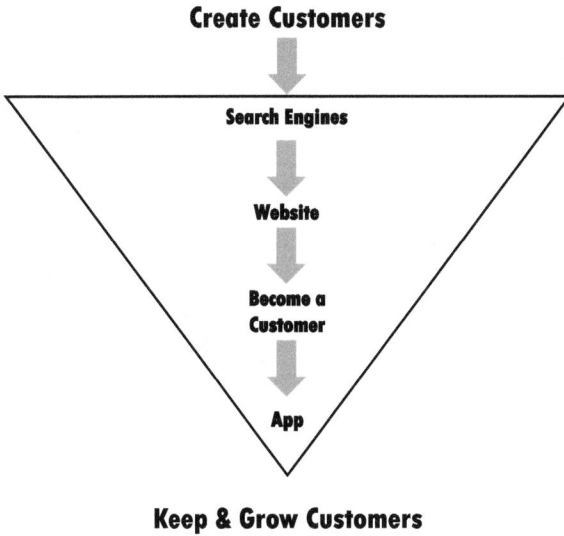

Figure 2.9: Sorting the customer touchpoints by their position in the acquisition funnel.

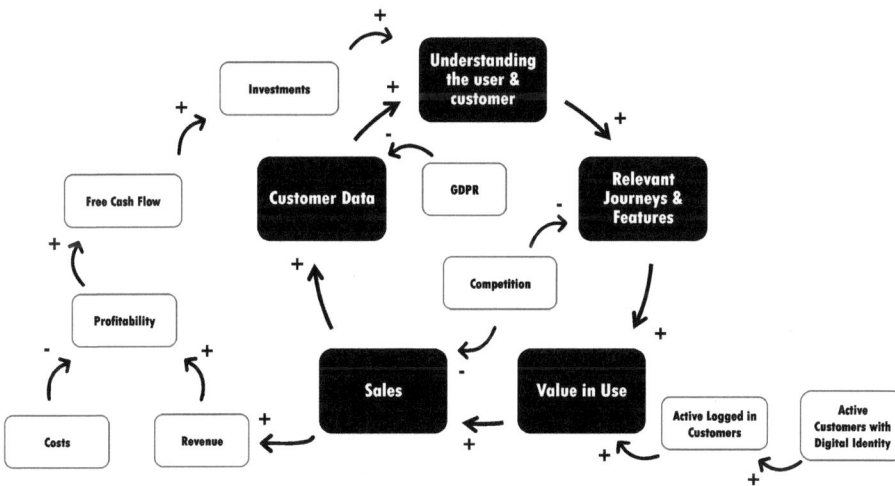

Figure 2.10: A typical success engine for a digital product such as an app.

retention is the main goal, and it will be achieved by providing Value in Use. This principle creates stickiness and pays into long-term loyalty of the customers.

In the next step of the system definition process, the network diagram in Figure 2.10 was produced to understand the "success engine" (black colored cycle) of the mobile app.

A big advantage of network diagrams is the ease and elegance of describing complexity, and reciprocity with only a few elements. Additionally, this network is totally focused on directly related aspects, but not on the big picture in terms of the wider ecosystem like technological progress or corporate purpose. Therefore, the deduction of early warning indicators in such a concise network proves to be relatively easy, as will be shown in the second step of our methodology.

Case study: "Living composition in the machinery industry"

In the realm of **strategic management**, a case study from the machinery industry will discuss topics of the positioning of a worldwide active Swiss company in general and issues arising in its business in Russia in the context of the war in Ukraine. This case study covers the lower right quadrant of Figure 2.2, where participants are challenged by enabling "living composition," the production and reproduction of an autopoietic system. It is based on extensive interviews with the Chairman of the Board of Bucher Industries, Philip Mosimann, to whom we are deeply indebted for his cooperation.

Bucher Industries (www.bucherindustries.com) started in Switzerland in 1807 as a small blacksmith's shop and has been built over several generations into a globally active technology group for machinery and professional vehicle construction. In 2022, Bucher Industries reported sales of $3.9 billion and 13,560 employees worldwide. They are publicly listed on the SIX Swiss Exchange in Zurich with a long-term oriented anchor shareholder.

The current business focus of Bucher Industries lies on agricultural machinery, municipal cleaning vehicles, hydraulic components, glass container manufacturing, and beverage processing. They have manufacturing and distribution companies in over 50 countries. The operations in Russia are mainly concentrated on agricultural machines with sales of $50 million and municipal cleaning vehicles with sales of $40 million.

To start the case study, the arguments for identifying Bucher Industries as an autopoietic system are stated. Next, the concept of "living composition," developed by Marjetta Maula (2006), is presented, and adapted to the present situation of Bucher Industries. Finally, the stage is set by defining the system and by identifying its boundaries.

Bucher Industries complies with the following group principles:

> We are a long-term oriented industrial group seeking technological and market leadership in industrialized and emerging markets worldwide. Publicly listed on the SIX Swiss Exchange, the long-term oriented anchor shareholder supports our efforts to increase the enterprise value to the benefit of all stakeholders. We remain committed to using the natural resources responsibly and being a fair group to all our business partners. Bucher Industries: Internal Memo

By implementing these basic principles, Bucher Industries meets the **criteria of an autopoietic system**: the company sustains a unique identity, experiences a strong internal support from an anchor shareholder and sustainably co-evolves with its business, societal, and natural environment. Therefore, Bucher will be explored in the following according to Koskinen's (2013, 146) advice: "The idea of a firm as a goal-setting system based on normative models should be abandoned. We should work with empirical descriptions of how firms operate their production and reproduction."

The strategic components of **an autopoietic system shaped as a living composition** are illustrated in Figure 2.11 and will be characterized for our case.

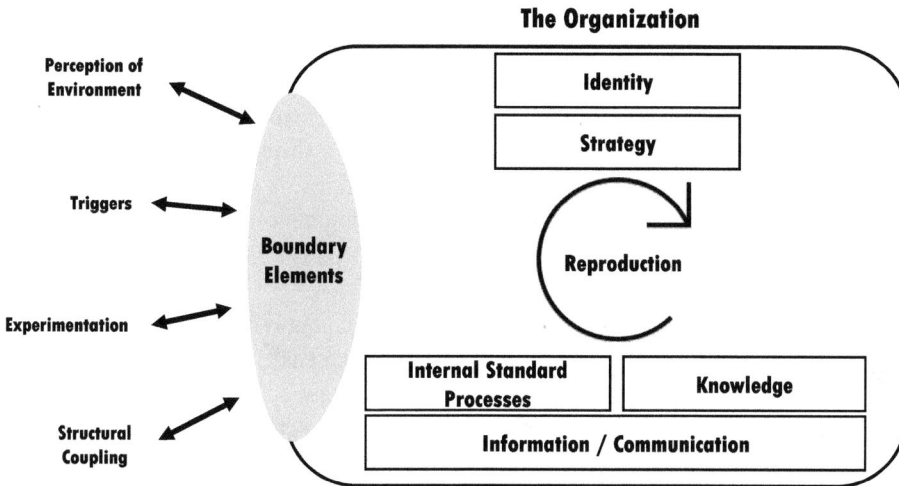

The Organization

Figure 2.11: The concept of living composition (adapted after Maula, 2006, 80).

Bucher Industries' elements of living composition are characterized as follows:
- Identity: their purpose of deploying "simply great machines" for industrialized as well as emerging markets, and to be a fair group to all business partners as well as to the environment, gives Bucher a unique identity.
- Reproduction: Bucher Industries reinvents itself by continuous improvement in everything they do. They aim for profitable organic growth, enhanced by selected acquisitions. With a decentralized management and result responsibility they operate close to their customers. Management on all levels fosters an entrepreneurial spirit and is committed to ethical principles and participative decision-making.
- Strategy: the long-term industrial orientation is based on perseverance, innovation, and operational excellence. Bucher Industries has a diversified portfolio of industrial activities in over 50 countries worldwide. They seek to achieve technology and market leadership, mainly by organic growth.
- Internal Standard Processes: on Group level, the annual Strategy Process consists of a revolving standard sequence. Financial KPIs of each business segment are reviewed and analyzed by product families, market areas, applications, life cycle status and cost structures. The monthly and quarterly Management Reporting is highly standardized worldwide, allowing timely and efficient analysis. The centralized Treasury System, where the Group acts as the inhouse bank of the divi-

sions and business units, completes the three main standardized processes. Furthermore, being close to its respective markets and customers, each Division has its own R&D processes including midterm development plans.

- Knowledge: while conserving knowhow from generation to generation, based on the value principles of decentralizing activities and responsibilities involves the employees in a sharing work environment, new knowledge is developed internally and by acquiring small and even start-up companies.
- Information/communication: in the bi-annual Group Meeting, 60 top managers from all continents get together and exchange learnings across all functions. Once per year, selected managers participate in a Group training, learning and sharing management principles and value systems of the company. A smaller group of talents participate in the Group's development training. Corporate Communication addresses financial analysts and journalists, while the divisions focus on the customers and employees.
- Perception of the environment: Bucher Industries aims at co-evolving with its business, societal, and natural environment. This process is guided by the spirit of enhancing Bucher Industries' identity, rather than by adapting to the (seemingly inevitable) forces reigning outside the enterprise. The company's highest impact to preserve the environment is granted by its products, e.g., fertilizer spreaders and plant protection sprayers using latest IoT and GPS technologies with the aim of applying precision farming, placing the lowest needed amount of fertilizer or pesticide at the right place. Another example is the "end-to-end" technology applied in the production of glass containers, increasing the "pack to melt" ratio and reducing the energy consumption of the energy intensive production process.
- Triggers: Bucher is permanently faced with disturbances from the outside world, be it high currency fluctuations, protectionist decisions of governments requesting higher than 50% local production content, nonproductive union activism, sanctions and restrictions (USA, EU, China), and excessive reporting requirements. These triggers are interpreted in terms of Bucher Industries' own identity and responded by strategic moves to surprise the competition.
- Experimentation: strategic planning provides an established framework for Bucher Industries to deal with the outside world. But small experiments which are not endangering the business and come as a surprise to the competition complement the strategy process. Before electric driving became the standard for modern municipal vehicles, the company developed a H2/fuel cell electric compact sweeper which was tested in various cities in Switzerland. This experiment surprised the competition and the customers. It paved the way for battery driven electric sweepers of today.
- Structural coupling: autopoietic systems are closed with respect to reproducing their identity, but they are open to people, material, and information. Bucher uses these channels to build up first-class logistical and information systems by regular exchanges with universities, startup clusters, research organizations, and IoT/data management experts.

This illustration of Bucher's living composition sets the stage for further elaboration and defines the system in focus. In the next step of the methodology, weak signals must be detected at the system's edge.

2.3 Step 2: "Edges": Searching the periphery for weak signals

Conceptual foundations

Once the system in focus is identified or discovered, the search for weak signals can get started. In the next three steps of the methodology, the process of **perception**, introduced in Figure 2.12, will be elaborated and illustrated.

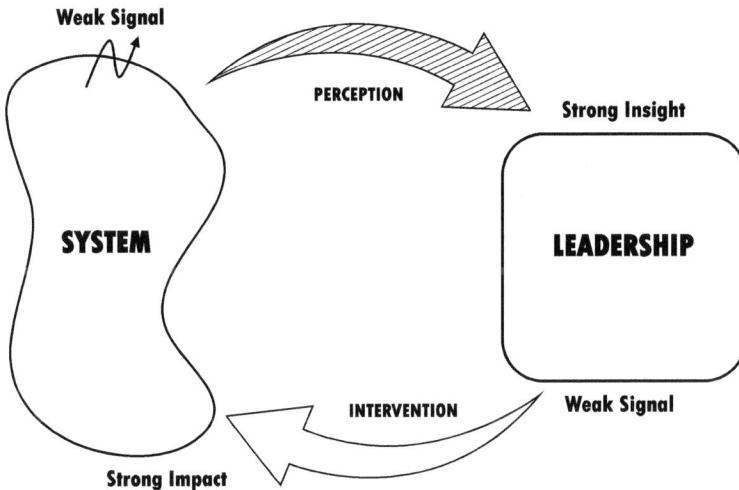

Figure 2.12: Leading by Weak Signals – The perception phase.

Why do complex systems deserve a special treatment? They are difficult to understand through our common thinking routines, as well as through classical approaches of the natural and economic sciences. Cleveland et al. provide the following insights:

> Complexity theory teaches us that systems of all types only grow and evolve when they migrate to the 'edge of chaos' – tearing apart old structures, but retaining enough coherence to take advantage of the disequilibrium and use it to innovate, to reinvent, to renew at higher levels of complexity and depth . . . A vibrant democracy is an 'edge of chaos' form of governance; a healthy market is an 'edge of chaos' form of economics; a flexible and adaptive organization or network is an 'edge of chaos' institution; and a mature, well-developed personality is an 'edge of chaos' psyche. (Cleveland et al. 2020, 14 and 19)

As argued in the first chapter, complex systems often cannot be accessed directly from the outside. The only way to learn about their functioning mode is by getting some indirect information, especially in the form of weak signals.

To guide this process, three questions arise: **where** to look for weak signals, **what** form do they take, and **how** can they be identified?

Where is the "edge of chaos" to be found? Cleveland et al. (2020, 41) identify three rules which are followed by systems in this stage:
-   Let autonomous agents follow simple rules
-   Create moderately dense connections among agents
-   Feed the fringe and nurture innovation

Systems on the edge always look like swarms, with lots of agents acting independently, but sharing few common rules. They experiment profusely with rigorous feedback to build on the most promising options. They initiate tiny shifts which have the potential for causing huge changes. These rules are followed by **Disney** and by **Google** with their organizationally decoupled innovation teams in the environment of leading Swiss universities or by the pharmaceutical company **Roche** successfully acquiring **Genentech** to enter new areas of biotech.

As a rule, the "edge of chaos" is mostly localized at the boundary of the system. In **input-output systems**, the organization is often characterized by free floating units at its borders which are deliberately designed to experiment with new forms and procedures. In **autopoietic systems**, the "edge of chaos" is normally found around the sensors at their boundary which enable the co-evolution with the environment, as will be illustrated below.

Once the place to search for information is specified, the next question arises: **what** form do weak signals take? It is vital to distinguish signals from data and to create a meaningful taxonomy which will guide us through the book. How can we make such a distinction, and is data as "independent" and "objective" as it appears to be? We argue that signals and data are always observer-dependent. Therefore, it is inevitable to emphasize the danger of forgetting the context of signal collection and data selection – and this needs to be mitigated. Without context, we could fall into the trap of trivializing the complexities of our life by looking at data as some sort of "truth."

From data to "capta"
Peter Checkland and Sue Holwell (2006) replace the term data with "capta." They differentiate between the potential amount of data points as such, and the amount of data points that we as humans are able and willing to observe and process. "Capta" is taken from the Latin word capere, which means 'to take.' This idea of the subjective nature of data is closely related to Ansoff's idea of information filtering and the surveillance filter, shown in Figure 2.13.

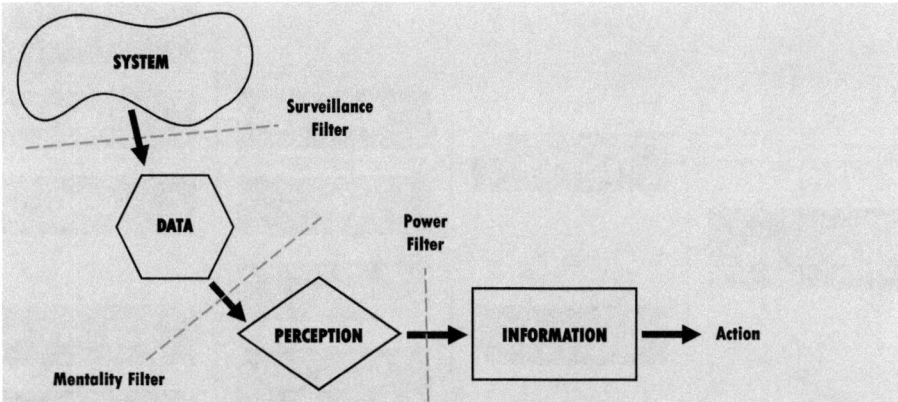

Figure 2.13: Information filtering, according to Ansoff (1984, 335).

Data are inherently coupled to their selection. Therefore, when using the term "data," "capta" should come to mind, considering the fact that data was "sensed and selected." Figure 2.14 illustrates how the cognitive structuring process can be used as a distinction criterion.

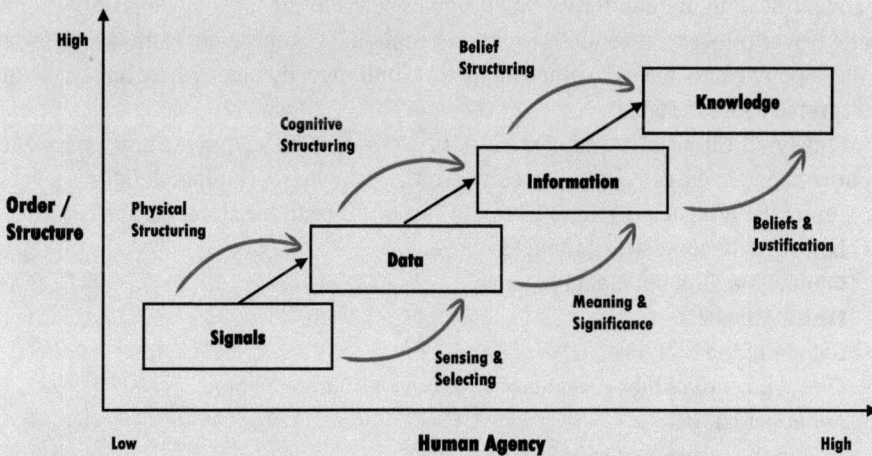

Figure 2.14: From signals to knowledge – a structuring process (Choo, 2006, 131).

Another aspect is crucial to lever the potential of weak signals: to capture qualitative weak signals like obscure stories or strange narratives is one thing, but to work with quantitative data points is another. Outliers in data sets represent special qualities of a weak signal, e.g., a peak in a periodic pattern. These anomalies generate attention about imminent change in a system. When working with quantitative data sets, one needs a "driver tree" to understand how "the numbers" are connected, as will be illustrated in section 2.4. The best-known driver tree is the DuPont diagram in Figure 2.15:

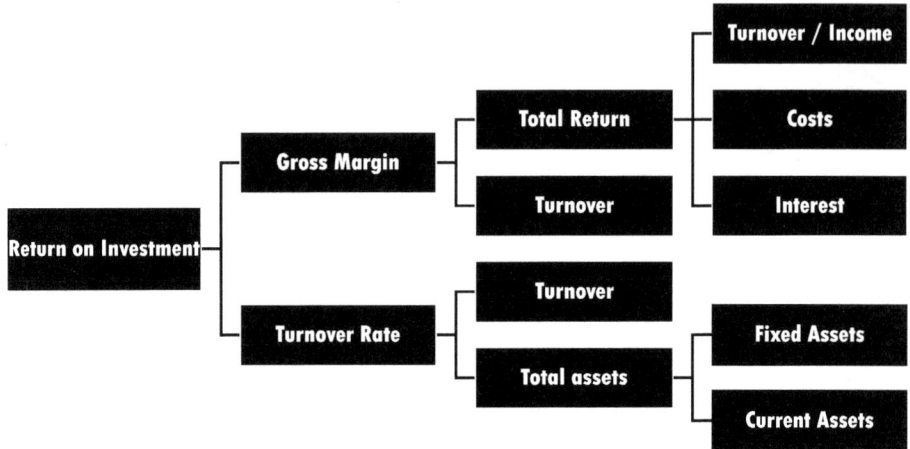

Figure 2.15: The "mother" of all driver trees – the DuPont scheme (simplified version), https://en.wikipedia.org/wiki/DuPont_analysis, accessed December 17, 2022.

The identification of quantitative weak signals starts at the most obvious entry points of the driver tree, e.g., revenues or working capital. If no imminent change is detected at these points, one moves to other indicators, until new dynamics are discovered and interpreted as weak signals.

Finally, in the managerial context, Rita McGrath (2019, 27) gives practical advice on **how** to detect weak signals. She comes to the following recommendations:
– Direct the information flows from the corner office to the street corner
– Leverage the diversity of thought
– Empower agility but create balance
– Foster little bets
– Get out of the building
– Create incentives that reveal useful, if awkward, information
– Avoid denial
– Talk to the future that is unfolding now

Methodology and tools

The identification of the system in focus and the delineation of its boundaries has prepared the ground for the search of potential weak signals. Here again the distinction between input-output systems and autopoietic systems, as well as the differentiation between observer/coach and participant/player, will guide the search process. In the case of **input-output systems,** the elements and their relationships are clearly defined. This enables the positioning of **early-warning signals** by working backwards in the circular network, following those critical loops determining the desired outcome of the system. Searching for weak signals in this kind of system means detecting indicators which reveal relevant changes even before the early-warning signals act. **Autopoietic systems** are the main territory of **weak signals**, as their organization is not accessible from the outside. Information from the edge of the system is prerequisite for changing the system's course. For participants/ players, weak signals are also of importance, as the internal reproduction process often changes in an unpredictable way.

In the introductory theoretical part, the questions of why, what, where, and how were addressed when dealing with weak signals. The focus so far was on the why and the what, in the following the **where** – the process of **scoping** – and the **how** – the process of **scanning** – will now be presented in more detail.

The **scoping process** to specify early-warning indicators and discover weak signals is guided by concepts and tools shown in Figure 2.16.

	Observer/Coach	Participant/Player
Input-Output System	Defining early-warning indicators **High Reliability Organizations**	Exploring time-delays in circular networks **Dynamics of Circular Networks**
Autopoietic System	Structural coupling at the edges of the system **Swarm Intelligence**	Monitoring co-evolution and reproduction **Living Composition**

Figure 2.16: Scoping for weak signals: Concepts and tools.

Observers/coaches facing input-output systems: High Reliability Organizations

The circular network of internal driving forces developed in Step 1 defines the "arena" for the search of early-warning indicators. Here the concept of "High Reliability Organizations," developed by Weick and Sutcliffe as a guide for specifying warning signals in an input-output setting, comes into play.

> Managing the unexpected is an ongoing effort to define and monitor weak signals . . . managing is an active process that is spread over time as the signals and situations change . . . "High Reliability Organizations" are characterized by following five basic principles: Preoccupation with failure, reluctance to simplify, sensitivity to operations, commitment to resilience, deference to expertise. (Weick and Sutcliffe 2015, 3 and 7)

Preoccupation with failure directs attention to symptoms of malfunction, small errors that could spread or a gradual shift of complacency. Reluctance to simplify means, paraphrasing Einstein, to see things as simple as possible, but not too simple. This presupposes the creation of nuanced pictures of the system at hand, as illustrated above by circular networks. Sensitivity to operations is secured by familiarity with the "machine room" of the corporation; strategic management without traction in operations proves to be futile. Commitment to resilience characterizes the capability to recover after a major mishap, by distinguishing different modes of operation: normal, up-tempo, and crisis. Deference to expertise finally means pushing decision-making down to the front line and migrating people with the most expertise. Weick and Sutcliffe are not intending to present a checklist for identifying weak signals or – as they call them – early-warning indicators, they rather encourage collective sensemaking: "Mindfulness preserves the capability to see the significance of weak signals and to respond vigorously" (2015, 17). As a side note, mindfulness can be abused in many ways, therefore it is necessary to add the aspect of situational awareness to fully grasp the idea. The capability to detect weak signals should not be reduced to superficial babble but be understood as a very serious state of perceiving "what is happening around us."

Designing the circular network of High Reliability Organizations (HRO)
The following list of questions is designed to incorporate the deciding aspects for HROs, even though it is not of prescriptive nature.
- Which failures would be lethal or severely damaging for the system, and which nodes represent these failures in the network? Working **backward** the circles connecting to these nodes, where should attention be given to symptoms or small errors acting as weak signals?
- Is the circular network "as simple as possible, but not too simple," does it provide a nuanced picture of the system's driving forces?
- Are the driving forces of operations represented adequately in the network? Where should weak signals be placed to provide sensitivity?
- Does the network contain circles handling a potential crisis, and which are weak signals to activate this mode?
- Does the network reflect special expertise, and how is it related to early signals?

Participant/player in input-output systems: Time-delays in circular networks
Discovering **early-warning indicators in circular networks** requires working backwards the circles which end up in performance indicators. Prerequisite is knowledge about the **time-delays** implicit to singular circles. This process is illustrated in Figure 2.17 by a circular network from the information-processing industry:

To be ahead of the competition, the corporation was looking for early-warning signals indicating a business downturn. Sales and profits were designated as classical performance indicators. There was information at hand about the time-delays in the circular relationships. Three elements were identified to be potential early-warning signals: demand for specialties, image with customers, and image with employees. The corporation had set up a sophisticated inquiry system about customer and employee satisfaction. But it turned out to be too slow to serve the purpose, with a time-delay of up to two years to indicate substantial changes. The corporation then focused on their sales of specialty parts and their impact on overall sales. They found out that a drop in specialty sales predicted – nine months in advance – a drop in overall sales. To the sur-

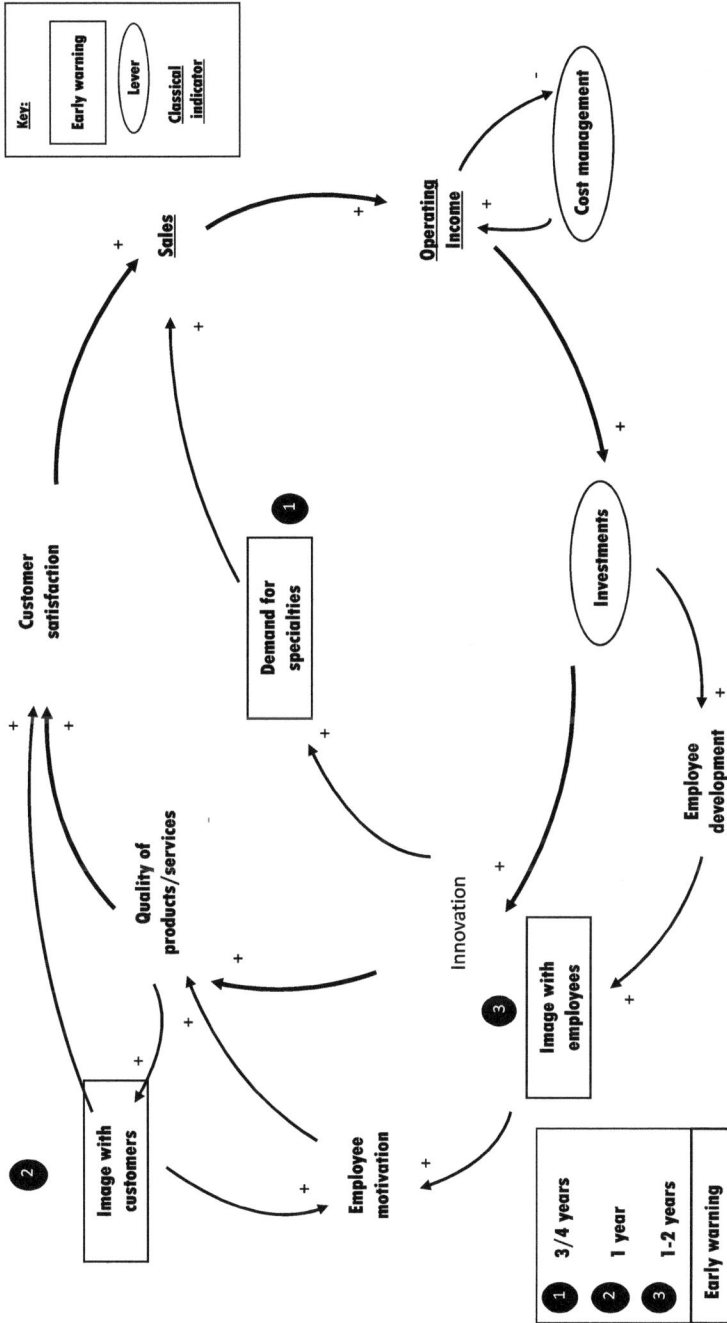

Figure 2.17: Time-delays in circular networks (Gomez, Lambertz, and Meynhardt 2019, 150).

prise of the industry, which were not aware of this early-warning signal, they stopped hiring personnel and releasing investments to avoid a loss. Specifying early-warning signals of this kind is only possible in input-output systems where elements and relationships are known and relatively stable over time, which is not the case in autopoietic systems.

Observers/coaches facing autopoietic systems: Swarm intelligence

As illustrated above, autopoietic systems on the edge of chaos are characterized by swarms of agents at their boundaries, acting independently but sharing few common rules. They experiment profusely with rigorous feedback to build on the most promising options. They trigger tiny shifts which have the potential for causing huge internal changes. How can this knowledge be used by observers/coaches to get access to the system? Here the concepts of **swarm intelligence** and **structural coupling** come into play. Autopoietic systems are closed to beliefs, decision-making, communication, and knowledge. But they are open to people, information, energy, and material. They use these elements for structural coupling with the environment, by establishing sensors at their boundaries to enable co-evolution. But these sensors can also be used as an entry portal for observers or coaches, which may detect weak signals of upcoming changes. An example from the automotive industry may illustrate this logic. Corporations in this industry are anxious to protect their business secrets and patents. But a total foreclosure would be lethal, as basic changes in the environment could not be matched by co-evolution. To be part of the electrification mainstream, these corporations establish swarms of autonomous, loosely coupled innovative agents and teams at their boundaries ("their edge of chaos") to contribute to and profit from these developments. Digital innovations or new forms of automation might provoke internal impulses to challenge basic beliefs. The car is no longer seen as a technical masterpiece, but as a lifestyle product to please digital forerunners. This could lead to a change in the CEO position from one with a technical background to one with special marketing skills in a digital world. This means a tiny shift at the edge has led to a basic change in the internal reproduction process of the system. For observers or coaches, a unique opportunity to access the system arises when their weak signals are placed in the right environment of the innovative swarm activities.

How to "manage" a swarm

In their book *The Wisdom of the Many*, Fladerer and Kurzmann (2019) illustrate the organization of heterarchical systems where there is neither superiority nor inferiority among the individual members. These properties make them special, compared to hierarchical systems, which are often illustrated with the famous top-down-organizational chart.

The swarm has no leader, the **relevant information** fulfills this role. If such information is available to a selected small number – in business at least five of 100 employees of a small to mid-size company – self-organization gets initiated. The authors illustrate this process with pedestrians, which set a whole crowd in motion when crossing a street at the red light. The relevant information could be knowledge about surveillance cameras or about drivers being used to people crossing at the red light. In nature, a flock of birds is organized by a simple "rule," the constant distance from one bird to another.

But what are the mechanisms that trigger relevant information in business? Such information can be of widespread origin, but nobody knows in advance whether it will become relevant one day. People typically communicate via pictograms, which compress information and thereby enhance relevance. Mastering such pictograms could be the key to shaping swarms. But here again, autopoiesis comes into play, the process of self-reproduction determines information relevance – and also the "simple rules" of swarm intelligence at the edge of chaos referred to above.

One potential way to foster relevance is to use the Power Law of "Contagion Theory" to be discussed in the next step of the methodology. It allows to understand that a group of people can be influenced by memes. Consultants often use this "propaganda" tactic to stimulate discussions within client organizations – and challenge existing paradigms and language patterns, as will be shown in step 3.

Participant/players in autopoietic systems: Living Composition

Cleveland et al. propose the following questions to initiate the process to discover weak signals at the "edge of chaos":
- How close to the edge is the system currently?
- What forces are pushing towards order? Towards chaos?
- What would "reshaping at a higher level of fitness with its environment" mean for the system?
- Who has how much autonomy in the system?
- Who might be loosed to be autonomous?

(Cleveland et al., 2020, 46)

The answers are fundamental for leadership in autopoietic systems. They help specify weak signals which draw the attention to imminent change at the earliest possible stage. Marjatta Maula (2006, 77) describes this identification process by pointing to 10 strategic components of a living composition, four of which are illustrated by the example of Ernst and Young (Maula 2006, 156):
- Identity: our purpose is to create value for clients by pursuing thought leadership and developing new ideas, methodologies, and solutions.
- Boundary elements: capture tacit knowledge from the interaction with clients by documenting it. Pack and store knowledge into power packs and global-knowledge bases. Trace knowledge by using knowledge navigation tools.
- Triggers: global center monitoring trends, web scans round the clock, external databases.
- Experimentation: specialized units, success stories, facilitated by "productive chaos."

Internal weak signals are tailored by these components to enhance an effective process of reproduction.

After finding the right scope, the **process of scanning** must be initiated and optimized. This process is equally suited for all four areas discussed above. In the following, three promising scanning approaches are presented in due brevity:
– Vigilance
– CIPHER
– Peripheral Vision

George Day and Paul Schoemaker (2019, 12) characterize their **Vigilance** approach as follows: "Vigilance means sensing, probing, and interpreting weak signals from both inside and outside the organization." The problem is not the lack of data, but the lack of good questions. And when faced with weak signals, one must not jump to conclusions, but generate multiple hypotheses. For Day and Schoemaker (2019, 95), there are five robust ways to separate signals from noise: canvass the wisdom of the crowd, leverage the extended network, apply successive filters, explore diverse angles, and catch smoldering crises. In Appendix A of their book (Day and Schoemaker, 2019, 186) they offer a diagnostic tool which allows to explore the state of vigilance in a very detailed way.

Amy Webb (2016, 150) proposes the **CIPHER** concept to detect weak signals: Contradictions, inflections, practices, hacks, extremes, rarities. She illustrates these points with the following examples (Webb 2016, 151): contradictions appear when a node in an organization becomes connected to another one while this connection had been shunned away or prohibited in the past. Inflections are the signal of a great acceleration in emerging research. Practices change when a new technology threatens the established orthodoxy. Hacks are the result of frustrating experiences with new media that lead to smarter, more intuitive products. Extremes are biohackers who are using themselves as test subjects to reach new frontiers. Rarities are social movements so unusual and unique that they seem meaningless but solve fundamental needs.

In their book *Peripheral Vision*, George Day and Paul Schoemaker take vision as a metaphor for organization. For treating poor peripheral vision, they give the following advice:
– Transplanting good retinal cells from donors (hiring individual employees or consultants to offer new insights)
– Transplanting whole new eyes (bringing in a new CEO or initiating a substantial restructuring to change perspectives)
– Using stem cells to encourage growth of ocular tissue (creating internal educational programs and initiatives to build broader perspectives in the existing organization)
– Using electronic or artificial aids (using technology to augment, amplify, and organize information from the environment to challenge existing perspectives)

Day and Schoemaker (2006, 171)

Managerial practice

Case study: "Mobile App development in the wholesale industry"

To continue the case of the wholesale industry, the process of weak signal detection is illustrated in the context of developing and implementing an app strategy. This topic must get adequate attention considering which impact on revenues such a digital touchpoint has – especially in a typical "brick and mortar" business like Cash and Carry. Its global revenue can be compared to the turnover of a medium country of the group (middle nine-digit numbers in Euros). The discovery of weak signals started with the selection of the participants – in this case exactly two. It may sound surprising, but two well experienced persons were enough to cope with the guiding questions since these persons brought a lot of situational awareness into the game. The definition of Amy Webb was provided upfront to give the "carriers of knowledge" the chance to show up prepared for the face-to-face session. The scope of the territory to be explored was not limited to the app and the wholesale industry as such, but it was kept as open as possible to widen the field of view. One could claim that we tried to enhance our ability of peripheral vision as much as possible.

Their procedure was very simple: preparing ideas on sticky notes, presentation and initial clustering, deep dive, fine tuning. The weak signals were clustered into three areas:

The signal of the **unexpected trust in the brand** of the firm was the most remarkable. This signal was based on the sheer amount of people who are giving a tracking permission when logging into the app (on a global scale more than 70%). This indicates that a lot of people trust the brand and understand the benefits of personalized offers and vouchers. That insight was confirmed later by a brand study. Therefore, these kinds of signals provide a lot of opportunities to interact with those customers in a personalized way. One could even say: these B2B customers expect to be treated individually! It is not a bug, but a feature that should be exploited! During the process this signal was selected as the most important one, because it "felt" like it contains the highest variety of potential gains in the future.

Besides this signal, the two others appeared to be too fuzzy to be exploited. For the sake of completeness, we want to share them with the readers to provide more concrete ideas on what weak signals look like.

- A **new alliance of companies** which have not been perceived as competitors so far: a food delivery service which cooperates with a meal delivery service. Such an alliance could be optimized for small order volumes – the exact opposite of what the wholesale company focused on "getting the truck full." The potential benefits for hotels, restaurants, and caterers are evident: you need less suppliers to get your resources into the kitchen and deliver the prepared dishes to the customers. Furthermore, they need less storage space – and it would probably reduce the number of wasted resources (especially when dealing with ultra-fresh food assortment like fish).

– Technological progress that would allow to convert IT solutions into a holistic customer experience like never before: one of the obvious ideas would be a personalized AI chat bot, which could compliment certain services usually done by humans – to free up capacity of the sales force for interesting interactions like presenting samples of the own brand assortment, e.g., a wine tasting. B2B customers expect service excellence, this is not about cost saving, but rather augmenting the interactions and letting the customer decide which kind of contact experience she or he prefers.

As mentioned before the two latter signals were dropped, since they were too big to be tackled – but the trust in the brand is valuable, because that is something that the company can control (more or less).

In the next step, it was crucial to connect existing data points with discovered weak signals. To which extent is it possible to relate the rather fuzzy topic of weak signals with the operational reality? The app already existed for three years with certain open questions as the "pink elephant in the room." Everybody knows about the need to create transparency and clarify open points – and on the other hand everyone is too busy with daily operations. Dancing with the complex tides of unplanned work and "changing the engines while flying" absorbs the available capacity, which is needed to anticipate the future. Therefore, these kinds of topics were collected and sorted out according to the Three Horizon Model (which will be presented in section 2.4). This approach was very helpful to set the focus on urgent matters and map the topics to the overall strategy of the company. Furthermore, this procedure clarified questions of the following type: what about the integration of three different business models – one app for all or one app per business model? How important is it to replace the physical card with the digital version in the app? Which of the three business models has priority?

App strategy development is still underway, but the idea of referring to weak signals brought new dynamics into an otherwise very traditional way of strategizing.

Situational Awareness and Cognitive Biases

There is no better model to understand the nature of situational awareness than John Boyd's OODA loop shown in Figure 2.18.

To grasp the general idea requires going back to the Korean war. John Boyd was studying the fact that a significant amount of US jets was returning to the home base, while many North Korean fighter jets were shot down. Relying on practical experience, he was able to derive a universal pattern by linking the ability to perceive operational reality with a solid way to gain control over a combat situation. This led him to the OODA loop: the more you can observe (with the widefield cupola of US jets), the easier it is to orient yourself in space and time, to decide, and finally to act. In a classical "dog fight"

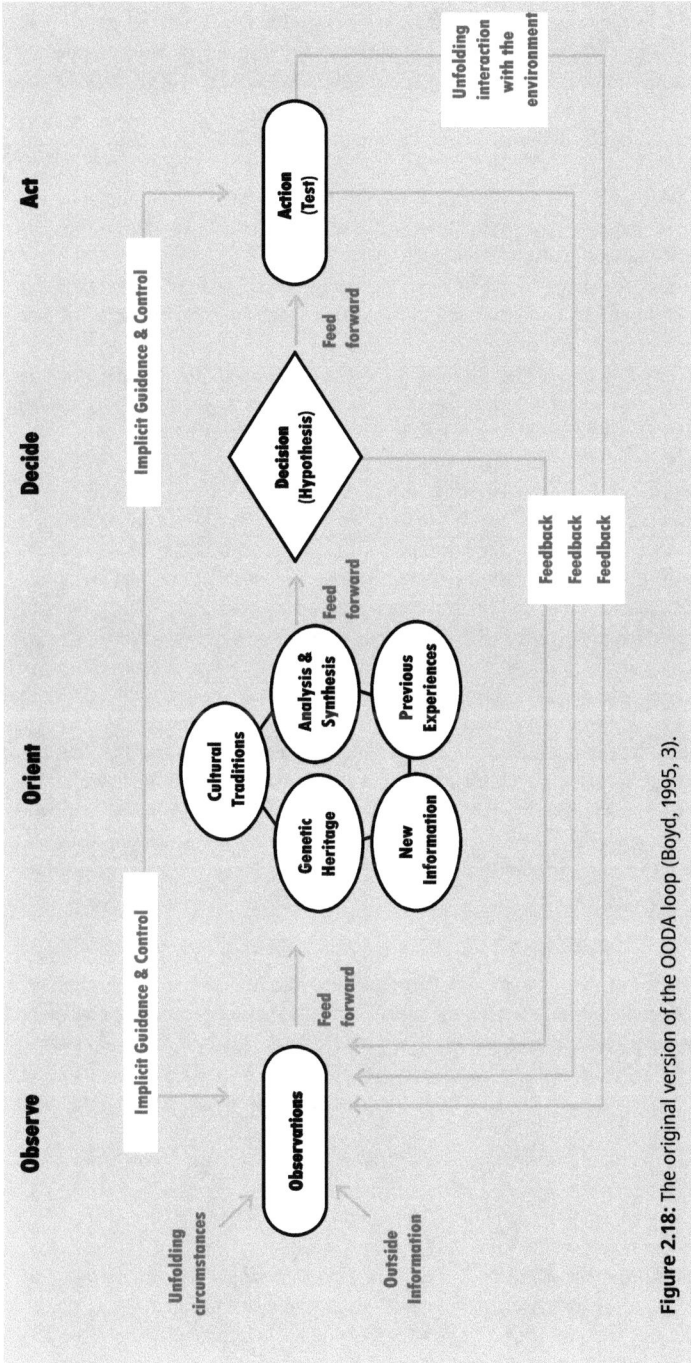

Figure 2.18: The original version of the OODA loop (Boyd, 1995, 3).

this means to be behind the enemy and pull the trigger earlier than the opponent. The overall message is simple: create a situation which distracts or consumes the cognitive energy of your opponent and never let them come to a point where they can decide. Be faster in your own OODA loop and break the OODA loop of your competitor.

In particular, the **"orient" phase** of the loop contains important hints about detecting or missing weak signals:

- Cultural traditions, which mirror socially accepted ways of thinking, often based on morale and "good behavior." It can be as simple as a different cultural understanding of colors, signs, and symbols (e.g., the color white can mean "mourning" in China).
- Analysis and synthesis are related to cognitive abilities and the capability of critical thinking, which is especially important when putting the puzzle pieces together. Although an assembled picture might look plausible, it still can be total nonsense.
- Previous experiences can be tricky when evaluating a new situation and are a strong driver for cognitive biases. While well thought-through heuristics can be of enormous value to understand unknown territory, unreflected experience can lead to the neglection of new information.
- New information may create the possibility to strengthen the "difference that makes a difference" and to structure contexts and to create hierarchies of meaning.
- Genetic heritage describes the fact that our DNA determines, up to a certain level, our capability to understand and use observations during the orient phase. This aspect might sound very biological – but it is indeed meant this way. For sure, the research about the impact of our genome on our mental possibilities is quite dynamic and the estimated percentages differ a lot. Still, it cannot be ignored that the distribution of the results of a typical IQ test look like a Gaussian bell curve.

The importance of the loop cannot be underestimated, as the following quote from General Maxwell Taylor on the Vietnam war states:

> First, we didn't know ourselves. We thought we were going into another Korean War, but this was a different country. Secondly, we didn't understand our Vietnamese allies. We never understood them, and that was another surprise. And we knew even less about North Vietnam. Who was Ho Chi Minh? Nobody really knew. So, until we know the enemy and know our allies and know ourselves, we'd better keep out of this dirty kind of business. It is very dangerous. (Karnow 1984)

This leads us directly to the next topic: why do we miss to observe weak signals with our mental apparatus? Why are weak signals always easy to explain retrospectively? This is all due to cognitive biases. Top managers and executives barely reflect on these biases and how they influence decision-making processes, let alone how these filters affect their ability to perceive weak signals. A very good starting point is the Cognitive Bias Codex (https://en.wikipedia.org/wiki/Cognitive_bias, accessed July 8, 2022), as it provides a hands-on categorization of the different types of biases. It shows how we are fooling ourselves:

- How do we remember events correctly? Memorizing "facts" is an active construction process and not just "accessing a hard drive."
- How are we easily overwhelmed by too much information? Because our working memory can process only two to four objects at the same time.
- How do we deal with situations which do not provide enough meaning? By adding meaning, which seems to be the human (or evolutionary?) need to closed contexts operationally.
- How does time pressure create the urgency to act fast? By filtering information and focusing only on certain parts of the situation, and therefore missing important aspects.

All these aspects need to be reflected on before one starts to collect weak signals – it is truly a meta-cognition exercise. Finally, another quality should be present to be able to harvest weak signals out of all the surrounding noise. Traditional managers have the tendency to disregard the power of imagining potential futures. This capability is only accepted when a vision ought to be developed. Otherwise "visionary" people are seen as outliers – far away from the social median. However, this capability is very important to connect the dots and think the "unthinkable," e.g., create extreme scenarios in your mind, by combining different signals. A simple trick is to use the Walt Disney method to stimulate the creativity. Basically, you want to change perspectives regarding a certain problem or question, and by this enrich the idea space to come up with a better (more creative) solution. In this methodology, you look at the given context from the perspective of . . .
 – The dreamer: What would be possible if there are no limits?
 – The critique: Which impediments or problems exist?
 – The realist: Who integrates the dreamer and critique to a solution?

Case study: "Living composition in the machinery industry"

In Figure 2.11, the boundary elements – the sensors towards the environment – of Bucher Industries, as an autopoietic system from the perspective of a participant, were identified:
 – Perception of the environment
 – Triggers
 – Experimentation
 – Structural coupling

But in the special case of a player in a closed system, the other components must also be investigated as sources for weak signals:
 – Identity
 – Reproduction
 – Strategy
 – Operations (standard processes, knowledge, information)

These components of living composition are loosely interconnected, which allows a better access to weak signals, as the following pairings show:

 – Perception of the environment and strategy
Scanning the environment for opportunities and threats is the main task of strategic management. But in the case of autopoiesis, its options are limited, because the co-evolution with the environment serves the purpose to the system's identity. Therefore, weak signals must be placed at the boundary of the system as well as at the re-production process of the identity. The following questions must be answered in this context: which weak signal indicates environmental change that might influence our

identity? Which weak signal of change in our identity might cause a different strategic approach to co-evolve with the environment?

In the beverage packing industry, PET bottles were gaining market share due to its light weight, easy logistics, and consumer handling. News of plastic waste in the oceans, rivers, and beaches changed consumer behavior helping the glass container revival. Later, the focus on CO2 emissions made the context more complex as single use glass containers have a higher CO2 footprint than PET containers, but multi-use glass containers have the lowest CO2 footprint. Today, plastic pollution and CO2 footprint of beverage containers are strong signals; years ago they started as weak signals. Bucher reacts on these trends, seeing as an opportunity by promoting the "end to end" strategy.

– Structural coupling and operations

To get access to technological advances in logistics, informatics, and manufacturing, structural coupling with relevant providers must be established to acquire the necessary know how and procedures. Here the following questions are important: where to position weak signals to detect opportunities to acquire state-of-the art technology, and how to make sure that weak signals indicate early enough when we fall behind technologically? The H2/fuel cell sweeper development followed the very early weak signal of electrification. Partnerships with H2 producers, fuel cell manufacturers, and technical universities provided access to latest state of the art technologies and allowed Bucher to act as vehicle integrator. This concept was unique in the industry.

– Triggers/experimentation and identity/reproduction

The reproduction of identity requires an adequate perception of disturbances from the outside and experimentation with measures to cope with them. Here the following questions arise: which weak signals distinguish relevant disturbances from the obsolete, and which weak signals measure the proficiency of the experimentation process? The interpretation of weak signals relevance can only be achieved by experimenting in the market, which finally leads to an entrepreneurial judgement. Risk taking is an attitude for Bucher, it reflects the spirit of aiming for technological leadership. The H2/fuel cell project finally led to battery driven, electrical vehicles where today the company holds the leading market position in Europe. For the H2/fuel cell concept, the public infrastructure is not ready yet and will take some more years for the breakthrough.

2.4 Step 3: "Patterns": Detecting regularities and power laws

Conceptual foundations

Weak signals are signs of fundamental change in the system under observation. This change is not easily detectable in managerial practice, due to the system's complicatedness or complexity. Searching for patterns behind the change will provide new insights, as Peter Drucker (1980, 2) states: "Turbulence, by definition, is irregular, non-linear, erratic. But its underlying causes can be analyzed, predicted, managed." Patterns are regularities driving the evolution of a system, shaped by universal laws of nature, and empirically validated causal relationships. They are often called "power laws."

To get deeper insights into the process of pattern recognition, three questions must be answered:

- Which type of "power laws" might be the causing the patterns behind weak signals?
- Do these patterns reflect a dynamic development – in the form of a prototypic/universal curve?
- How are specific "power laws" attributed to weak signals? Is it possible to derive a causal relationship?

We call this process **"exploring the curve,"** and the logic behind it is illustrated by the case of a pharmaceutical company in Figure 2.19.

PHARMACEUTICAL COMPANY

POWER LAW	PATTERN	WEAK SIGNAL

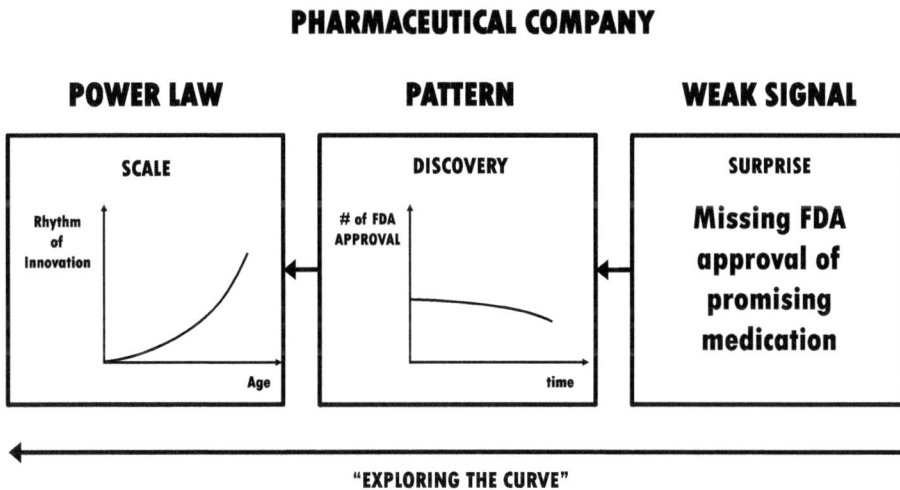

Figure 2.19: "Exploring the curve" – an example from the pharmaceutical industry.

The company was taken by surprise when the US Food and Drug Administration FDA rejected approval of a promising new medication. During the research process of more than a decade, the management was convinced it would be a successful outcome, therefore the disappointment was big. But after an in-depth analysis, they judged this unfortunate threat as an opportunity, announced by this "weak signal." They investigated their history with the FDA and found out that in the last decade that not only was their number of applications on a slowdown, but also the approval-rates had decreased. This pattern made them search for the optimal evolutionary curve for pharmaceutical products.

First, they did a competitive analysis with their peers, but due to main differences in their research processes they didn't make much progress. Then they came up with the idea to search for universal regularities or "power laws" which govern such processes. They discovered the universal law of "Scale" which postulates that to sustain continuous growth, the time between successive innovations must get shorter and shorter (West 2017, 379). They redesigned their processes along the lines of this power law, and they started to "ride this curve," as will be shown in the next step of our methodology.

What is new about this approach? Instead of asking how business genes could be changed or how to differentiate to become a better competitor, the focus shifts to steering the growth path of a business when scale is becoming critical or when the innovative rhythm is too slow for an aging company. But answering such questions requires in-depth knowledge of power laws, of their logic, and of their fit to specific situations.

The **distinction between complicated and complex systems** is again of importance in the process of selecting "power laws," as is shown in Figure 2.20.

	Universal Natural Laws	Empirical Business Laws
Complicated Systems	Laws of motion, gravity, heredity, and survival by differentiation	High reliability organizations, Predictable surprises, Normal accidents
Complex Systems	Laws of Growth, Scaling, Critical transitions, Punctuated equilibrium	Power curve of economic profit

Figure 2.20: Exemplary classification of power laws.

Power laws for complicated systems

A variety of universal laws are related to complicated settings in nature, such as Newton's laws of motion and gravity, Mendel's laws of heredity or Gause's Law of survival by differentiation (see Koch 2020). In the business context, complicated situations are present mainly on the operational level. Using universal laws of nature for these kinds of problem situations can provide insights not available in the business logic. However, relying solely on analogy can also pose a potential danger, as the context differs considerably. And often, the results of such a process prove to be quite trivial. Therefore, when dealing with complicated business situations, "power laws" developed based on sound empirical research or derived from narrative approaches provide much better results:

– High reliability organizations
– Predictable surprises
– Normal accidents

The concept of **"high reliability organizations"** (Weick and Sutcliffe 2015) was introduced and illustrated in section 2.3, *Methods and Tools* in the context of identifying early-warning indicators of Input-Output Systems. Behind these indicators, relevant patterns of behavior in five areas are readily available and illustrated by a rich set of examples: preoccupation with failure, reluctance to simplify, sensitivity to operations, commitment to resilience, and deference to expertise. Are these standards fulfilled, could they even be improved, and which measures could be taken in case of failure?

The concept of **"predictable surprises"** (Bazerman and Watkins 2004) deals with developments that cause surprise, despite prior awareness of all the information necessary to anticipate these events. The authors distinguish cognitive roots (biases), organizational roots (institutional failure), and political roots (special-interest groups). And they suggest three ways of prevention: recognition, prioritization, mobilization.

The concept of **"normal accidents"** (Perrow, 1984) deals with the relationship of a system's complicatedness and the structural coupling of its parts. If complicatedness increases and the coupling of the parts becomes tighter, the danger of disasters rises. The author's advice: higher complicatedness must be coped with more autonomy and loose coupling of the parts – intelligence must be distributed over the system!

Power laws for complex systems

"Power laws" that shape a complex situation provide invaluable insights to understand its evolutionary dynamics. A set of power laws relevant for managerial practice will now be discussed in detail, and their application will be illustrated. But first – to gain an intuitive preunderstanding – the function of power laws in the process of pattern recognition and interpreting weak signals must be illustrated. Therefore, two power laws which have proven their effectiveness in managerial practice will serve as an example: the universal natural law of **"Scaling"** and the empirically validated **"Power curve of economic profit"**:

> **Scaling** simply refers, . . ., to how a system responds when its size changes. What happens to a city or a company if its size is doubled? Or to a building, an airplane, an economy, or an animal if its size is halved? . . . Scaling arguments have led to a deep understanding of the dynamics of tipping points and phase transitions (. . .), chaotic phenomena (. . .), the discovery of quarks (. . .), the unification of the fundamental forces of nature, and the evolution of the universe after the Big Bang. (West 2017, 15)

Understanding the laws of scaling helps to design the structures of increasingly large and complex social systems. And with respect to weak signals, it not only allows detecting a critical change in the size of a system, but also how this change might lead to new organizational constellations or a breakdown of the system.

The **"power curve of economic profit"** is the result of an extensive empirical study of 2,500 worldwide leading companies over a time span of 15 years (Bradley, Hirt, and Smit 2018). The authors show how successful companies created value by optimizing ten basic variables or levers (size, debt, research, industry trends, geographic trends, acquisitions, resources allocation, capital investment, productivity, differentiation). The companies are positioned in five zones of corporate success ("quantiles"). The law assigns probabilities of success for companies to move from one quantile to the next by optimizing a certain combination of variables. These empirical results are not to be considered equal to universal natural laws, but are the result of sound socio-economic research and, therefore, well-founded heuristics. With respect to finding "leading indicators," these business laws give indications of change in the composition of variables as well as change in the size of singular variables. And they also advise how to correct the composition at the earliest possible moment to avoid backdrops or to boost value.

The following table in Figure 2.21 shows a combined application of the power curve of economic profit and the laws of scaling to a managerial context. First, the main levers in the process of changing the business must be identified. The power curve of economic profit distinguishes ten such levers or variables, whose objectives must be defined in line with empirical findings. For **"size,"** the objective is "the bigger, the better." To corroborate this insight, the universal natural law of scaling is applied with respect to the size of the company. Here the basic principle states that economies of scale are more important than returns or innovations. The objective would be to sustain steady but slow exponential growth.

To facilitate the tracking of the entries in Figure 2.21, the basic findings of the two power laws are summarized in the following:

Bradley, Hirt, and Smit present the following empirical findings of the "**power curve of economic profit**":

1. Size of the corporation: The bigger, the better
2. Debt-to-Equity ratio: Top 40 of your industry
3. R&D to sales: Top 40 of your industry
4. Industry growth 10 years: Minimum one quantile
5. Geographic trend GDP: World-wide countries top 40
6. Acquisitions 10 years: Market capitalization >30%
7. Resource re-allocation: >50% in 10 years
8. Capital expenditure to sales: Top 20 of your industry
9. Productivity increase: Top 30 of your industry
10. Growth margin: Top 30 of your industry

(Bradley, Hirt, and Smit 2018, 99)

The basic principles of the **universal natural law of "scaling,"** applied to business on an empirical basis, can be summarized as follows:

- Companies are scaled self-similar versions of one another, they scale following simple power laws.
- Economies of scale are more important than increasing returns or innovation.
- If metabolism (sales) and maintenance (expenses) both develop in a linear fashion, this leads to exponential growth.

- To sustain continuous growth, the time between successive innovations has to get shorter and shorter.
- Surviving companies settle down to a steady but slow exponential growth.
- Companies become vulnerable if they are unable to keep up with the growth of the market.
- Only about half of companies survive for more than ten years.
- The risk of a company dying does not depend on its age or size.

(West, 2017, 379)

Methodology and tools

This illustration of applying power laws in a business context prepared the foundation for the introduction of the set of laws predestined to support the process of Leading by Weak Signals. The starting point of our presentation is a word of caution. This section appears to be – at first sight – very technical. Therefore, instead of diving directly into the details of the individual charts and curves and maybe getting lost, a metaphor might shed some light on the idea behind this approach: look at this collection of power laws – in a playful way – as a deck of cards. There are 34 cards in the deck, each depicting a fully elaborated power law. In the process of allocating power laws to weak signals, one selects first the card which appears to be the best fit. As this is only a first educated guess, it could fail, and another card must be drawn. As it would be quite tiring to learn all the details of the power law cards in advance, a playful approach proves to be preferable, especially if you want to use this deck of cards with a group of people. Various ideas about implementing the deck of cards will be explained in this chapter, as well as advice on where to download free formats of the cards.

The set of power laws (our "deck of cards") predestined for Leading by Weak Signals falls into the following categories:

Generic Curve Shapes – a family of dynamic patterns which are well known in mathematics, e.g., the exponential curve.

Universal Natural Laws – which explain scaling and other phenomena omnipresent in the cosmos, independent of being micro or macro structures.

Cybernetic Laws – basic structures of control and self-regulation to enhance viability in all kinds of systems.

Empirical Business Laws – heuristics based on empirical research on businesses developing over time.

Technology Laws – basic knowledge on how technologies emerge and how they diffuse in societies.

Each law will be presented according to the following logic: name, visualization, discovery, application, description.

ECONOMIC POWER CURVE (Bradley et al)	2400 firms over 15 years	SCALE POWER LAWS (Geoffrey West)	Universal laws of scaling
MAIN LEVERS	**OBJECTIVES**	**BASIC PRINCIPLES**	**OBJECTIVES**
1. SIZE	The bigger the better	Economies of Scale	Steady but exponential growth
2. DEBT	D:E, better than industrial avg.	Maintenance	Linear development
3. INNOVATION	High R&D investments	Innovation Cycles	High rhythm with age
4. INDUSTRY TREND	Growing industry	Growth	Higher than market
5. ECONOMY TREND	Growing Economy	Growth	Higher than economy
6. ACQUISITIONS	Programmatic M&A	Size	Sustained exponential growth
7. RESOURCE ALLOCATION	Re-Allocation > 50% p. 10 yrs	Growth	See above
8. CAPITAL INVESTMENT	Top of industry	Growth	See above
9. PRODUCTIVITY	Δ Top of industry	Metabolism	Higher than maintenance
10. Differentiation	Margin Growth	Metabolism	Higher than maintenance

Figure 2.21: Power laws of "scaling" (West 2017) and "power curve of economic profit" (Bradley, Hirt, and Smit 2018): a comparison.

It is important to keep in mind that the different power laws can be combined to understand a certain curve, especially when it is about "riding the curve into potential futures." For instance, it is possible to connect an oscillation with a goal seeking function. Alternatively, you could combine the Innovation Distribution Bell Curve with the Three Horizon Model. Of course, the reader is invited to add her or his own power laws! The compilation of power laws can be downloaded at www.leadingbyweaksig nals.com where you find different digital assets to be used as printed versions or pixel graphics for virtual whiteboard.

Finally, please note that detailed references to literature are only made for authors of our time.

Generic Curve Shapes

The detection of these generic curve shapes is facilitated by developing a circular network, as illustrated above. Knowing a system's elements and their relationships is fundamental to identify weak signals.

Name: **Exponential Growth**

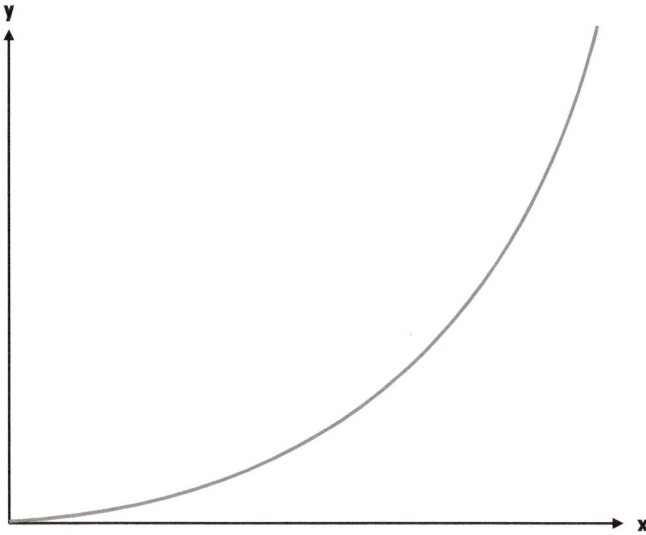

Figure 2.22: The exponential growth curve.

Discovery: Sissa ibn Dahir (legendary, between 400 and 600 AD)
Application: Startups, Innovation, Growth

Description: This curve represents the idea of unlimited exponential growth – and only a few phenomena can be described in this way (see card Phi M). Often only a particular phase of an evolutionary path is purely exponential because any system has a maximum carrying capacity. If one observes such a curve shape, it is wise to look out for dampening factors or inflections points (see also Logistic Growth).

Example: In the managerial context, this curve is characteristic for the introduction of new technologies, for new business models, and for market trends (e.g., web bubble of the early 2000s, transfer sums for soccer players, growth of stock value of Apple or Google). The same applies for the tulip mania in the Netherlands in 1637, which was based on speculation and greed, driven by a self-reinforcing loop of the availability of a product and its price. Obviously, this logic works in abstract domains like money flows, but natural systems have built in constraints which prevent endless growth (besides the aforementioned card Phi M). A good weak signal would be the discovery of elements in a system which are structurally too tightly coupled which reinforce each other's growth. A regulating element is missing in the scene.

Name: **Logistic Growth, S-Curve**

Growth

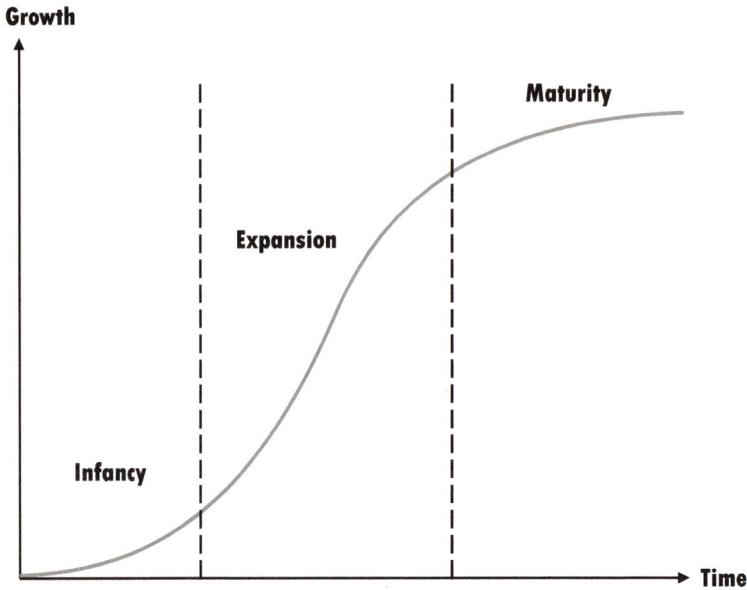

Figure 2.23: The famous S-curve, constrained by a given carrying capacity.

Discovery: Gompertz 1825 and Verhulst 1837
Application: life cycle of a company, product or service, market saturation

Description: the sigmoid shape can be found in many contexts (the growth rate of cells or the population of a species in an environment with a given carrying capacity). It is possible to model this function with different approaches. Still, the message always stays the same: growth starts slowly in the beginning, then a phase of exponential growth follows, after which a saturation effect comes into play.

Example: this is probably the most common curve type for all sorts of organizations, from biological, over economical, to social systems. To spot weak signals for this shape, it makes sense to understand the environment of the observed system. In the economic domain: which factors determine the maximum size of an ecosystem? How is energy flowing through the elements? Is there a certain degree of friction that determines the maximum capacity? How big is the market, e.g., the maximum number of customers or the availability of a resource? By understanding the boundaries of the systems, one can estimate the expected curve shape over time.

Name: **Strategic Inflection Point**

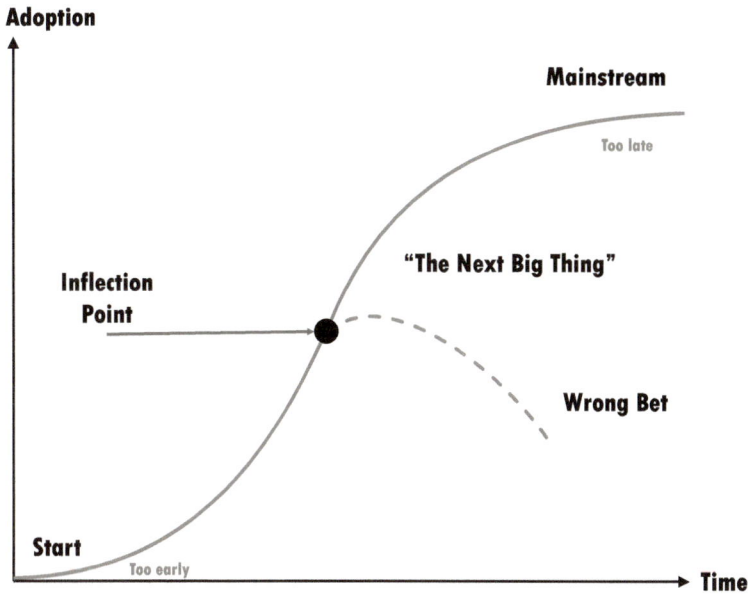

Figure 2.24: The turning of a curve is always critical, but it is the question whether this is a good or a bad thing.

Discovery: Andy Grove 1996 (in the business context)
Application: Strategy, Change, Business Models

Description: an inflection point is a marker for the change of a curve. From a mathematical perspective, it shows how a shape transforms from concave upwards to concave downwards or vice versa. In business, it is crucial for the business to discover these points as soon as possible to be able to cope with the upcoming change and to have enough time to prepare for the impact.

Example: the interpretation of an inflection point can be manifold, as it depends on the specific context. A company might have reached its highest revenue growth rate and starts to slow down towards its boundaries (the middle of a S-curve). But an inflection point can be also related to bad product reviews, as a quality initiative is showing its effect. The detection of a weak signal is very challenging because it is mathematically impossible to calculate the inflection point without a complete data set. A circular network could be promising to acquire an understanding of the given situation and to detect the deciding levers that will drive the inflection point. Unfortunately, this is the hardest law when working with weak signals and associated power laws.

Name: **Oscillation**

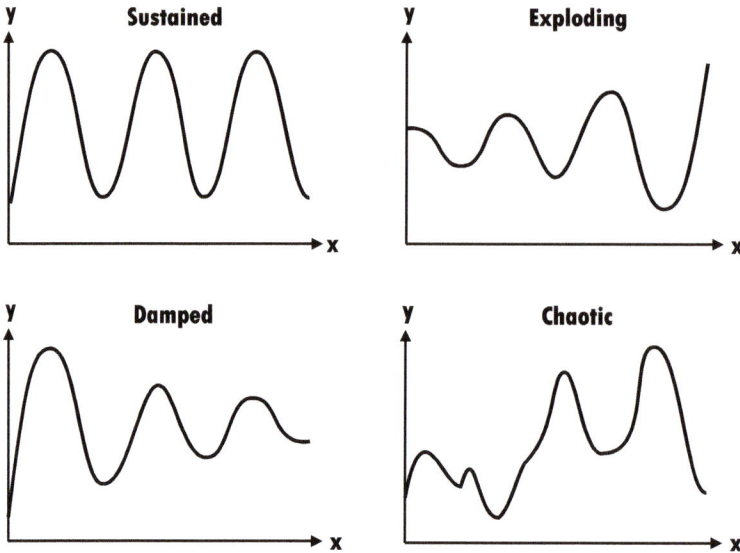

Figure 2.25: When is an oscillation healthy or pathological?.

Discovery: Christiaan Huygens, 1673
Application: Seasonality, Cycles, Resilience

Description: oscillations usually reveal a periodicity in a system and therefore show seasonality and overarching cycles in the business. If this shape is observed, it can be helpful to examine how regular the oscillation seems to be. Is it stable (sustained) within a certain range, or are there fluctuations (see also perturbation card)? Furthermore, are the oscillations converging, diverging, or even chaotic? In a nutshell: extreme oscillations are usually either a sign of an ongoing crisis or some sort of trial-and-error process.

Example: recurring events like Black Friday or Christmas are highly welcomed by retailers and online shops as they promise a nice peak in sales. This type is unproblematic because it is known in advance and can be planned. But if a seasonal trigger is not known, it makes sense to find the path that shall lead to its source. Due to the general nature of this curve, a weak signal can have various reasons. This applies also to the exploding or the damped oscillation – a (hidden) system element is intervening, either in a self-reinforcing or a self-balancing way. A chaotic oscillation must depict a chaotic weak signal as source – inherently, such a weak signal can only be explained retrospectively.

Name: **Goal Seeking**

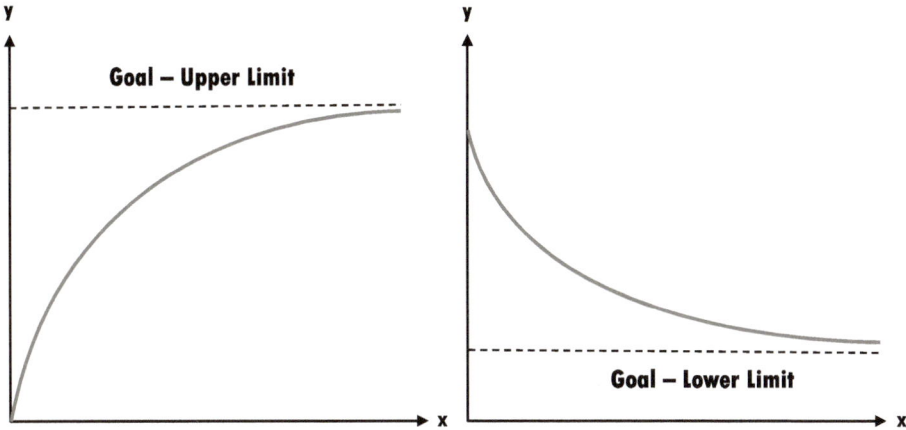

Figure 2.26: Goal seeking shapes indicate a regulator in the background.

Discovery: Archimedes, 287–211 BCE
Application: Goal Seeking, Stabilization, Control, Stagnation

Description: converging curves indicate a goal-seeking behavior, typically influenced by the dampening effect of a negative feedback loop in the system. In business, this shape can be related to the end of the life cycle of a product (sunset phase) and the maturity of a product (e.g., all feasible features are built, nothing is left to iterate). That phenomenon is also known as the marginal benefit curve.

Example: goal seeking shapes are closely related to the start and the end of a S-curve, as some sort of saturation effect is entering. A typical example is an enterprise reaching its maximum market position. On the other hand, we can find curves which converge towards a minimum limit, in situations where the lowest cost level has been reached (given the existing technology is not progressing). Weak signals for this type of curve must be found, in the truest meaning of the word, at the edges of the observed system, no matter if it is adjacent to a whole ecosystem, to a specific niche-market or to the company itself. The guiding questions are about the upper and lower limits of the observed variable, and again a circular network can be useful to identify the influencing weak signals.

Name: **Chaos**

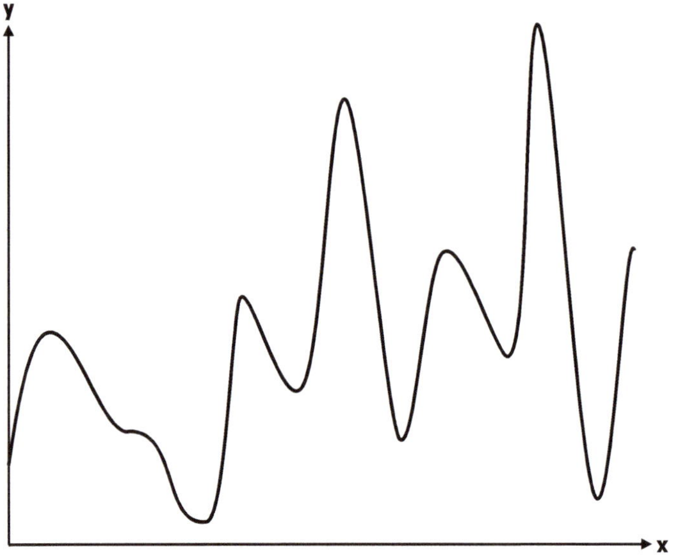

Figure 2.27: If patterns show no regularity, we call them chaotic, a pure random function.

Discovery: Newton, 1680s (Three Body Problem)
Application: Unstable system detection, Collapse, Warning Signs

Description: chaotic patterns point towards situations which call for immediate action. Let's take the example of a burning house as a chaotic situation, where it is necessary to evacuate – and where one needs a lot of training to survive such an incident (with a high likelihood). In a timeseries a chaotic pattern can be understood as a creative process, where a new behavior is about to emerge. It represents the edge of knowledge.

Example: a chaotic pattern in the economic sphere is often related to the fact that something new is going on. This curve can be found in start-ups which are still in the infant stage of company development. A new company is rarely perfectly organized, a lot of value is delivered initially, but the performance is too low, due to the lack of knowledge about the customer or the production process. The weak signals can have many sources, and usually they interact in a non-predictable way – otherwise it would not be a chaotic pattern.

Universal Natural Laws

These laws are omnipresent, independent of the industry or area of expertise. The question must be answered to what extent a company stays on a healthy evolutionary path. This requires a comparison of actual data with forecasts based on universal natural laws. A deviation from a predicted curve is investigated by looking for weak signals and the natural laws behind.

Name: **Punctuated Equilibrium**

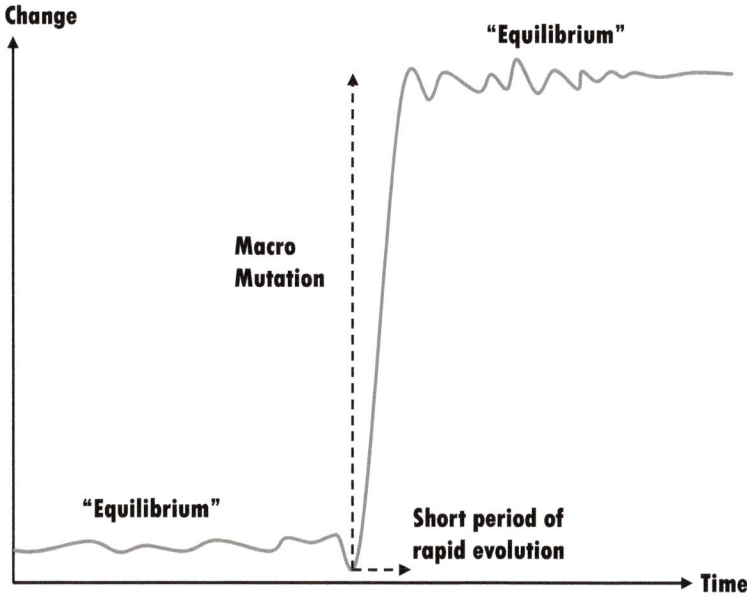

Figure 2.28: A sudden change could indicate an evolutionary shift.

Discovery: Eldredge and Gould, 1972
Application: Discovering Wildcards, Sudden Shifts in Markets, Macro Economic Changes

Description: the punctuated equilibrium represents a rapid change in a very short amount of time. These kinds of jumps can be observed when relevant internal or external factors change, which are leading to new behaviors or structural characteristics. A typical example would be a drop of stock value because of a pandemic situation, or a stock rises because of new customer preferences.

Example: this shape can be characterized as a "wildcard event," caused by a competitor which deploys a completely new technology that directly attracts a lot of customers. Alternatively, a sudden peak can also be affected by an emergent behavior of various actors in a system, e.g., when different players in a market decide to switch to a new standard. Suddenly, the old solution is obsolete and the new one is leading.

Name: **Critical Transitions**

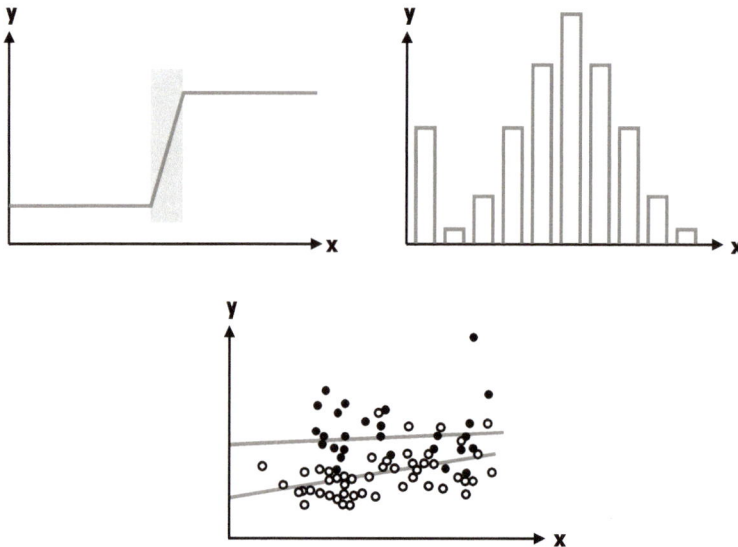

Figure 2.29: Critical transitions can show up in different forms.

Discovery: Marten Scheffer 2009
Business Application: Anticipating fundamental changes, especially catastrophes

---

Description: it is possible to anticipate critical transitions before they happen, by identifying "alternative attractors" in a system. This could be a shift in a time series (see also Punctuated Equilibrium), a multimodal distribution, or a dual relationship to a controlling factor. The term critical transition does not imply that a catastrophic event will happen – it can be also a positive outcome (anastrophe).

Example: in managerial practice, this kind of transition appears in various forms. The adoption rate of a new competitive solution could be the control parameter which leads to a dual relationship of two variables, e.g., the number of lost customers and the overall growth of a new market. This control parameter must be identified early as a weak signal, to adapt quickly to the upcoming change. A multimodal distribution is another indicator for an upcoming transition, e.g., a change in preferences of customers and expectations about a special feature of the product. This kind of change can be identified by weak signals about trend setters and influencers in social media and equivalent sources. One needs to find out the highly connected players in a social network which decide about "hot or not"?

Name: **Scaling of Units and Size**

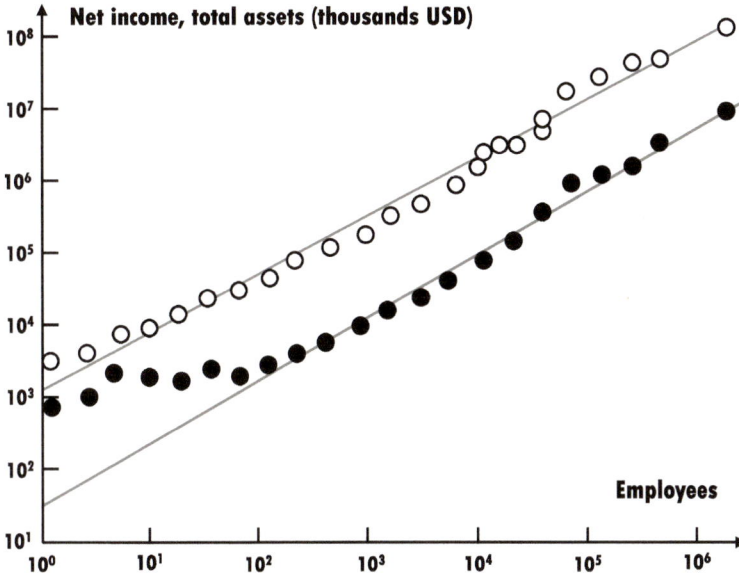

Net income, total assets (thousands USD)

Employees

Figure 2.30: The correlation between the number of employees and the net income. The black and white dots represent two different companies in the same market.

Discovery: Geoffrey West 2017
Business Application: Understanding Growth of an Organization

---

Description: the visualization shows on a logarithmic scale the relationship between "units" (number of employees) and the "size" (net income in dollars). This proportion represents a sublinear scaling, which can be also found in mammals, where the size is proportional to the number of cells. The quarter-power scaling law derives its magic number 4 from our three-dimensional world in space plus one time dimension.

Example: to understand the scaling of units and sizes, weak signals can provide valuable information about change or evolution over time. For example, if one detects a weak signal indicating a greater popularity of a product, one can use this information to predict its demand, which may require adjusting your production or supply chain to accommodate this larger demand.

Name: **Metabolic Rate of Natural Systems**

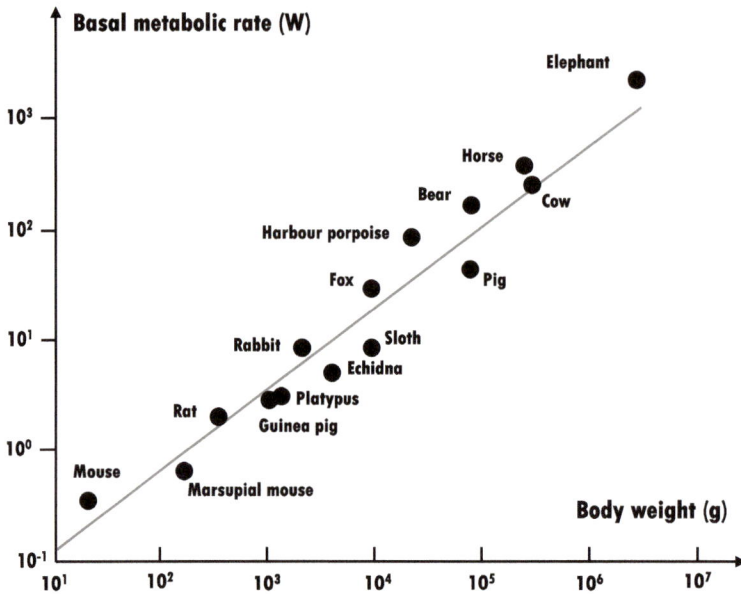

Figure 2.31: The proportional relationship of body weight and basal metabolism rate.

Discovery: Geoffrey West 2017
Application: Check healthiness of the proportion of size and maintenance efforts

Description: the graph shows on a logarithmic scale how body weight (100%) and metabolic rate (75%) are related to each other. One could roughly say that per size doubling the heart rate is scaled by the exponent −1/4. This relationship can be found across mammals in nature.

Example: in the context of this power law, weak signals could refer to small changes in an organization: changes in "body weight" (e.g., number of employees) which are not easily noticeable but affect their "basal metabolic rate" (e.g., total workplace costs). An organization which loses a small number of employees may have a slightly lower metabolic rate, but this change may not be immediately apparent. It is important for organizations to pay attention to these weak signals and make workflow changes to maintain a healthy body weight and metabolic rate.

Name: **Size & Scaling Human Made Systems**

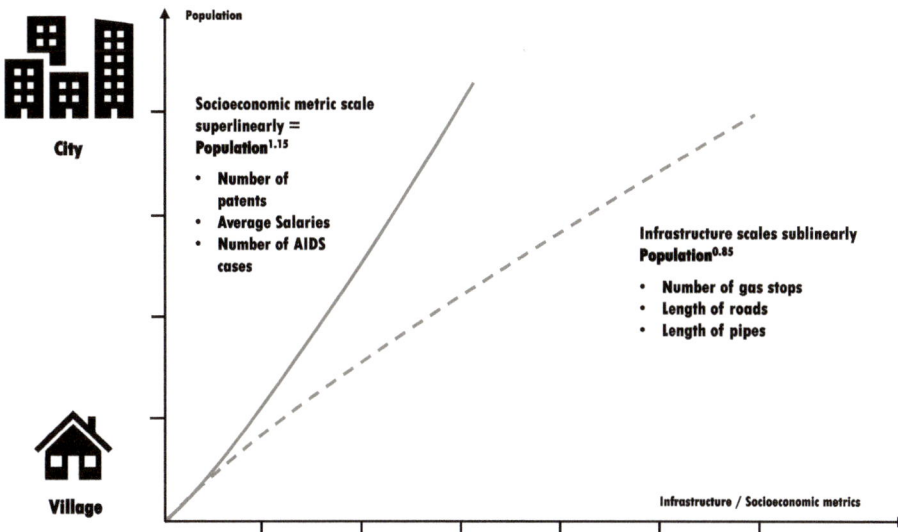

Figure 2.32: The benefits of size: While the infrastructure scales sublinearly, the socioeconomic growth scales superlinearly.

Discovery: Geoffrey West 2017
Application: Check healthiness of the proportion of infrastructure costs and benefits of scaling effects

---

Description: this law is valid for socio-economic contexts, and it describes two growth factors which are also relevant for companies. For sustainable growth, the scaling of the infrastructure costs (including maintenance) should be sublinear ($^{0.85}$). The benefits of a bigger organization (network effects) are expressed via a superlinear scaling of $^{1.15}$. The known limits of this law can be observed when looking at the biggest cities in the world.

Example: size has several benefits, such as a sublinear scaling of the infrastructure. For example, a company with 10,000 employees may require a certain number of computers, utilities, and other infrastructure to support it. As the number grows to 100,000, the infrastructure required increases at a much slower rate. Furthermore, large systems can be more effective at detecting and responding to weak signals, because they have more and better data, which can help to identify and address issues before they become major problems.

Name: **Network Invariants**

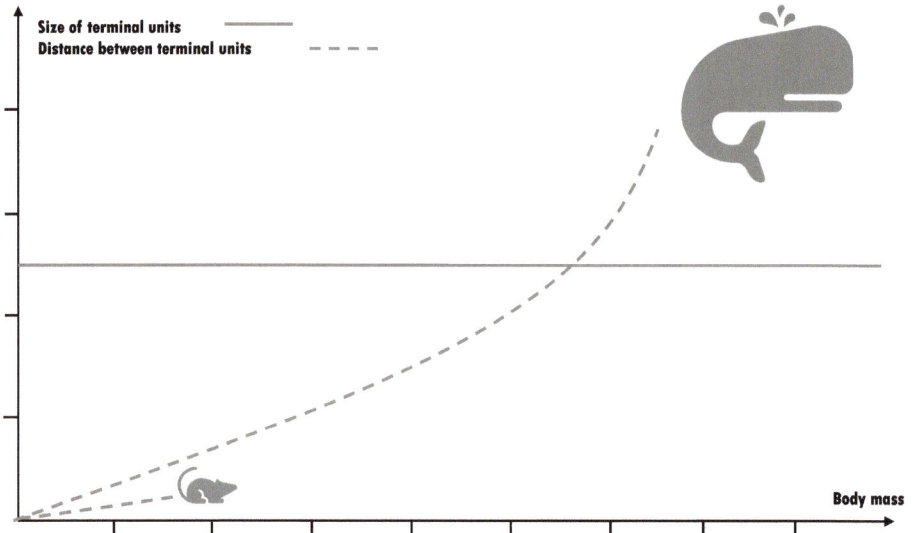

Figure 2.33: Some variables are invariant in a network, other traits scale with size.

Discovery: Geoffrey West 2017
Application: Understanding Networks, Market fit, Interoperability

Description: in each network/system, like the human body or a house, the "end pieces" are invariant. That means they are all of the same size, depending on the specific "piece type." In a house, the electric plug sockets are all the same size, and this applies also for water appliances. The capillaries of the blood system are another example: the "last meter" has always the same size. Insight: when designing networks, these terminal units define the constraints of the network (e.g., the flow rate in the capillary system). But the distance between the terminal units will scale differently.

Example: invariant variables can help to identify weak signals because they provide a consistent and stable reference point to be compared with changes in the network. For example, if a network has an invariant variable that measures the average number of connections between nodes, a change in this variable over time could indicate the presence of weak signals, such as the emergence of new connections or the loss of existing ones. By analyzing these changes, it is possible to identify new trends or problems that may require further investigation or action. E.g., the scaling of the distance could be detected via minor changes in the DNA.

Name: **Phi M, Rising Complexity**

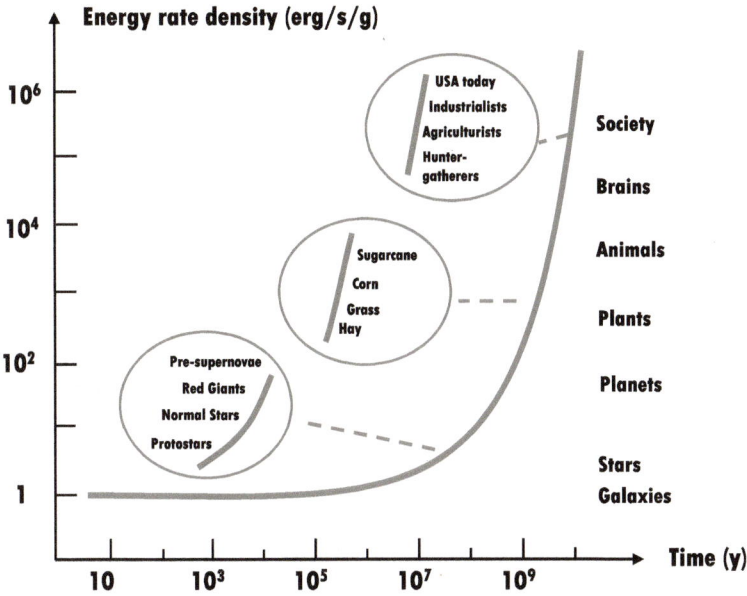

Figure 2.34: The ever-increasing complexity in the cosmos and how "pockets of complexity" evolve.

Discovery: Eric Chaisson 1996
Application: Unterstanding of Cosmological Evolution and New Technologies

---

Description: the ever-increasing complexity over time can be understood via the energy flow (information) rate density, which is called Phi M. It is a measure of the rate of evolution in a complex system and expresses the energy flow in a given space per time interval. Therefore, the Phi M value of a sunflower is much higher compared to the value of the sun – the plant is much more complex than our "hydrogen oven."

Example: when a complex system is operating at a low Phi M, weak signals may indicate a slowing down rate of evolution. The reasons can be manifold, e.g., inadequate or ineffective leadership or lack of clear objectives, which makes it difficult for the system to prioritize its efforts and resources. Finally, the lack of diversity or innovation within the system can prevent it from exploring new ideas or approaches favoring new growth and development.

Name: **Contagion Theory**

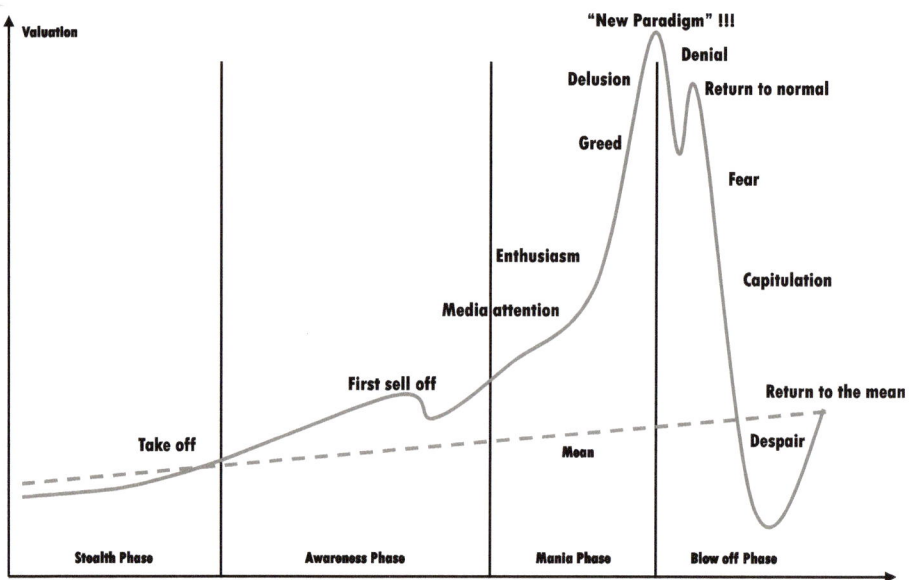

Figure 2.35: The distribution of contagious "material," here as a curve according to the four phases of a bubble (Jean-Paul Rodrigue).

Discovery: Starting with Lotka 1907 and for Business: Kucharski 2020
Application: Distribution of ideas, products, or services in networks

---

Description: the idea of contagious ideas, also known as memes, is well known. With this card, one shall be inspired to look at a times series like an epidemiologist and ask yourself: what are the drivers behind the basic reproduction number, aka R0? Kucharski offers this formula as a guideline:

$$R = D \times O \times T \times S$$

(Duration × Opportunities × Transmissibility × Susceptibility).

Example: all factors (D, O, T, S) can be important to predict how a message, e.g., a new hype (like Bitcoin), will spread through from early investors to the public – or how it could be stopped if one of the factors equals zero. Therefore, weak signals help to identify the probability that a message will travel through the network. While it is obvious that the time of exposure is key for duration, opportunities always depend on people in each space. Transmissibility and susceptibility are rather qualitative indicators in the social context, which are based on norms and questions around the topic of identity.

Cybernetic Laws

Communication and control are the main foci of cybernetic laws. They describe basic principles of organization and help to identify generic problems. The laws provide weak signals as a "solution" when the question about a problem arises. As cybernetic laws are often hidden in plain sight, they can show up in all sorts of curve shapes, even though the cause always remains the same.

Name: **Loose Coupling, High Cohesion**

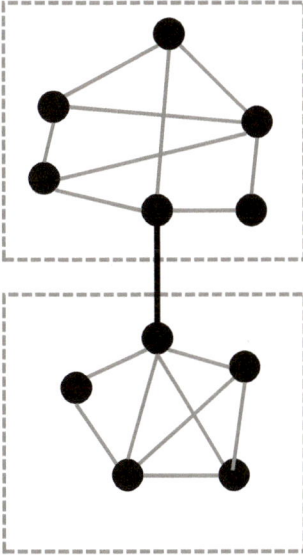

a) **Loose coupling, high cohesion**   b) **High coupling, low cohesion**

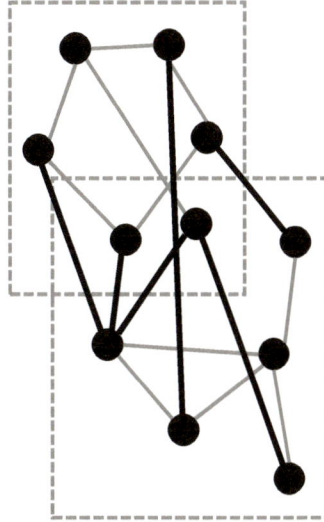

Figure 2.36: Loosely coupled systems are more resilient (variant a).

Discovery: Stevens, Myers, Constantine 1974
Application: Product-, service-, or organization design

Description: this law (or design principle) was described first in the context of programming and information systems design. It aims at robustness and reliability. It is easier to balance a system that is loosely coupled while showing a high level of cohesion. Systems that follow this approach require fewer dependencies and coordination efforts. Systems that claim to be modular need to follow this approach to be "truly" interchangeable.

Example: complex systems which are characterized by high coupling of their parts and little cohesion of the whole are doomed to failure. Catastrophes are looming when chain reactions destabilize a company acting in a complex environment. Weak signals can reveal inefficient or ineffective processes within the enterprise. Another structural reason could be long lead times for change or transformation, due to external perturbations from new competitors entering a market. Tight coupling leads to a lack of adaptability or flexibility within the system, which can prevent it from responding quickly and effectively to changing conditions. On the social level, conflicts among departments or teams are also a source of weak signals, which point to their ability to work together effectively.

Name: **Perturbation Recovery Time**

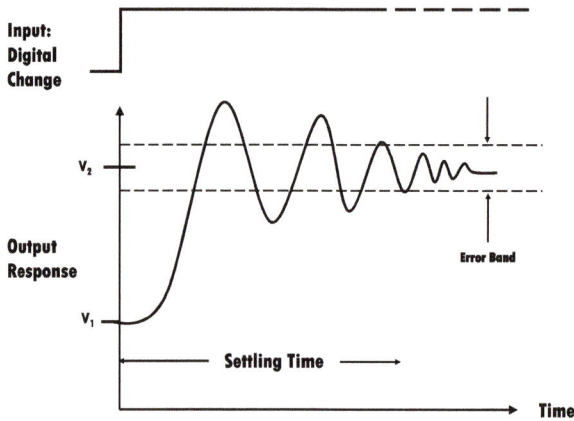

Figure 2.37: After a perturbation it takes some time to settle the output (from V1 to V2).

Discovery: Euler, La Place, Lagrange, 1748ff (Perturbation Theory)
Application: Interventions, Relaxation Time, Resilience

Description: many systems are exposed to internal and external perturbations. Usually, they use internal regulatory processes to find the desired stable state. But if the frequency of the perturbations is higher than the system's ability to compensate against them, it will be impossible to reach the equilibrium. Escalating positive feedback loops are a typical cause for perturbations.

Example: this law and the related weak signals have a strong link to the power law of "loose coupling and high cohesion." If a company operates this way, it will be resilient to deal with perturbations. Thus, the weak signals are very similar, but rephrased to emphasize the importance of a company's ability to cope with disruptions: watch out for interdependencies and conflicts, manage interfaces between departments or teams according to the concept of minimal necessary exchange, while ensuring the highest level of completeness to fulfill the purpose of the managed interface.

Name: **OODA loop**

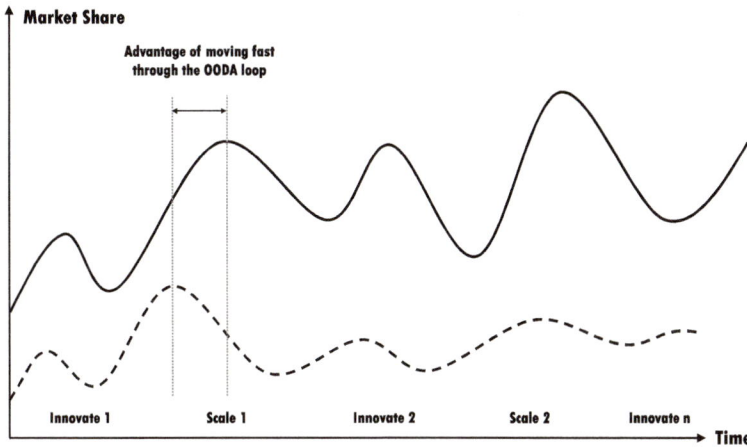

Figure 2.38: Illustrative visualization how moving fast through the OODA loop (Figure 2.18) creates a competitive advantage.

Discovery: Boyd 1995 (first PowerPoint visualization)
Application: Perception, Weak Signal Detection, Winning

Description: the OODA loop always needs a defined opponent (or enemy) to use it in the context of a timeseries. One scenario would be a comparison of the adoption rate (see Innovation Distribution) of new technologies, processes, or business models, with that of competitor XYZ. It makes sense to move as fast as possible through your own loop and to disrupt the challenger's loop by not letting them come to the decision point. That's the essence of winning or losing.

Example: this law points to a wide range of sources of weak signals. Any activity of a competitor related to gain higher market shares can be a weak signal, e.g., knowledge from market research about testing new products, or from a competitor starting strategic acquisitions. Furthermore, brand reputation can be an important source of weak signals as it provides hints about the speed of looping through the OODA sequence. For example, a sentiment analysis in social media helps to understand how new marketing efforts are perceived. Typical quantitative metrics like "likes" or shares are other indicators about the pace in the market race. Moreover, the reputation among "social influencers" is crucial.

Name: **Channel Capacity & Signal to Noise Ratio**

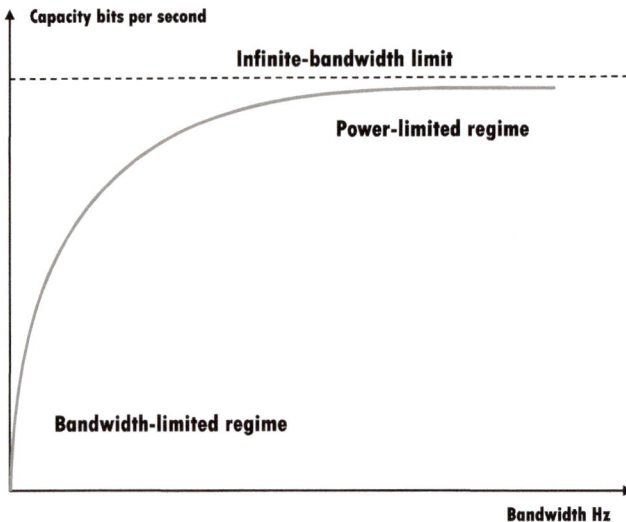

Figure 2.39: Every channel can carry only a certain bandwidth of information.

Discovery: Shannon-Hartley-Theorem 1948
Application: Communication Design, Information Transmission

Description: the law describes the relationship between a given channel and its inherent capacity to transmit information (e.g., bit/s). There is an upper limit, and the realized transmission rate is not only relevant for the signal as such, but also for "noise" (erroneous information, bias, etc.). Furthermore, the signal-to-noise ratio (SNR) reminds of the ever-present "unknown unknowns" in any data.

Example: in economic contexts, the Shannon-Hartley theorem is useful to understand the communicative performance of an organization. Any weak signal that could compromise channel capacity needs to be observed to ensure the optimal transmission rate. The signal-noise-ratio is an indicator of how well the real signal (e.g., reputation of a company) can be distinguished from noise. Are "error-correcting codes" in place that allow a better transmission to spot weak signals? Alternatively, are enough "antennas" available to cover a large area when receiving communication? Complementarily, how strong is the transmitter? All these aspects are crucial when applying this law.

Name: **Autonomy & Cohesion, first Axiom of Management**

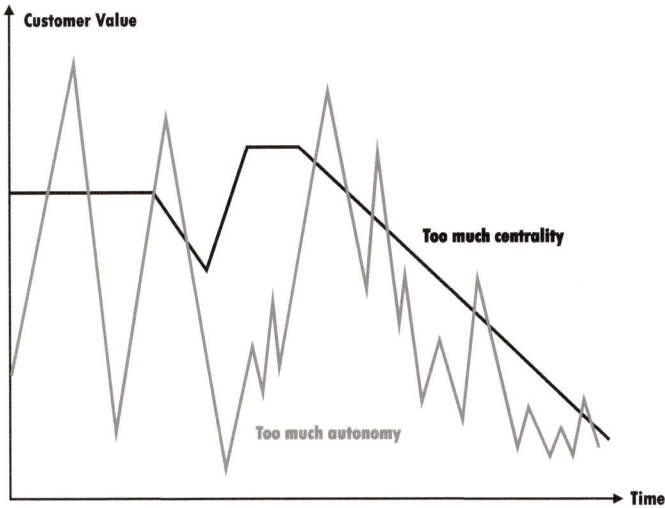

Figure 2.40: The essential balance of local autonomy and overarching cohesion, reflected as value delivered to customers.

Discovery: Beer 1985
Application: Enable healthy self-organization, prevent over- or under-engineering of control

---

Description: Stafford Beer described with this law the universal insight that autonomy (self-organization) and cohesion (corporate interventions) need to be contextually balanced. If centrality is too high, it will be impossible to deliver customer value (bureaucracy). If autonomy is too high, it will be hard to deliver customer value in a relatively stable way (chaos). The effect of this axiom can be only found indirectly in a time series.

Example: weak signals resulting from this law can be found in any organization. If there are too many and too detailed policies and normative guardrails in place, the autonomy of the value generating units will be limited, which endangers success at the customer interface. If it is not possible to act fast when problems occur (e.g., a quality issue), the value for the customer will decrease and they will churn. Alternatively, if the degree of freedom of the value generating units is too high, it might be arguably possible to achieve a local optimum, but it will be impossible to achieve a global one. An indicator are dominating business divisions within a group, which dictate their interests to the whole enterprise.

Name: **Strategic and Tactical Fit, Second Axiom of Management**

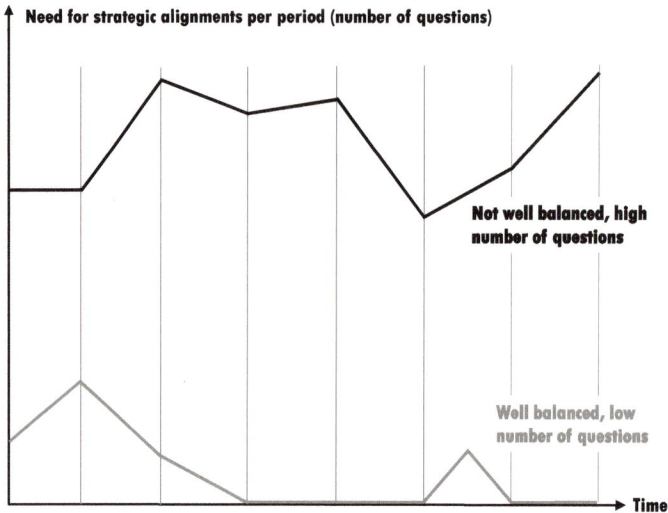

Figure 2.41: If the business strategy is not clear, it will create a communicative overhead and time lags (which affects the ability to go fast through the OODA loop).

Discovery: Beer 1985
Application: Balance the "inside and now" versus "outside and then," also known as Exploitation vs. Exploration

---

Description: the second axiom points out that management must take care of different levels (strategic and tactical), and that each management level needs to take care of its scope. In short, the strategic function takes care of new ideas, insights, and prototypes, and it acts in the interest of the greater whole to adapt to new conditions. The tactical and operational levels are close to the customers and provide them with the best possible value.

Example: the most common weak signal for this law is reflected by the following statement: "I cannot make tactical decisions, because I do not know the business strategy." Another indicator could be missing trust in leadership or resistance to implement a strategy. The sharing of operational budgets and strategic investments is another source for weak signals. In general, when one constantly encounters misunderstandings, demoralization, or confusion in the business, it is likely that this loop is not well balanced.

Name: **Maintain the Whole, Third Axiom of Management**

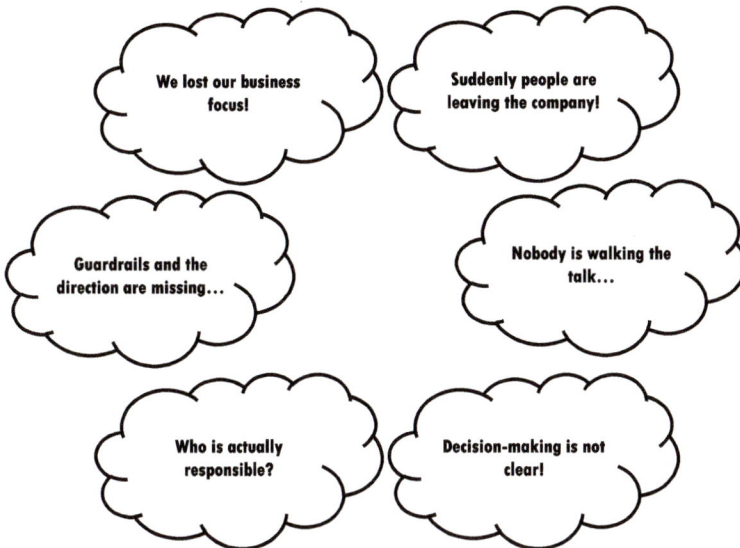

We lost our business focus!

Suddenly people are leaving the company!

Guardrails and the direction are missing...

Nobody is walking the talk...

Who is actually responsible?

Decision-making is not clear!

Figure 2.42: In this context it is not feasible to show a time series since this type has very strong qualitative aspects in it.

Discovery: Beer, 1985
Application: Identity, Vision, Purpose, and Mission, Policies and Norms

---

Description: any decision can ultimately be derived from underlying ethical values and basic beliefs which determine cost structures, value creation, and the capability to maintain the existence in a turbulent environment. The viability of a system is defined in essence by this loops and all the explicit and implicit decisions.

Example: weak signals are basically connected with the identity of a business in a formal and an informal way. On the formal side, these signals point to a lack of artifacts, like a statement of purpose, a vision, a mission. On the other hand, weak signals can be found in the informal realm, when people complain about the company culture, when they can't remember their company's vision by heart. Those weak signals are clearly an expression of companies' autopoietic nature.

Empirical Business Laws

As the name suggests, these laws are based on empirical evidence. Each law is specific regarding context and curve shape, which facilitates the allocation of these laws to generate insights (e.g., the Hype Cycle and how innovation develops over time). Weak signals can be of quantitative and qualitative nature, as will be illustrated later.

Name: **Power Curve of Economic Profit**

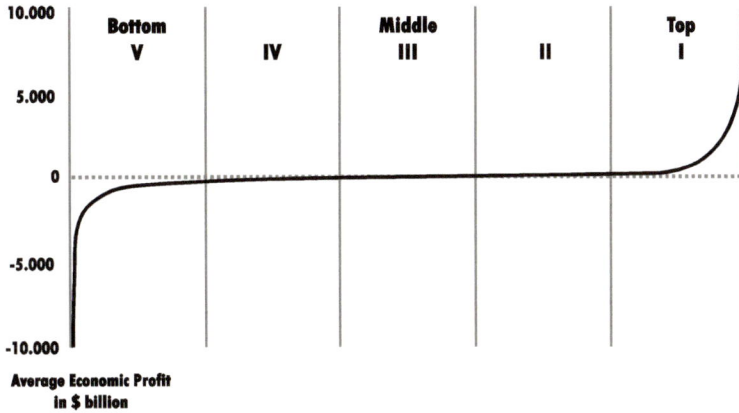

Figure 2.43: The power curve of economic profit.

Discovery: Bradley, Hirt, and Smit 2018
Application: Strategic positioning, competitive advantage

Description: empirical study of 2,500 worldwide leading companies over a time span of 15 years. It shows how successful companies created value by optimizing ten basic variables or levers (size, debt, research, industry trends, geographic trends, acquisitions, resources allocation, capital investment, productivity, differentiation). The companies are positioned in five quantiles of corporate success. The law assigns probabilities for companies to move from one quantile to the next by optimizing a certain combination of variables. As illustrated in Figure 2.21, this law has much in common with the natural universal law of Scale (growth proportion of Units and Size) and may be applied in combination.

Example: to move from quantile II to I, a company in a growing industry in worldwide leading countries decides to focus the strategy on a combination of improving research and development, forcing acquisitions, and optimizing the debt-equity ratio. To achieve optimal results, the law proposes to speed up R&D in line with the aging process of the company, to focus on programmatic (rather than growth-driven) acquisitions and to achieve a debt-equity ratio superior to the industry.

Name: **Disruptive Innovation**

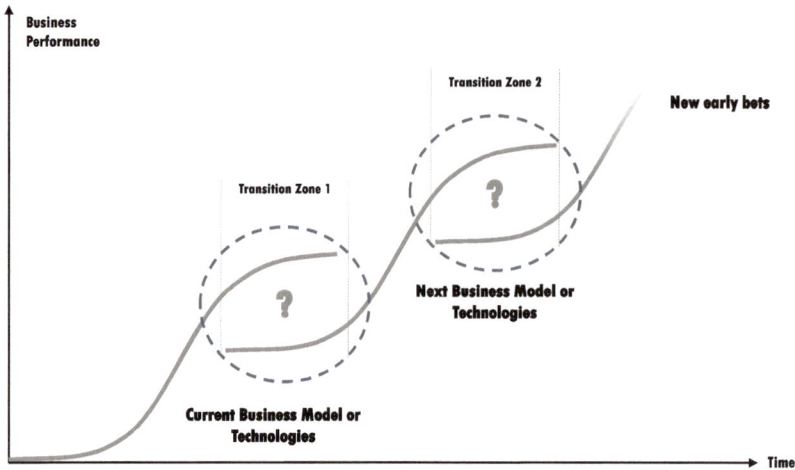

Figure 2.44: Combining S-curves allow us to understand continuous disruption.

Discovery: Clayton Christensen, Innovators' Dilemma, 1997 (in the business context)
Business: Application: Innovation, Change, Disruptive Technologies

---

Description: Christensen coined the term "disruptive technologies" (later: disruptive innovation) to explain why big firms often fail to deal with new technologies. It explains how young companies can bypass mature businesses because they can better implement innovative business models which are enabled by new technologies (see also Logistic Growth). De Sola Price's work can be seen as the foundation because he is a co-inventor of scientometrics (science about science).

Example: the range of potential sources for weak signals is as rich as any approach that deals with the dynamics of markets and changing preferences of customers. The concept is related to the OODA loop and the S-curve. Next to market and customer surveys, trade shows and industry conferences are a valuable source of signals. Furthermore, industry publications, blogs, social media, patents, and patent applications can provide information about new products. The same applies for government reports because they contain hints about upcoming regulatory changes. Partnerships with universities are also an interesting source.

Name: **Hype Cycle**

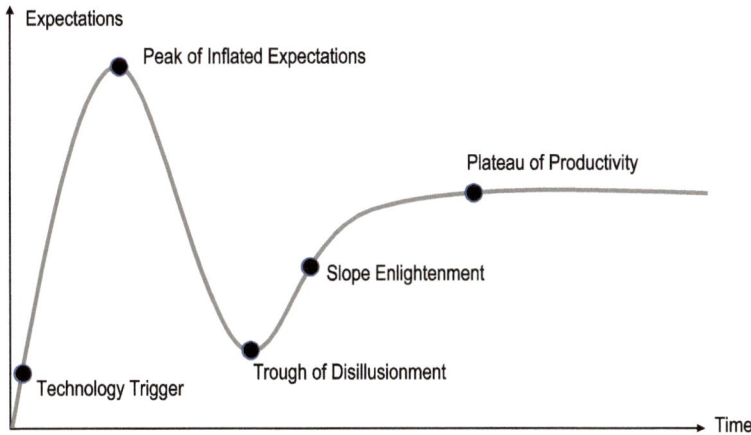

Figure 2.45: The classic pattern of new ideas which generate high expectations, till they reach a productive stage.

Discovery: Jackie Fenn at Gartner 1995
Application: Innovation, Tech Strategy, Long-term Planning

Description: the emergence of new technologies can be assigned to different stages: from the initial trigger, up to the peak of inflated expectations, down the through of disillusionment, upwards to the slope of enlightenment, it finally reaches the plateau of productivity. Its shape looks like an overshooting, goal-seeking curve. This heuristic can be combined with the Bass Distribution of Innovation, as it reflects the very early market penetration and the adoption rate of new a product or service.

Example: as this law has the quality of a universal natural law, weak signals are positioned to predict deviations from the idealized curve. The clue is to understand why an organization is over- or under-delivering innovation. On the one hand, customers do not perceive the problem yet. On the other hand, the added value delivered comes too late.

Name: **Little's Law**

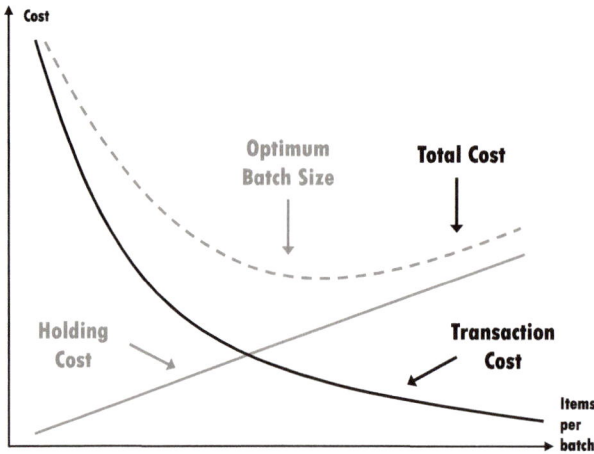

Figure 2.46: With this law we can find the sweet spot between holding and transactions costs to balance out the optimum batch size.

Discovery: Alan Cobham 1954
Application: Flow, Lead Time Optimization, Constraints Management

Description: this law provides one of the most underrated insights in business: generate flow by limiting the work in progress, because cycle time and queue depend on each other. It is connected to the Theory of Constraints which explains how to create flow in a system by focusing on the bottlenecks. Please keep in mind: Little's Law works only well for "relatively" stable systems. In complex environment, the math collapses exponentially.

Example: the detection of weak signals depends on the ability to reveal small changes in the grow rate of the queue in a production line. The potential impact of disruptions on its operations could be measured based on Little's Law. This could involve estimating the average arrival rate of the disruption, as well as the average time it would take for the company to respond and adapt to it.

Name: **Three Horizons**

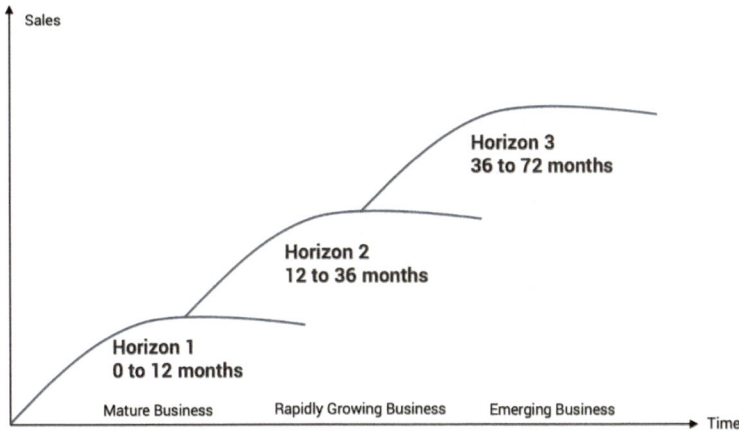

Figure 2.47: The visualization looks like a stacked version of the upper shapes of the disruption model of Christensen (S-curves).

Discovery: Baghai, Coley, and White 2000
Application: Innovation, Strategy, Business Development

Description: the horizon model could be interpreted as an extended version of Christensen's Disruptive Innovation S-curves. The three horizons represent three time-related perspectives: Horizon 1 focuses on the extension of the current value proposition (operators); Horizon 2 looks at the strategic dimension (builders); finally, Horizon 3 is reserved to visionary ideas to build viable options.

Example: the three horizons serve as a criterion to find weak signals for rapidly growing and emerging businesses. In each of the horizons it is possible to discover relevant hints regarding opportunities and threats. Again, this type of law is related to any other power law that addresses the competition and other environmental factors. The general question remains the same: what is happening around us that could accelerate or slow down the process of gaining a good position in the market in relation to "here," "later," and "one day," or "must," "should," and "could"?

Name: **Innovation Distribution**

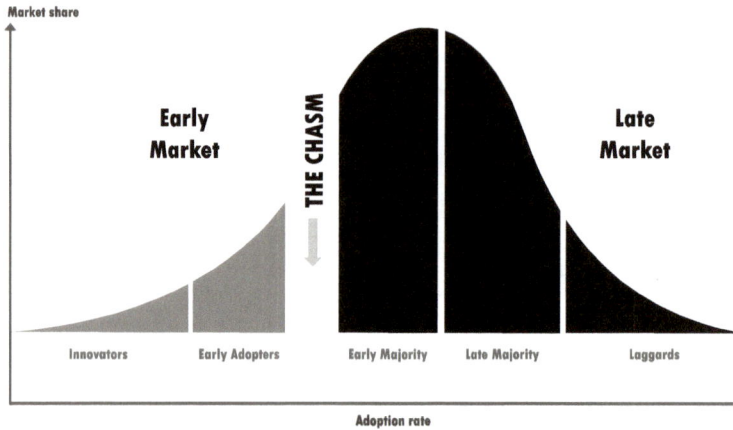

Figure 2.48: Typical phases of innovation adoption including the challenge of bridging the chasm.

Discovery: Geoffrey Moore, Crossing the Chasm, 1991
Business: Application: Trend Adoption, Innovation, Product or Service Development

---

Description: the distribution of innovation depends on adoption rates across a given population. According to Rodgers it is the key to "bridge the chasm" between early adopters and the early majority in a market. According to this theorem it is critical to excite not only the inventors and "tech nerds" but convince customers close to the "average" (majority). This distribution is closely connected to the Gartner Hype Cycle. This also implies a different marketing message to the different types. Early adaptors prefer other messages than the late majority.

Example: since adoption rates are the distinctive criterion of this law, all weak signals must be connected to the perception of the value in use of a company's products or services. It is essential to differentiate between new, loyal, or lost customers to gain insights on how to stay ahead in the race for adoption rates of new solutions.

Name: **Zipf Principle of Least Effort**

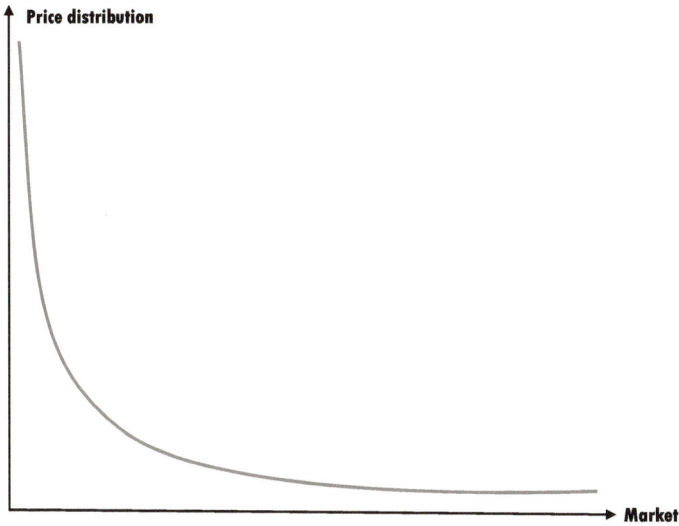

Figure 2.49: The typical shape of the Zipf distribution, as it can be found in the distribution of prices in a certain market.

Discovery: Zipf 1949
Application: Understanding harmonic distributions, Optimization

---

Description: the Zipf Law originates from the examination of the word frequency in English. It states that in a given text, the frequency of a word is inversely proportional to its rank in the frequency table. In other words, the most common word will occur about twice as often as the second most common word, three times as often as the third most common word, and so on. It reminds us that nature tries to find the optimal balance between effort and outcome. This kind of distribution can be also found when examining city sizes, the structure of markets and industries, the distribution of prices or the distribution of wealth and income in societies.

Example: weak signals are related in terms of the relative frequency or prevalence of different types of signals within a dataset. If the distribution of signals follows Zipf's law, then this could suggest that a small number of signals are much more common or prevalent than most signals. In this case, the weak signals might be the ones that are less common or less prevalent and might be more difficult to detect or identify. If the distribution of signals follows this power law, then this could suggest that a small number of signals have a much greater impact or influence on the system being studied, while the majority of signals have a much smaller impact. In this case, the weak signals might be the ones that have a smaller impact or influence and might be more easily overlooked or discounted.

Technology Laws

The last set of power laws is devoted to constants of technological progress. Like the universal natural laws, this type serves to compare the company's performance with evolutionary forces of scientific and engineering progress. The detection of weak signals originates in an observed deviation from actual data and the trajectory predicted by the law, demanding an explanation for the gap.

Name: **Wright's Law**

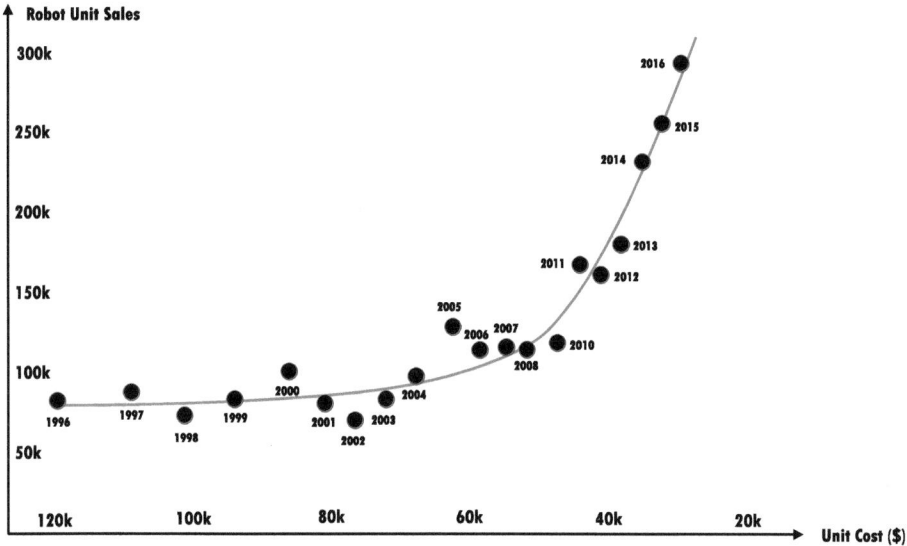

Figure 2.50: Wright's law in action in the context of robot unit sales and unit costs – the non-linear learning curve can be easily identified.

Discovery: Wright 1936
Application: Learning Curve, Diminishing Costs, Increasing Returns

---

Description: this law is the origin of most other technology laws. It has proven to be more reliable than Moore's Law and helps to understand the exploitation of a given technology (or business model). The learning curve can be explained by scaling effects, new materials, or processes. It is closely related to the Laws of Increasing Returns and Marginal Benefit Function.

Example: Wright's law and weak signals are related in an indirect way. For example, an organization might use Wright's law to predict the future cost of a product or to anticipate potential trends that could impact the demand for this product. In this way, Wright's law and weak signals could be used together to inform strategic planning and decision making.

Name: **Koomey's Law**

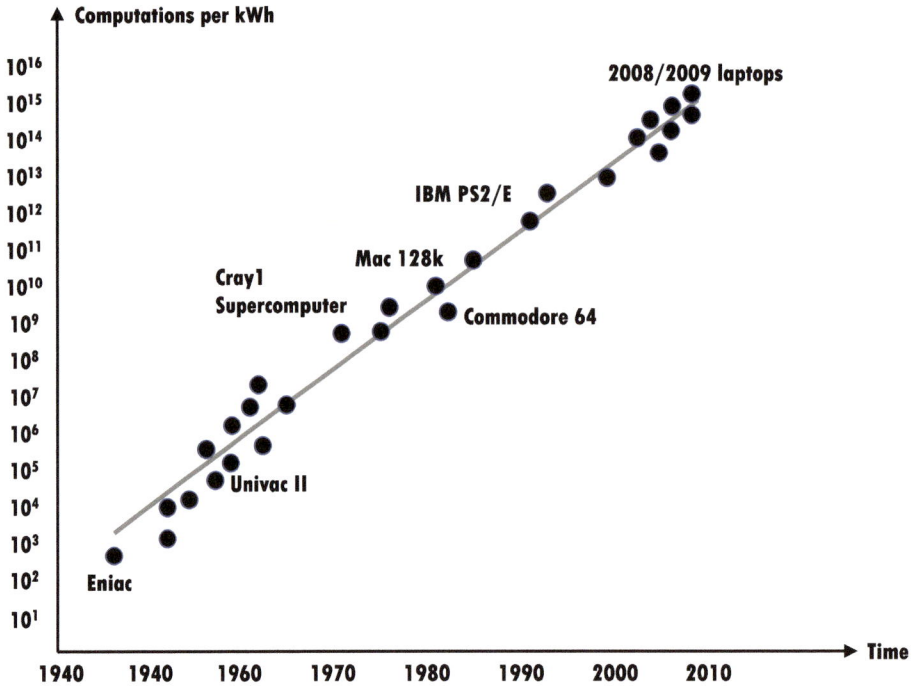

Figure 2.51: The exponential relationship between energy consumption and computation, demonstrated with some legendary computer systems.

Discovery: Koomey 2010
Application: Hardware Design, Energy Optimization, Technological Progress

Description: while computational speed is important when assessing technological progress, it is also essential to optimize the energy consumption of computation. That is why Koomey examined the relationship of computations per kWh (or joule) over time. This law is even more precise than Moore's Law, even though the growth has slowed down since 2010.

Example: this law reflects the state-of-the-art technology to build computer chips. Any indication of a slowing pace indicates that technology is progressing beyond the known limits. This insight is useful to anticipate paradigmatic shifts. Koomey's law could be considered a weak signal in this field, as it provides an early indication of future developments in energy efficiency and computing power. With respect to better material properties, any signal pointing to new architectures could be worth following. While hardware topics are important, one should also focus on software, because it helps to ensure exponential growth.

Name: **Metcalfe's Law**

Visualization:

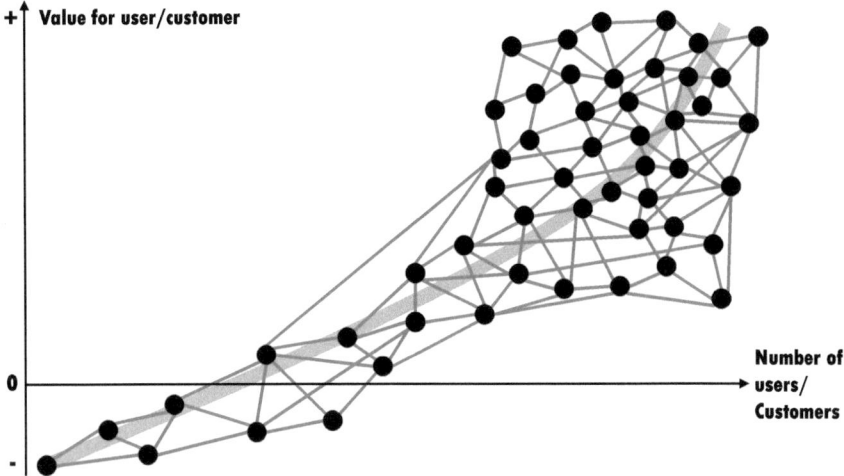

Figure 2.52: The higher the number of participants in a network, the higher the value for the participants.

Discovery: Metcalfe 1980
Application: Business Modelling, Creating Critical Mass, Growth Strategies

---

Description: originally this law was developed to express the value of technology compared to the number of connected devices (here: fax machines!). Later it was applied to interpret social networks. It also explains why internet startups often take economic losses in the early growth phase into account to achieve the critical mass of users – and create some sort of social "lock-in effect." The costs to switch to a new platform are too high.

Example: this law is closely related to the concept of economies of scale, which depicts the dynamics of non-linear growth effects. A weak signal for this type of phenomena can be found in the adoption rate of new services and products, or the number of new users on a particular platform. The growth rate of connections between the users is also of importance. Other weak signals could be recommendations by influencers, or other types of early product reviews, e.g., social media "likes" or shares of a post. Overall, all metrics related to the attractiveness of new services, compared to competitors, are an interesting source of signals that help to understand if this law is acting in the background.

Name: **Keck's Law**

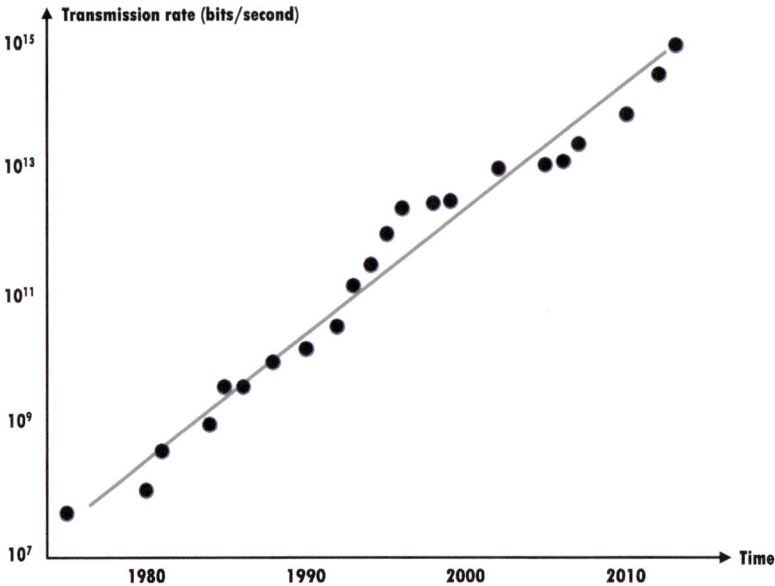

Figure 2.53: The exponential growth of the transmission speed in glass fiber systems.

Discovery: Donald Keck, early 1970s
Application: Communication Systems, Transmission Speed of Data

Description: the exponential growth of the transmission rate in fiber optics reminds us of the ongoing technological progress (like Moore's or Koomey's Law). It enhances the idea of an evolutionary process which designates transmission of data as being of the same criticality as the computational power or the energy consumption of computation. A recent example of this trend is called "data center as computer" (scale every essential aspect as you need it).

Example: to understand this evolutionary heuristic, deviations from the ideal plot are examined, with special focus on the braking transmission speed: is it a design issue of the technical architecture, and is a specific product or service even close to physical boundaries? Is it possible to compensate physical constraints with an optimized technical structure? Weak signals indicate technical protocol issues to control the transmission of data. At a metaphorical level this law can be inspiring to discover signals about human-to-human communication and what it means to exchange information in times of technological acceleration.

Name: **Kondratieff Waves**

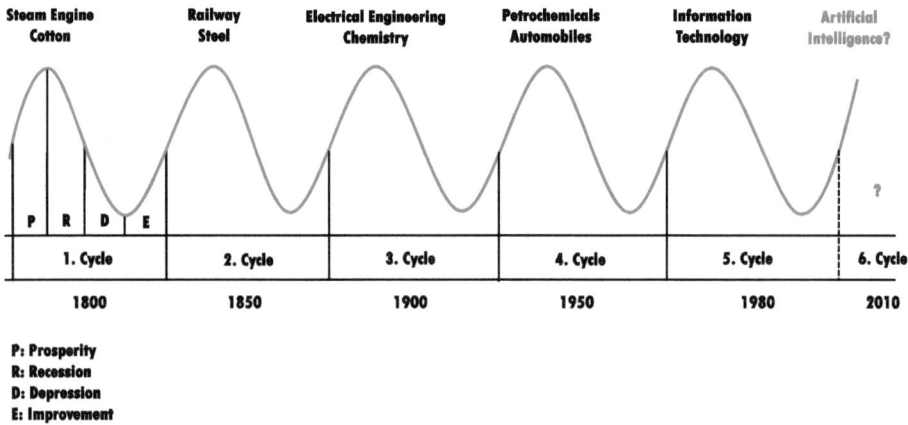

Steam Engine Cotton	Railway Steel	Electrical Engineering Chemistry	Petrochemicals Automobiles	Information Technology	Artificial Intelligence?
1. Cycle	2. Cycle	3. Cycle	4. Cycle	5. Cycle	6. Cycle
1800	1850	1900	1950	1980	2010

P: Prosperity
R: Recession
D: Depression
E: Improvement

Figure 2.54: Scientific breakthroughs create long lasting economic cycles, but the intervals are becoming shorter and shorter.

Discovery: Kondratieff 1935
Application: Macroeconomic Understanding, Break-through Innovation

---

Description: "Long waves" of technological advances can be observed and mapped towards the economic stages of prosperity, recession, depression, and recovery. Typically, each wave is about 50 to 60 years long. The big question (and opportunity for entrepreneurs) is: what will follow information technology? Is it "Green tech"? Synthetic Biology? Artificial General Intelligence? Or something completely different?

Example: here weak signals need to be explored along all possible scenarios and their respective trajectories. It is more about general futuring than applying a law with a specific scope. Structural changes in industries, in global trade patterns, and in the transformation of social or cultural norms typically indicate "long waves." The next wave will probably be dominated by Artificial General Intelligence (AGI) because this type of breakthrough is necessary to augmented scientific discoveries (by the factor 10 to 100). In return it opens the opportunity that fundamental crisis' topics like climate change or the breakdown of supply chains can be resolved. Therefore, any weak signal coming from AGI is significant to anticipate the future, e.g., the number of newly published papers, reduction of training costs for new algorithms, and multimodality (text, image, or video input for model training).

Name: **Moore's Law**

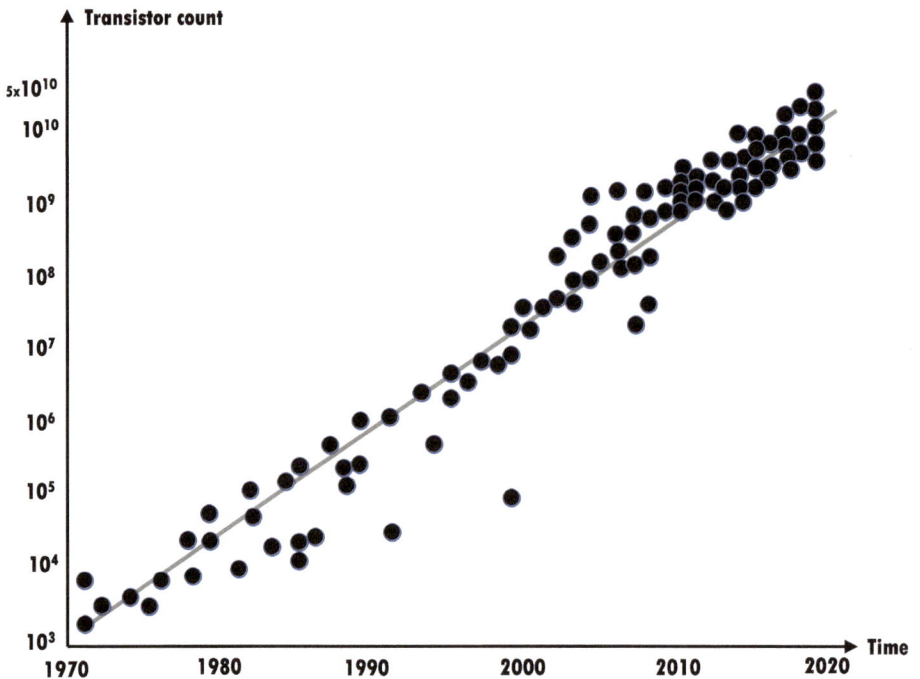

Figure 2.55: This law is often used to illustrate the technological progress.

Discovery: Moore 1965
Application: Hardware Design, Business Modelling

Description: faster computation allows more detailed models, no matter if they are of mathematical nature, or if it is a 3D-visualization. This law is useful to extrapolate upcoming technologies and it can be used to trigger the imagination of an entrepreneur. It fits Koomey's and Keck's Law and the underlying learning curve based on Wright's Law. Even if the growth is slowing down, the law as such is still applicable due to advancements in chip design and mathematical models.

Example: weak signals arise by comparing this curve with the performance of one's own products – and with that of the competition. They can be derived from the development of material science (alternatives to silicone), nano technology, or quantum computing. The occurrence of innovations and patents can serve as an indicator about ongoing improvements in those sectors, especially in the field of graphic chips, which are heavily used in the field of machine and deep learning.

To conclude this presentation of power laws, the attention must be drawn to their potential overlap. This should be seen as a feature of the laws and not a flaw. For example, the exponential growth curve is related to the S-shaped growth curve of natural systems – both curves and underlying power laws share the same shape of the starting part. The same phenomenon can be found when looking at Wright's Law (the learning curve) and the right side of the S-shaped growth curve – both curves converge towards a certain value. Therefore, the power laws should be used as a source of inspiration! It is not a prescriptive list but the starting point for a discovery journey.

With the "deck of cards" of the 34 power laws, executives are well equipped to discover the origin and the pattern of the change brought to the open by weak signals. In the following, the use of these power laws will be illustrated. But first, the **collection and perception of data** must be addressed.

If data do not comply with certain quality standards, the attribution of power laws is doomed to failure. One must be extremely careful about the context of the data – it is all about "the data of the data"! Here are three typical traps one wants to avoid.

How was the data measured? There is a tendency in managerial practice to attribute a high level of accuracy to a data point when it is displayed as an exact number – but the exactness can seduce to believe in this number, disregarding how good the measurement was. Imagine you measure the voltage of a battery with a digital voltmeter. The display shows 1.47 volt. Now imagine using an analogue voltmeter, which is harder to read, because one must find the right position of the needle on the scale. After some attempts, 1.4 turns up. Now the question arises, which measurement was better? Which result will be considered? The answer is quite simple: one needs to know which sensor and measurement technology is more reliable, independent of the result measured.

When was the data captured, and in which meso- and macroscopic conditions was the measurement embedded? A fascinating feature of human nature is the ability to forget about a given timeframe when data was collected, as the following anecdote from personal experience illustrates. When working for a car manufacturer, every four years the same question popped up: "Why do we have a decrease of test drive requests during this specific summer?" "Well, this summer was dominated by one topic, the soccer world championship! People were busy watching the games, BBQing, and having a beer. They were not searching for a new car – and by the way, using Google Trends, we noticed this phenomenon for all car brands." This illustrates that **metadata** is crucial to contextualize data and derive the correct insights from it. Therefore, one should write a "metadata logfile" when collecting data.

Will the data influence the decision? There are more sensors and data-collecting devices at hand than ever before. It is quite easy to get digitized bits and pieces of each and everything, but the question remains: will the data influence a decision? In other words: is it necessary to collect data, or can an insights be derived by pure deduction? Connected to this complex is the question of whether it is necessary to have a high degree of accuracy. In other words: is it necessary to know how many grapes went into the wine? As William Bruce Cameron (1963, 13) said: "It would be nice if all the data which sociologists require could be enumerated because then we could run them through IBM machines and draw charts as the economists do. However, not everything that can be counted counts, and not everything that counts can be counted."

The human attention filter selects from all facts the ones which are most dramatic. The following rules of thumb for "factfulness" should be considered when dealing with data:

– The gap instinct: we are over-evaluating polarities when we should look to balance the perception – and reduce the drama.
– The negativity instinct: bad news is spreading wider and faster than good news. This can be tackled by expecting bad news and looking out for gradual improvements.
– The straight-line instinct: it represents our way of linear thinking. We should remember that curves come in different shapes.
– The fear instinct: we overestimate risks. Make no decisions when in panic!
– The size instinct: big numbers are very impressive. If you divide them by another meaningful number, you create smaller proportions.
– The generalization instinct: when something looks strange, be curious, humble and think, in which way is this a smart solution?
– The destiny instinct: if one assumes that cultures are not changing, because change is happening so slowly, focus on small changes to overcome this barrier.
– The single perspective instinct: we can't be experts in everything which reminds us to be humble and to collect many perspectives when looking at a problem.
– The blame instinct: we look out for the villain and favor heroes, even though we should look at the system and its rules and structure.
– The urgency instinct: it leads to decisions that neglect the wholeness of a situation. Take a breath, insist on data and beware of fortune tellers.

(https://gapminder.org/factfulness, accessed 10.07.22)

Once sufficient attention is given to the quality of the data, the use of power laws in the context of the methodology can be addressed.

How to start the search

First, different sorts of data should be at hand – and different types of visualizations. Although more data means more opportunities to discover weak signals, it comes at the cost of being overwhelmed. Thus, the following list will serve as inspiration to differentiate between types of data sources which help to understand of "what is going on." A distinction between external and internal sources is made, which will be further differentiated for illustrative purposes.

External Perspective:
– Emergence of new technologies and use cases (business models) which integrate climate issues
– Societal trends (from fashion to sport, everything that influences customer preferences and the decision-making logic)
– Political trends (law and regulation)
– Ecological trends, like biodiversity or the actual quantity of CO_2 in the atmosphere (measured in ppm)

> -   Competitor's behavior (from a measurable brand reputation to voluntary recommendations in the social media)
>
> Internal Perspective:
> -   Sales, especially the sales pipeline (number of hot leads)
> -   Marketing effectiveness (customer acquisition costs and customer lifetime value)
> -   Supply chain (availability, delivery time, fulfillment ratio)
> -   Finance (profitability to maintenance costs, free cash flow, stock price)
>
> It is important to visualize the data, to reduce complexity, and to digest a big amount of input.

There are a variety of options of applying power laws in a specific context:
1.   Individual application in a personalized context
2.   Workshops, offsites or similar meeting types
3.   Prediction tournaments

To take the corporate strategizing process for illustration: it is relatively easy to start off with a selection of power laws, but it needs focus and discipline to develop scenarios ("riding the curve"), to select leading indicators and to determine the measures. Therefore, no matter which type of work mode you are selecting, it is all about keeping a regular inspect and adapt-cycle alive. Only then will you be able to integrate learnings and synchronize them with other planning cycles, like the OKR framework to be discussed later.

To make the different work modes more tangible, a manual including a step-by-step guide will now be presented. However, this guidance can and should be adapted according to the needs of the specific situation.

Individual application in a personalized context

Preparation
-   At first, be aware of the system you are examining (autopoietic/closed or input-output/open) and about your role (player/participant or coach/observer) – this step will help you to develop the required sensitivity to detect weak signals.
-   A driver tree of your most important metrics, as illustrated above by the Du Pont scheme, will be the basis for identifying weak signals. You start off with the most obvious entry point of this tree, e.g., revenues or customer reviews. If no imminent change is detected at this point, move on to other indicators until you discover a change that might be a weak signal.
-   Access the data, in the best case timeseries plots of important data points that are relevant for business success.
-   Have a suitable power law at hand, be it the version from the book, or the downloaded files from www.leadingbyweaksignals.com.

"Exploring the curve" – applying power laws
In this step we recommend starting with power laws that fit your context. If you are looking at organizational data, it makes sense to start with cybernetic laws. If you are in the technological domain, then the corresponding technological laws might provide insights of what is going on behind the curtain. The same applies for scaling laws, and when trying to understand if the company's performance is on a healthy growth curve. Additionally, it is possible to combine different types of laws, which means you can use them like building bricks.

The sequence in a nutshell: from a weak signal (qualitative or quantitative) to a business metric (visualized as a timeseries) to a power law (whose curve could/would fit to explain the future development).

Workshop usage

Preparation
- The preparation is basically the same, but you need to socialize the experience and create a workshop that provides a dense interaction pattern to bring the participants into a high-performance mode.
- As a good practice we want to recommend using a mix of frontal input sequences and working in groups. This ensures a well-informed group, which is then able to work on the application of the power laws.

Prototypical workshop structure to explore the curves
- Prepare a pre-read that explains the process and the desired results. In particular, share the collection of power laws up-front, so that it is not necessary to do it in the workshop.
- Welcome participants and set the context, use the TRIZ technique to create a collaborative atmosphere (expectation management and success criteria for the workshop).
- Share the collected weak signals (if the participants have not been part of the discovery process) and give enough space for clarification – but be mindful of the time available and prevent a repetition of topics which have been already discussed.
- Split the participants into smaller working groups and parallelize this way the application of the power laws.
- Come back into the plenum, share ideas, and get feedback to optimize the results per working group. This can be repeated up to three times to include an improvement cycle into the workshop.
- Last, find out if the results of the groups can be merged (or enriched), or if it is necessary to keep ideas separated (this is already very close to the following step called riding the curve).

- If you have too many ideas on how to apply the power laws, you can do simple dot voting, or any other prioritization technique, to reduce the amount of power laws you want to consider.
- Document the results in a way that they are easily accessible for the participants of the workshop. Nothing is more frustrating than having had a good workshop but then the results get lost "somehow." Keep the given technological constraints in mind and find the lowest common denominator.

Prediction Tournaments (inspired by Tetlock 2015)

The tournament mode represents the usage of all steps and not only the application of the power laws, even though this step is of course crucial. The basic difference to the aforementioned modus operandi: the tournament implies that a group of groups will work on exploring and riding the curves. Additionally, this implies that a tournament includes an inspect and adapt cycle, because otherwise you would not be able to compare the results and to find a winner.

Preparation

- The same preparation as for individual or workshop usage applies.
- Furthermore, you want to have a simple set of rules on how to determine the winner of a tournament (e.g., length of the tournament, fair access to data, how to determine the best deviation of a prediction, etc.).

Mass scaling of power law applications

- When dealing with many teams, the general logic of the usage in workshops can be applied per group. Of course, more facilitators are needed, usually one per group plus an additional facilitator for the overarching events is ideal to manage the interactions.
- It is possible to conduct the workshops of a tournament in parallel or sequentially. For the sake of fairness, a mass event is preferred (many workshops happening at the same time). Having said that, one needs to incorporate an additional meeting level, where all the teams meet in the same room (physical or virtual).
- The application of rules of the tournament implies that there is someone who takes over the role of a referee – this could be the facilitator for the overarching topics.
- The documentation of the results can be very challenging, when the participants are coming from different organizations, since this often means that the available technology and provisioning access rights are either very complicated or not possible. Therefore, it is necessary to introduce a new piece of technology to have a common platform.

Managerial practice

Case Study: "Mobile App Development in the Wholesale Industry"

With the "toolbox of power laws" at our disposition, the case of the wholesale industry can be continued. As a reminder, here are the weak signals which were identified as relevant for the process of attribution.

- The unexpected trust in the brand, detected by the high number of customers who, voluntarily, agreed to be tracked in the app – on a personal level!

First, the data were put into context. A "driver tree" for the development of the wholesale app was prepared up-front to get an overview of directly and indirectly influenceable factors. This tree cannot rely only on one coherent unit like Euros or Dollars (as the DuPont scheme does). A good portion of common sense was needed to create a suitable structure. It all started with a hidden complex called "Digital and Digitally Enabled Sales," which is clearly a lagging indicator, as many other aspects must have happened before to generate revenue in a digital way. We called it "hidden," because we wanted to keep this important complex in mind, but rather focus on different metrics that we could directly influence from our position. Corporate functions can only provide a frame for the local country organizations because those are earning the money.

The chosen metrics which pay into the overall metric of "Digital and Digitally Enabled Sales" are the following:

- Valuable Digital Interactions, like the usage of the digital customer card, which is needed when a customer wants to enter the physical store, or when a user is putting a product on a shopping list to prepare the next store visit.
- Logged-in Users, since it is the prerequisite to buy digitally – or to personalize the experience in the app and show relevant services, products, and promotional offers to the customers.
- Revenue per session, which was chosen to keep the app as conversion oriented as possible (that is why we passed on a classical metric like average order value).

Overall, one can say that we transformed a classical retail model into the digital world, from the perspective of corporate functions, as shown in Figure 2.56.

After setting up the driver logic, we connected the weak signals to the relevant metrics. We started by examining the global number of active users per month since it was launched in the first country a few years ago. At the beginning, the shape of the curve looked quite linear, but in the second half it turned to an exponential growth. The plot looked like Figure 2.57 where the number of customers is on the y-axis, defining as maximum value the global number of customers.

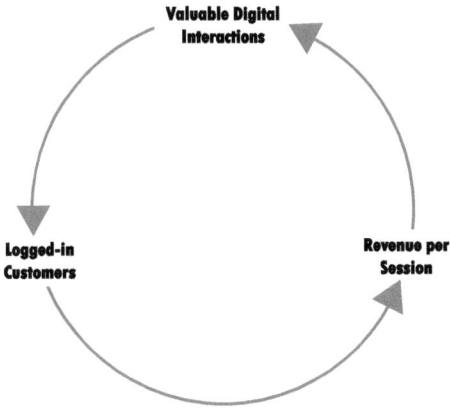

Figure 2.56: The drivers were connected in the logic of circular networks.

Number of app users

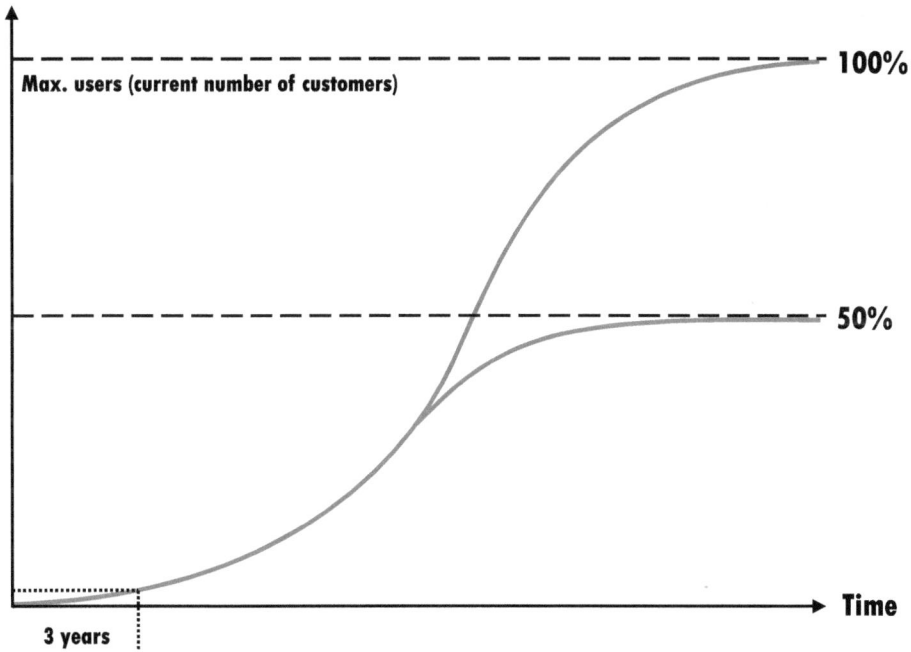

Figure 2.57: The logistic growth curve is a good starting point when exploring user related data.

It was feasible to think about it as the early stage of a S-curve. The only question was how long it would take until the inflection point turned up, and how many customers could be reached. Of course, this extrapolation was based on historical data and past action, but at least it gave an indication on how the growth of active users could continue if nothing would change (which is of course a naive belief).

We explored different S-curve shapes with a higher or lower customer reach and time horizons until a saturation effect was reached (if the maximum number of customers stays constant).

Coming from an explorative way of thinking we wanted to understand which levers promised the biggest impact on user growth, namely which features provided the highest value-in-use for the customers. This implied an in-depth analysis of the most used features (from a global angle, but also per country). The analysis focused on:

– Absolute number of interactions/taps of the users with a feature and the distribution as a bar diagram (which shows that three to five features are responsible for around 70% of the total interactions). This insight correlated with the weak signal of the high trust in the brand. It signaled: happy customers make use of the digitized purchasing process, e.g., using the digital customer card instead of the plastic type when entering the store and when paying at the cashier. Additionally, all activities regarding the preparation of the physical store visit where heavily used. Lastly, the digital invoice showed good access numbers, even though there is still room for improvement.
– Usage of features over the course of a year, which perfectly demonstrated the seasonality of the wholesale business, with peaks in almost all countries around Easter and Christmas.
– Usage of the features during a week, which nicely showed a correlation with the strong shopping days (Friday and Saturday), as well as when the local organization of the company in a country is communicating the new weekly offers to the customer base.

It was clear: the potential to activate even more customers seems to be huge, and different opportunities needed to be tested, especially because of the weak signal of regarding the high level of trust in the brand. That meant an almost revolutionary idea could be explored: what if the company, on a global level, would skip the distribution of physical plastic cards? For an outsider it might sound like an obvious thought, but within the system the idea to "de-prioritize" the almost "holy artifact" of the well-known customer card is very bold, because the idea of the card is deeply woven into the identity of the brick-and-mortar business.

On the other hand, the idea to serve to the customers primarily with the digital version via the app could be an inflection point for many other business opportunities, and consequently dramatically increase the number of active users. A very important side aspect must be mentioned to emphasize the potential impact: if all customers would use the app, all customers would make use of their digital identity (basically: a digital customer login, which is required to personalize the app and show the digital card). This simple fact would be the inflection point (another power law!) for the digitization of many core functions and processes of the wholesale business!

Case study: "Living composition in the machinery industry"

The process of detecting power laws for Bucher Industries will be illustrated by referring to three laws introduced above: Perturbation Recovery Time, Power Curve of Economic Profit, and the Hype Cycle.

– Perturbation Recovery Time (see Figure 2.37):
Bucher Industries experienced the worldwide financial crisis of 2008 as a massive downturn of the whole group. Within three months, the sales of its hydraulic division dropped almost by 40%. But within another year, they recovered to initial sales figures. In retrospect, this pattern had already been seen in former crises, and the shape of the curve reflected the power law of Perturbation Recovery time. Although the curve shape was often slightly different due to the specific context, its basic pattern remained invariant. This power law will be applied in the next steps of the methodology to illustrate the evolution of the Russian market in times of the Ukraine war.

– Power Curve of Economic Profit (see Figure 2.43)
With sales of $3.5 billion, Bucher Industries is not part of the empirical sample taken by Bradley, Hirt, and Smith (2018) to specify the power curve of economic profit. All the same, there are many similarities of its development, and the curve can serve as a benchmark, as an excerpt from relevant criteria shows (see Figure 2.21):
2. Debt-to-equity ratio: Top five of the industry
4. Industry growth 10 years: More than one quantile
5. Geographic trend GDP: Worldwide countries top 40
6. Acquisitions over 15 years: Market capitalization higher than 30%
9. Productivity increase: Top five of the industry
This means that Bucher Industries would be positioned in the second quantile of Figure 2.43, with the potential to be on the rise.

– Hype Cycle (see Figure 2.45)
As illustrated in Step 2 by the examples of the H2/fuel project and the beverage packaging industry, Bucher Industries is carefully monitoring the relevant curves of innovation. They rely on weak signals resulting from the hype cycle law to be ahead of critical developments.

In the following, the focus will be on **perturbation recovery time,** and it will be shown how the shape of the curve changes according to context, and how to "ride the curve."

3 Crafting "Leading indicators" and their narratives

3.1 Starting the exploration

System, Edge, Pattern – these three keywords characterize the previous process of leadership with weak signals. First, the system was identified and delimited by its boundaries. Second, weak signals of change were spotted at the edge of the system. Third, basic forces determining system dynamics – power laws and their patterns – were detected. The doors to dealing with complexity are now more than ajar.

In the phase of variety consolidation, the knowledge gained is converted into guidelines for leading change in uncertain times. "Leading indicators" will become the new compass for executives and employees, and tailor-made narratives will anchor the course taken. In the terminology of the management model shown in Figure 3.1, we are still gaining insight to achieve the optimal impact.

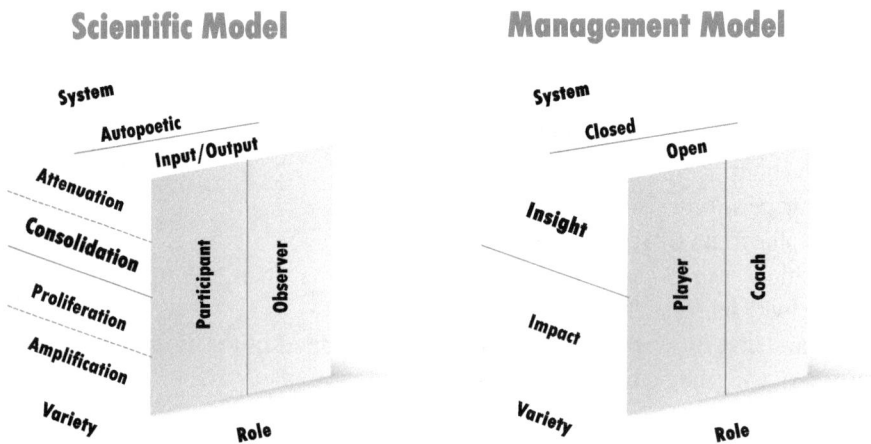

Figure 3.1: Scientific and managerial framework of Leading by Weak Signals.

The starting point is a look into the future, based on insights about the power laws governing the system's complexity and dynamics. Over the last number of decades, scenario planning has become the preferred instrument for management to deal with an uncertain future. Scenarios paint a picture of possible futures, and they develop narratives to cope with the unfolding change. They are either extrapolation of present paths of development, combining knowledge about technological and societal trends with a company's own capabilities and resources, or they just present phantasies about the world to be. There are no limits to creativity involved in such a process, but these scenarios remain somehow arbitrary. There is no empirical evidence to prefer

https://doi.org/10.1515/9783110797886-003

one to the other, and it is up to executive judgement to steer a company's growth path based on a specific scenario.

How could scenarios become more reliable and based on empirical evidence? The previous step of our methodology aimed at recognizing patterns and **discovering curves** of systemic evolution. This step of „exploiting" or "riding" **the curve**" is illustrated in Figure 3.2 by developing "power scenarios" along the curve and by specifying "leading indicators," their narratives, and objectives.

PHARMACEUTICAL COMPANY

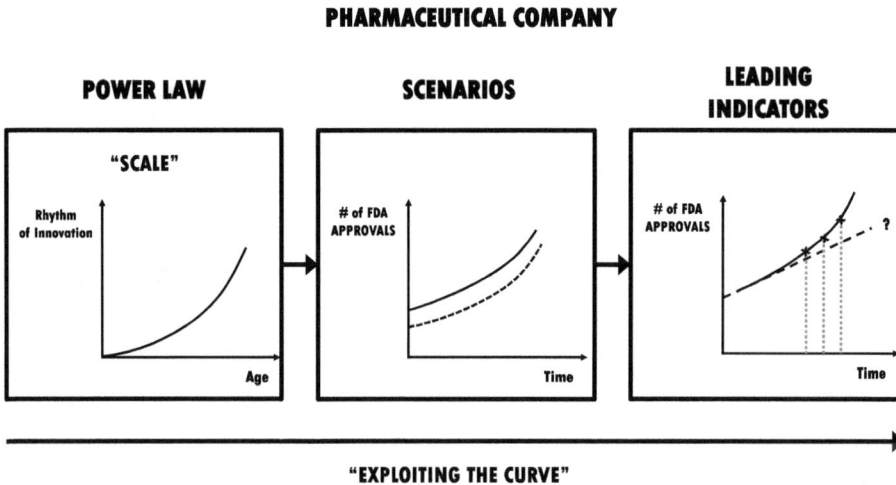

Figure 3.2: "Riding the curve": leading indicators.

"Power scenarios" tell the background story of selected data points on a curve, for instance events that point, well ahead of time, to an upcoming inflection point of a growth curve. "Leading indicators" transform insights from these scenarios into guiding principles and goals for the whole workforce. Contrary to "lagging indicators" (EBITDA, RONA) and "current indicators" (Operating cash flows, production costs), "leading indicators" represent things that are not facts yet but have the potential to become trustworthy guides in the leadership process (McGrath, 2019, 43). These "leading indicators" combine an appropriate metric with motivating narratives. They are found on the normative, the strategic as well as the operational level and have in common positions on power law curves well ahead of luring dangers or promising opportunities.

Machine learning and predictions
From artificial voice generation to dynamic image creation to natural language processing, the possibilities seem endless. Recent showcases demonstrate interesting use cases for AI-powered customer care services or even personalized erotica bots, which can stand the Turing test. These systems are

fascinating, and the combination of these technologies are very likely to create new business models – it is just a matter of time. Unfortunately, one aspect is often forgotten.

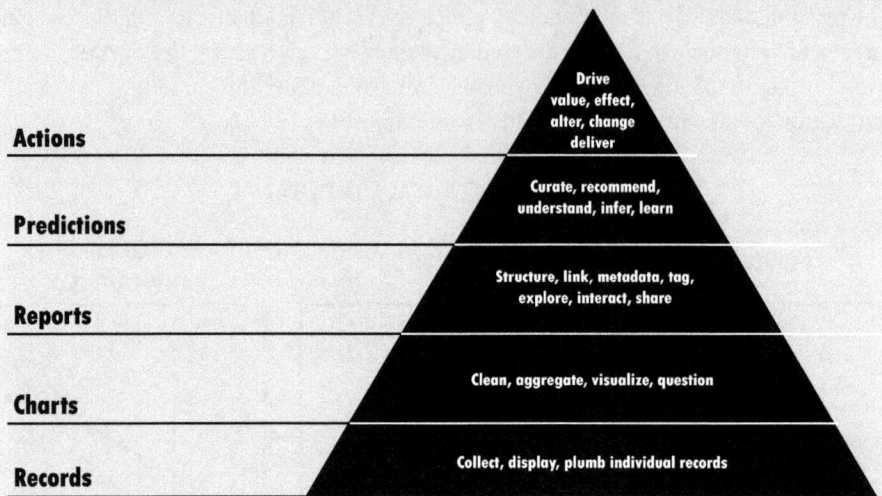

Actions — Drive value, effect, alter, change deliver

Predictions — Curate, recommend, understand, infer, learn

Reports — Structure, link, metadata, tag, explore, interact, share

Charts — Clean, aggregate, visualize, question

Records — Collect, display, plumb individual records

Figure 3.3: The Data Value pyramid (Jurney 2017, 124).

The Data Value pyramid in Figure 3.3 shows the basic steps that are typically conducted by any Data Science project to generate business value out of data. It explains the path from data collection, explorative analysis, reporting to predictions – which should finally lead to actions. For sure, this is an idealized model, because during such a project it is not that linear as it seems. For instance, when data is aggregated and visualized, it may reveal the need for further data collection. Similarly, if predictions are unreliable, it may be necessary to revisit the original question that the business stakeholders sought to answer.

But all in all, considering this approach, among many others, delivered in the end results and in the moment, we are living in an age where progress and news updates are rather measured in weeks and not in years, like it was during the AI winter in the 70s and 90s. In these days many concepts and promises have been developed, but the delivery rate was close to zero.

Due to new ideas on how to approach the neural network idea it was possible to accelerate in an astonishing speed. And it is worth noting that a new quality of inference capabilities has been developed. However, AI systems are not yet able to create "human layers of abstraction." Even if it is possible to code curiosity (up to a certain extent), it is very hard to create meaningful abstractions, which contain insights that in the end can drive decisions in the corporate world. For the moment, the entrepreneurial capability still sits in front of the screen – and not behind.

It is very likely that new AI solutions will emerge which are able to solve "high-order problems" – the question is how long it will take till systems are in place, which can invent reasoning frameworks like Pierce's Logic or Bayes' understanding of conditional probability.

3.2 Step 4: "Evolution": Developing scenarios of pattern dynamics

Conceptual foundations

Dependent on the context and the objective to investigate the future, scenarios differ in form and methodology, as illustrated in Figure 3.4.

	Strategic Reframing	Early Warning	Pattern Dynamics
Methodology	Planning	Detecting	Anticipating
Objective	**"Memories of the future"**	**"Changing Assumptions"**	**"Evolutionary Path"**
Approach	Oxford Ramirez/Wilkinson (2018)	Inflection Points McGrath (2019)	Power Laws see 2.4, step 3 of this book

Figure 3.4: Scenarios: Methodology, objective, and approach.

In the context of **strategic planning**, scenarios (represented here by the Oxford Scenario Planning Approach OSPA, see Ramirez and Wilkinson, 2016) play a central role in the process of investigating possible futures to test strategies virtually under varying circumstances. In the context of **early warning**, scenarios serve to identify inflection points due to basically changing assumptions of the business (McGrath, 2019). In the context of **pattern dynamics**, scenarios follow the evolutionary path generated by power laws with the objective to identify changes at the earliest possible instant.

Whereas the classical approach plays a subordinate role in the process of Leading by Weak Signals, the scenario approaches focused on early warning and on pattern dynamics must be elaborated in more detail, especially their differences.

The scenario approach to identify **early warning** signals serves to "spot inflections points in business before they happen" (McGrath, 2019). The process starts with observing changes at the edge of a system, extending those into the future by scenarios. For illustration, Rita McGrath chooses the topic of energy distribution. One of several scenarios she selects is **Time Zero Case**: "Two-thirds of energy investment is made in solar and wind" (McGrath 2021, 54). Working backwards from Time Zero, she identifies potential early warning signals six, 12 and 18 months before Time Zero, indicating, for instance, a change in government transitions or in incentives for renewables. These changes might falsify basic assumptions of the scenario or even point to an inflection point in the development curve projected by the scenario. In a final step, "leading indicators" are designed for these critical spots, and this in the form of special metrics and narratives to motivate the workforce.

Contrary to the early warning approach, the scenario process based on **pattern dynamics** is of prospective nature. The starting point is the present position on a system's evolutionary curve. Scenarios are developed along this curve and indicators positioned way ahead of critical transitions. In line with Rita McGrath's early warning approach, these indicators are designed as "leading indicators" to motivate executives and employees to detect basic changes early enough to initiate corrective activities.

The difference of the two approaches lies in the stance they take, as Figure 3.5 illustrates: Whereas early warning scenarios look back from the future (Time zero) to the present, pattern dynamics scenarios start from the present and follow the curve of a power law into the future. The corresponding questions are: "Do the assumptions of the scenario still hold?" versus "Are we still on track with the curve of the power law?" Whereas the first approach puts trust in one's own forecasting capabilities, the second relies on the optimal choice of a power law curve to follow the evolutionary path of the system.

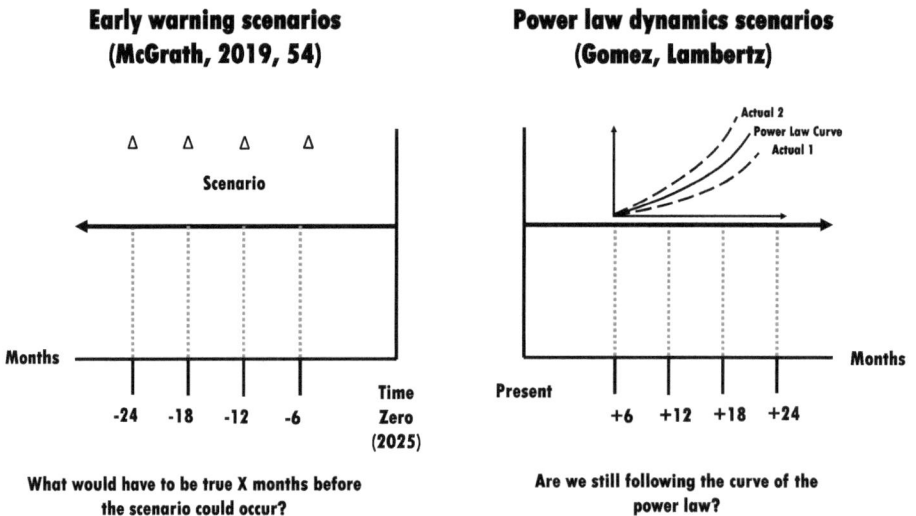

Figure 3.5: Early warning scenarios versus pattern dynamics scenarios.

Methodology and tools

A processual approach to developing scenarios in line with our methodology are **Wardley maps**. This framework bears the name of the inventor Simon Wardley (2020). There are different aspects that make this approach extremely fruitful, compared to other strategy tools, which often produce just "BLAHS" (Business Level Abstractions of a Healthy Strategy). Often, one ends up with generic statements which are characterized by an assemblage of keywords, but which often lack clarity to guide people in critical business situations.

A well-known example is the usage of SWOT analysis (Helms and Nixon, 2010), which should help the user to identify the Strengths, Weaknesses, Opportunities, and Threats of a given situation, and to derive insights that provide guidance regarding the long-term development of a topic or a strategy. Wardley offers in Figure 3.6 as an example the situation that Themistocles encountered when defending Greece against the Persian invaders (https://Medium.com/wardleymaps, accessed August 8, 2022). He demonstrates the fundamental difference between a map and its inherent qualities, compared to a typical SWOT matrix.

Figure 3.6: The difference between a visual map and a SWOT diagram is simple – but its impact is dramatic. Image credits: CC4.0-BY Simon Wardley.

The differences between a map and any kind of matrix can be summarized like this (https://medium.com/wardleymaps, accessed August 8, 2022):
- [Has a clear] Anchor
- [It is] Visual
- [Provides] Context
- [Space matters, so it allows playing with a] Position
- [Integrates] Movement
- [Contains value-generating] Components

These six aspects allow a completely different approach, which is close to the usage of real maps, as they are utilized in military contexts. Most important, one can simulate different positions and potential reactions of the competition on a map and you can get a much better overview about potential actions. A map is the foundation for the creation of scenarios – and to review a strategy cyclically. In this context he merges in Figure 3.7 the five factors of Sun Tzu with the previously mentioned OODA framework to emphasize the importance of Situational Awareness (https://medium.com/wardleymaps, accessed August 8, 22). It is about purpose, landscape, climate, leadership, and doctrine which are crucial to win. By integrating these factors, he provides another layer to gain a deep understanding on how stay one step ahead of competitors.

The significance of situational awareness can't be over-emphasized in the context of the detection and utilization of weak signals. It reflects the ability to scan and spot information that could be essential for the future development of the enterprise.

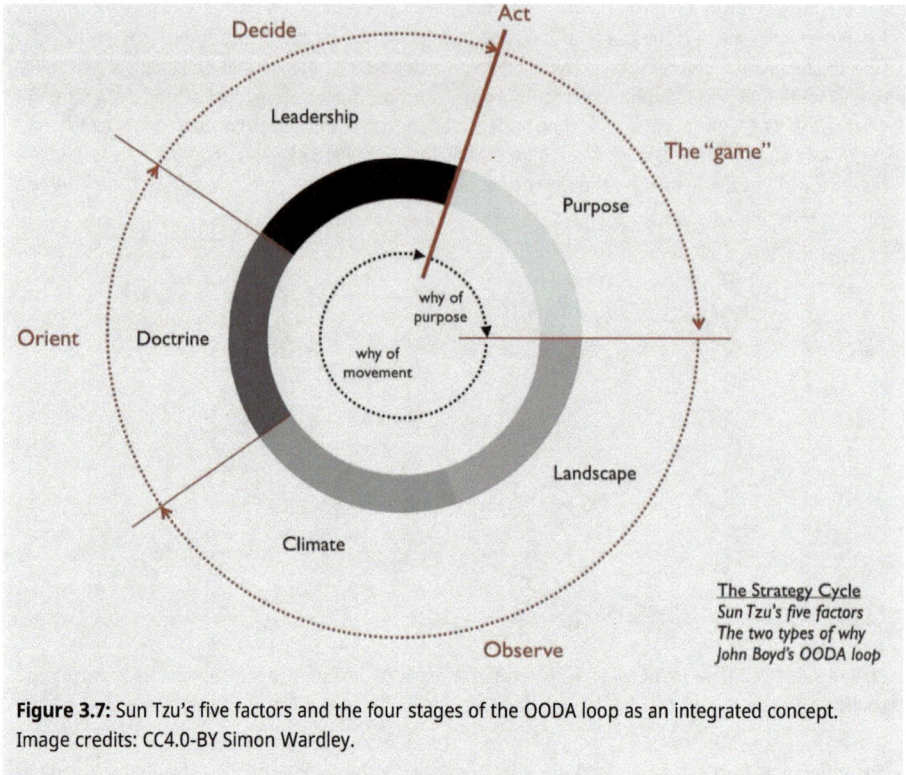

Figure 3.7: Sun Tzu's five factors and the four stages of the OODA loop as an integrated concept. Image credits: CC4.0-BY Simon Wardley.

A **Wardley map** uses two dimensions to create the playing field for scenario creation to run simulations for different strategic situations. It starts with the Y-axis which represents a typical value chain. The guiding idea: a map needs an anchor to be able to provide an orientation point. In the economic context this is of course the customer (or consumer) of a product or service, who has a certain need for "something." Usually, a customer needs a certain result that is fulfilled by using a product (or service), which needs other components to function holistically, that is something different than the sum of its elements. Another simple yet powerful aspect makes the idea of a value chain so special: the vertical sorting of the product (or service) components by its visibility towards the customers specifies the user interface (or the surface) of a good. It does not matter if it is a Google search bar or the cockpit of a car, the product's surface promotes all the settings and options to use the specific product – because the customer always needs value-in-use to achieve her or his goal. A simple explanation for this principle can be found in Figure 3.8 (Wardley, OSCON 2014, Keynote) which examines the typical British use case of . . . a cup of tea.

As you can see, the "cup of tea"-value chain is sorted by its visibility and structure into its components which need each other. One could say that this chain or tree-like structure represents the inherent dependencies of the components of a product to de-

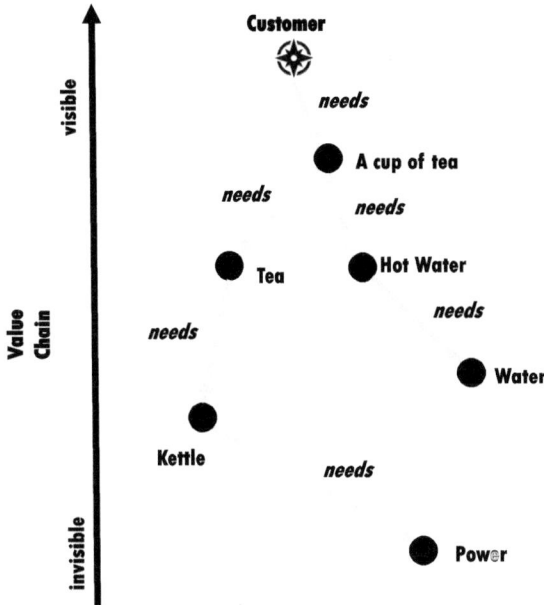

Figure 3.8: The Y-axis is defined by the value chain of a cup of tea, starting with the customer Image credits: CC4.0-BY Simon Wardley.

liver value-in-use for customers. Side note: other value chains exist which look more like a network structure, because they must accommodate the complexities of the composition of a good, driven by the customer and the corresponding ecosystem.

The second dimension of a Wardley map is defined by the product (or service) life cycle stages as a result of studying the history of product development and by considering the phenomena of "componentization." Wardley came up with four mayor stages that every component of every product will go through:

1) **Genesis.** This represents the unique, the very rare, the uncertain, the constantly changing, and the newly discovered. The focus is on exploration.
2) **Custom built**. This represents the very uncommon and that which we are still learning about. It is individually made and tailored for a specific environment. It is bespoke. It frequently changes. It is an artisan skill. You wouldn't expect to see two of these that are the same. Our focus is on learning and our craft.
3) **Product (including rental).** This represents the increasingly common, the manufactured through a repeatable process, the more defined, the better understood. Change becomes slower here. Whilst there exists differentiation particularly in the early stages there is increasing stability and sameness. You will often see many of the same product. Our focus is on refining and improving.
4) **Commodity (including utility).** This represents scale and volume operations of production, the highly standardized, the defined, the fixed, the undifferentiated,

the fit for a specific known purpose and repetition, repetition, and more repetition. Our focus is on ruthless removal of deviation, on industrialization, and operational efficiency. With time we become habituated to the act, it is increasingly less visible, and we often forget it's even there.

(https://medium.com/wardleymaps, accessed August 9, 2022)

These four stages are plotted on the Y-axis, so that the prototypical version of a Wardley map looks like Figure 3.9.

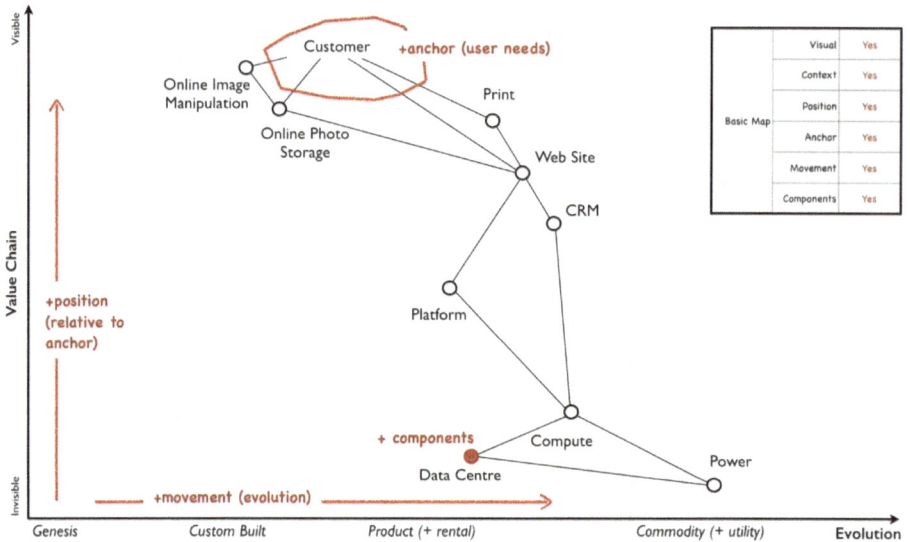

Figure 3.9: An exemplary Wardley map of a "Photo Online Service" (https://medium.com/wardleymaps, accessed 09.08.22). Image credits: CC4.0-BY Simon Wardley.

The map shows how the structure evolves from the anchor (the user needs), and how the internal dependencies are distributed over the four evolutionary stages of the product. Obviously, power is a commodity, while the Online Image Manipulation component is custom built – and there might be good reasons why you want this customer facing feature always as "agile developed" as possible, because you want to always experiment with new benefits to distinct yourself from the competition. But usually every component drifts over time to the right side of the map, because that is how innovation works: just imagine how the first batteries looked like at the end the nineteenth century, while we nowadays buy batteries in every supermarket.

The "gamification" aspect comes into play when you create scenarios with this framework. Basically, you can emulate two different types of component behavior with a Wardley map.

- How existing components will evolve, and especially how fast they will move from left to right.
- Which new components might emerge and how they will support the consolidation process.

Based on all these aspects it is possible to play with the maps. The following example deals with the question of to which extent it makes sense to move the platform component towards the commodity. The movement must take into consideration climate, doctrines, and other factors from Sun Tzu. One notices immediately that there is an incredibly slow modus operandi, also known as inertia, shown in Figure 3.10.

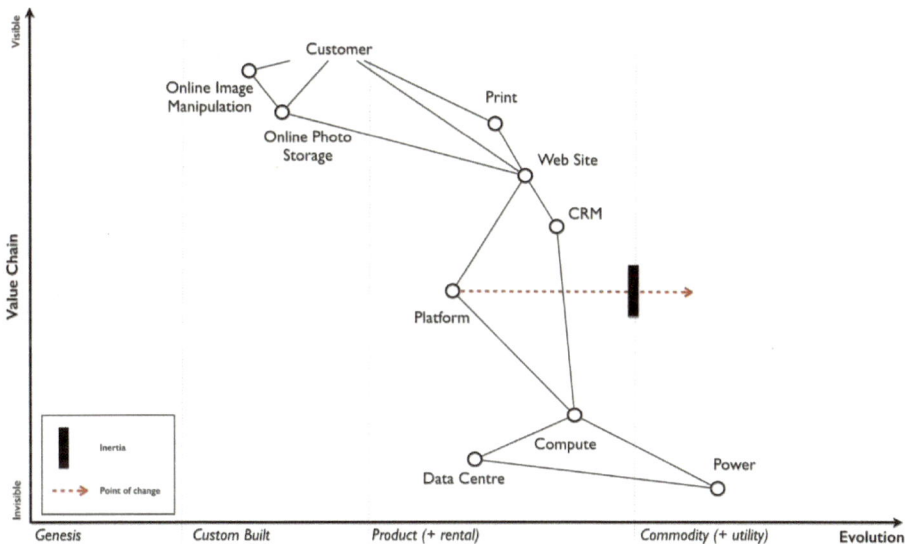

Figure 3.10: Incorporating obstacles which slow down the evolution towards a commodity (https://medium.com/wardleymaps, accessed August 9, 2022). Image credits: CC4.0-BY Simon Wardley.

Next, the scenarios of the Wardley map are combined with the power law curve selected in step 3 of the methodology. Here, the creativity of human beings to connect these two playgrounds comes into play. Just imagine that the movement of the Platform component would stay in the product (or rental) stage – that could imply a certain level of costs per user and is illustrated in Figure 3.11 as scenario A. But what if it would be possible to break through the "wall" between product and commodity? Then, in this example, it could be feasible to assume that the costs per user will decrease even stronger, because we see Wright's law (the learning curve which leads to decreasing unit costs) in its full beauty. This is scenario B in the graph.

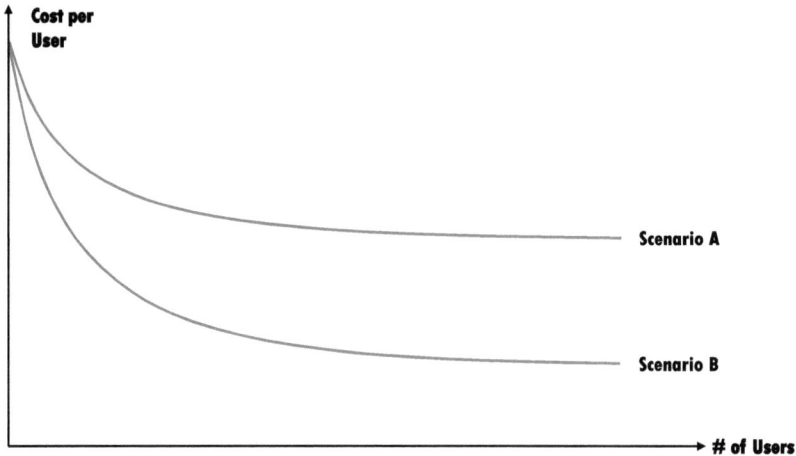

Figure 3.11: Power law scenarios and potential evolutionary paths – the case of Wright's law.

In a nutshell:
- First, use the Wardley map to understand the inherent value chain of the components which constitute a product or service – along the four evolutionary stages.
- Then use the playing field to try out different positions of the components on the map (Figure 3.10).
- Next, relate these positions to the discovered weak signal and the connected power law. This allows to anticipate the potential impact and to model different scenarios forward into the future (Figure 3.11).

How to design a workshop to specify the power curve
Developing scenarios
After identifying candidates for weak signals and associated power laws, the curves representing these laws must be specified by developing Wardley-scenarios and by answering "what if" questions: how will a specific position of your driver tree be influenced by the power law curve? Which factors could influence the selected metric? Can different shapes be extrapolated? What are potential reasons or events that could happen to explain the future development? The next step aims at shaping and marking influencing points on the curve (keeping the associated weak signals in mind). Work as visually as you can. Eventually, you discover a chain of events that needs to happen to make a scenario come true, e.g., if a competitor would behave like "that" and the customer's preferences would change to "this," then Metcalfe's law would make this scenario very attractive.

Confidence evaluation
After having created a set of scenarios they have to be evaluated. In this step one ranks the scenarios according to one's confidence that a certain law is "really" acting in the background – and that a certain development will really take place. A good practice is to use a simple percentage-based estimation of the likelihood of the scenario. Then you define a threshold that needs to be met to prioritize.

Managerial practice

Case study: "Mobile App development in the wholesale industry"

Let us summarize the whole sequence of steps to reflect where we are coming from, before we continue the wholesale industry case:

- Step 1: we started by defining the system and pointing to the input-output nature of the app, which is imbedded in the autopoietic system of a wholesaler (including all the typical frictions between the "brick and mortar" and the digital people in the organization).
- Step 2: three different weak signals were spotted, and one was selected as the most promising for further elaboration: the unexpected trust in the brand, due to the high number of customers who gave their consent for personalized tracking.
- Step 3: while looking at the data of the monthly active users of the app, we came up with the power law of the logistic growth curve (S-curve) and featured usage patterns. In short, we explored the curve.
- Step 4: Now we want to find out: which evolutionary path could result from proactively "riding the curve" of this law? In this step, the curve must be interpreted by scenarios to learn more about its evolutionary path. Additionally, we need to answer the question of which components of the app should be developed to comply with the selected power law and the corresponding metric (here: monthly active users). The Wardley map helps us to understand the range of measures that could be initiated to match the logistic growth curve.

First, the Wardley map process must be initiated to create the canvas on which the different options for product development can be drawn. It starts with the creation of the value chain, as shown in Figure 3.12. This activity provides a collateral benefit since it helps to identify the structural input-output nature of the app.

This mapping exercise was already interesting for the product team because they were aware that they depend on a high number of other internal products and service teams. One could say that the app is often just the interface to services like the electronic invoice or the product catalogue. However, they had not yet visualized these dependencies to engage in further discussions – especially with stakeholders within the organization (namely headquarters and local organizations).

After creating the value chain of the components, the evaluation of the component's maturity comes next, as shown in Figure 3.13 by mapping it on one of the four evolutionary stages.

In the next step we thought about component scenarios and how they could affect the power law of the logistic growth curve, which is related to the number of active users per month. Basically, we wanted to find out which of the features need to be "industrialized" so that the desired impact can be realized. Without going into too

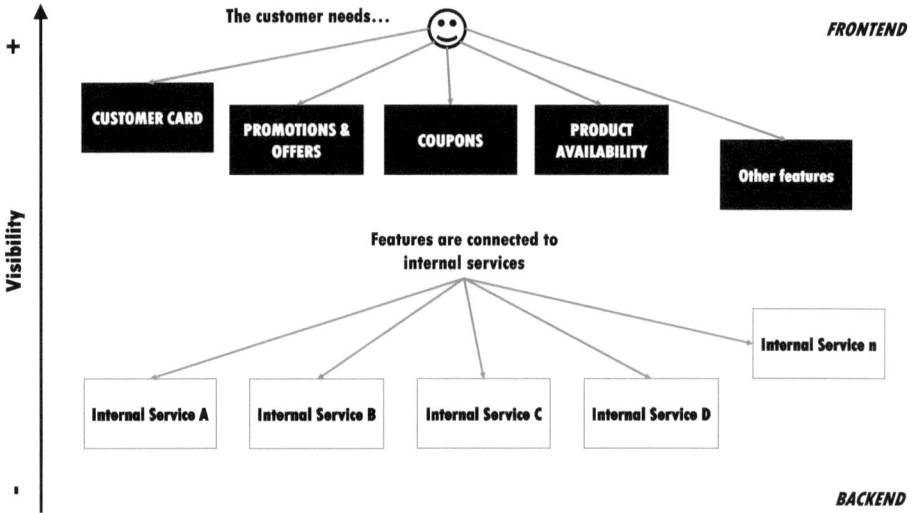

Figure 3.12: The value chain of the whole sale app (simplified version).

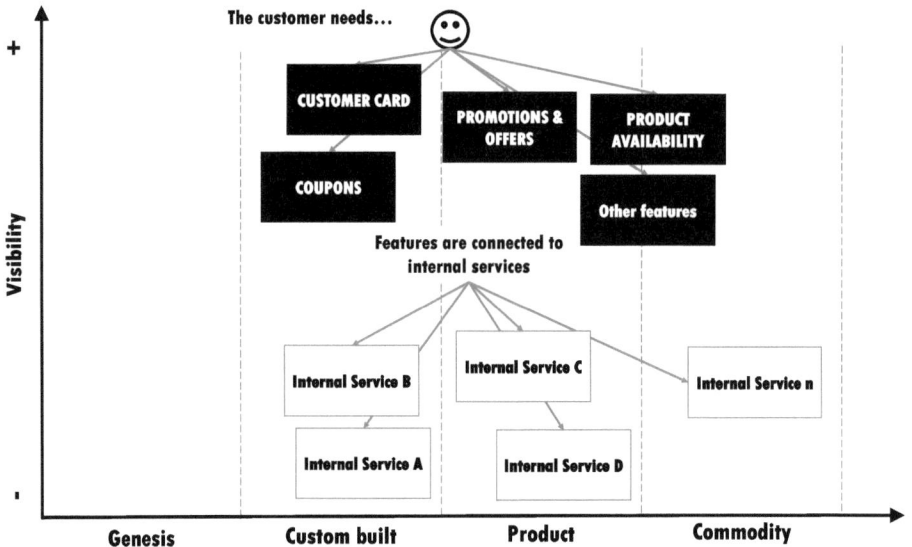

Figure 3.13: The Wardley map, showing the as-is situation (simplified version).

much technicalities, it is obvious that the strongest lever for growth would be the decision to position the digital card as the "new normal" to new and existing customers. The rationale: if customers would use per default the digital card, the app would be always used when visiting the physical store (which is related to the Cash and Carry business and proves to be extremely important for the revenue of the group). The chain of thoughts goes even further because the prerequisite of using the digital card is the existence of a digital customer identity (basically, a username and a password). Figure 3.14 shows that this would offer a whole new world of personalization opportunities to make not only the life of the customer easier, but also save money for the company, because marketing and sales measures could be conducted with much less wastage/loss spread due to better targeting possibilities.

As demonstrated in the methodology and tools section of this chapter, the clue is to connect the Wardley map scenarios with the potential power curve shapes, which of course depend on the power law you want to "ride." This means we want to be in the **mode of futuring and sensing forward.**

For our case, this means estimating how long it might take to make the digital card a normal part of customer experience. As mentioned before, the real challenge is not the technical creation of this feature and to make it a commodity, but how the organization will react on the change. This aspect points towards the autopoietic nature of the organization and its essential beliefs and its internal logic, including the legacy of thought that the physical business was the success factor in the past.

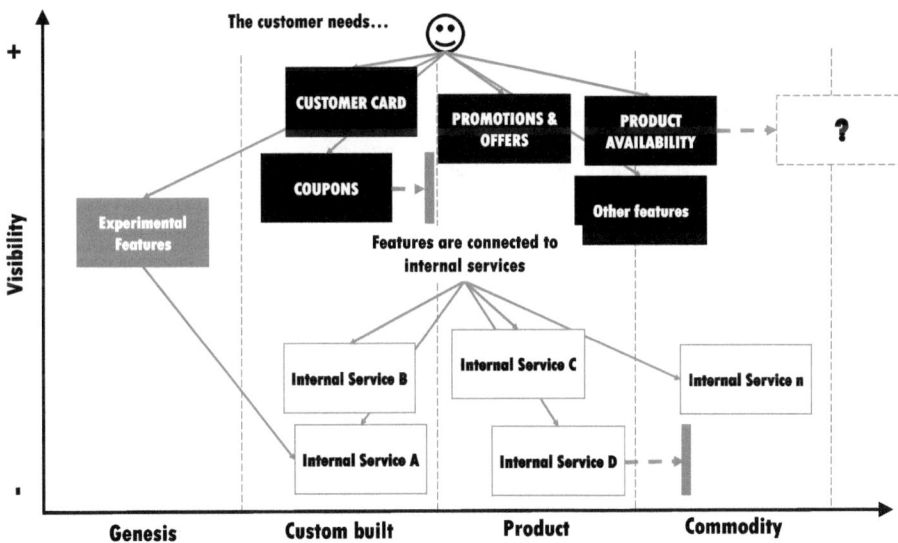

Figure 3.14: Different component positions can lead to different growth curves for the app, from new experimental features to identifying blockers.

Considering this background, the true challenge for the growth of monthly active users is to estimate the ability of the organization to change its position regarding a digital card – and to abandon (as much as possible) the good old plastic card, which has iconic qualities. It needs a very strong narrative to align a huge system towards the best scenario number three, as shown in Figure 3.15.

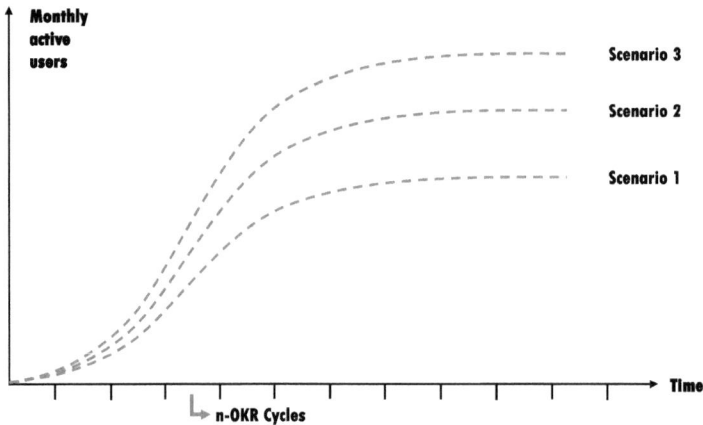

Figure 3.15: Different scenarios to reach a higher level of monthly active users.

Figure 3.15 could also be interpreted as curves correlating with the effort to change the basic cultural aspects which are part of the identity of the company: the higher the effort to change towards a digital mindset, the higher the amount of monthly active users in the app.

> A special note for readers with affinity for mathematics rounds off Step 4. They can build regression models which come as close as possible to the general S-curve power law, and they can calculate logistic functions which cover past data and extrapolate the anticipated evolutionary paths (=scenarios). Furthermore, these experts can help to experiment with mathematical parameters which are useful to increase the management's variety for the given situation.
>
> The mathematical modelling part is serving a very specific purpose: when defining the anticipated curve (= a formula), another activity needs to be initiated. It is about the confidence interval and the definition to which extent you want to tolerate deviations from the ideal plotted curve. This question is quite delicate because it defines the threshold that you want to comply with. If the threshold has been reached, one could say in such a moment: "Here we have a high level of deviation reached, that needs further investigation to understand if either our basic perception of the weak signal was wrong, or if something happened that led to a change of a variable in the function that describes the growth curve." That is why you want to define a border of acceptable oscillations.
>
> Without going into details, the accepted corridor for deviation (= confidence interval) in the App case was quite low (80%). While in scientific contexts one wants to start with 95% confidence, in business every value which is below the famous 95% can be acceptable, as long it is above 50%. That means it is better than throwing a coin to determine the chance for a reliable prediction. The derived results are the leading indicators to change the shape of the curve.

Finally, another interesting feature of Figure 3.15 is shown: The X-axis is sliced into chunks of time, which are labeled as "OKR cycles." In the next section, we will dive deeper into the question of dealing with the universal aspect of time, and how it can relate to the question of how to set qualitative and quantitative goals. But first let us continue the Bucher case which touches on the strategy of the whole enterprise.

Case study: "Living composition in the machinery industry"

In the previous step, the application of the power law of **perturbation recovery time** was illustrated in the context of Bucher Industries handling the financial crisis of 2008. To demonstrate the role of this law in the process of developing scenarios, Bucher Industries' evolutionary path in Russia over 10 years will be shown.

The operations in Russia comprise the production and the servicing of agricultural machines with sales of $50 million and municipal sweepers and equipment with sales of $40 million. There are three time periods to be documented, before 2014; (capture of Crimea by Russia); 2014–2022 (start of Ukrainian war); and 2022 to present. How can/could knowledge about perturbation recovery time enhance the development of scenarios?

In the time before 2014, there was no reason to be alerted, as the Russian market performed "business as usual." If there had been any market turbulence, perturbation recovery time would have been in line with the financial crisis experiences. As to weak signals, the options for an early discovery of emerging threats were limited before 2014. Today's instruments of data mining were not available then, so one had to rely on the usual market observations. Therefore, scenarios were made in a traditional manner by using the available forecasting data. The question arises of if the capture of the Crimea could have been foreseen by any means – for Bucher Industries this was out of question.

From 2014 to 2021, there was relative calm, as the global community tolerated the Russian invasion. But other developments gained importance. For foreign companies to build new production sites the process became more bureaucratic and time consuming with an uncertain outlook to get the needed certificates for operation. To mitigate the risk of wrong investment by buying a new site without infrastructure, Bucher requested from the Russian authorities to build the basic infrastructure first, after what delays took place. The legal requests for local production and added value increased which made a local production site mandatory. This meant that perturbation recovery time was increasing, the power law curve had to be adjusted, and the scenarios had to be refined. Towards the 2020s, the techniques of data mining made huge progress, which meant that weak signals gained in importance. Bucher Industries focused on searching the net for signs of change on the Russian side. Only towards the end of 2021 did they notice an increase in probability for an invasion of the Ukraine. But although their scenarios moved in the direction of the red zone, they were not able to react within a reasonable time span.

In February 2022, the Ukraine war started. The two industries of Bucher were hit differently by worldwide sanctions against Russia, with agricultural machines granted exemption whereas imports of municipal sweepers were hit accordingly, including the supply of spare parts for the large installed fleet. Furthermore, state expropriations threatened, and the Russian parliament ruled that in cases of misconduct the

CEO of the foreign company could be replaced by local executives within weeks, and in the extreme that local assets could be confiscated by the state. This unstable situation persists to these days. What does all this mean for the use of scenarios and weak signals? First of all, the Board of Bucher Industries decided to stay in the Russian markets, as their products and services have a direct influence on the wellbeing of Russian citizens. But again, the power curve of the perturbation recovery time had to be adapted to the restrictions of Russian authorities with respect to preliminary investments and to the lack of spare parts. And new types of weak signals had to be defined to detect impending expropriations and substitutions of executives as early as possible. By the end of 2022, the Russian municipal business is – under the given circumstances – strongly reduced but still in operation.

3.3 Step 5: "Indicators": Shaping metrics and their narratives

Conceptutal foundations

The concept of "leading indicators" has been introduced above in contrast to lagging and current indicators. Leading indicators are positioned at critical points of a system's evolutionary curve. To illustrate this logic, Figure 2.21 combining the universal natural law of "Scaling" and the empirical "Power Curve of Economic Profit" is supplemented in Figure 3.16 by examples of leading indicators.

To take lever 3 as an example: the **power curve of economic profit** focusses on "innovation" and specifies as an objective "high Research and Development investments." A leading indicator would be the development of the "top 50 of the industry." If the company starts to fall out of this bracket, action is required. On the same innovation issue, the **law of "scaling"** demands "high innovation cycles" with the objective of "higher rhythm with age." Here the "leading indicator" would be this rhythm, and its slowing would be a danger signal.

Another example is lever 6, addressing "acquisitions." Here, programmatic M&A is of great importance according to the power curve of economic profit. Therefore, a leading indicator of imminent danger would be a rising number of opportunistic M&A. The corresponding lever of the law of scaling is "size," with the objective of sustainable exponential growth. Here the leading indicator would be "phase transitions by size changes."

In a next step, the leading indicators must be translated into **narratives** to motivate the workforce to change the focus from the past to the future. And the **metrics** of performance must be developed in a wholistic manner, as Figure 3.17 illustrates.

MAIN LEVERS	ECONOMIC POWER CURVE (Bradley et al) OBJECTIVES	2400 firms over 15 years LEADING INDICATORS	BASIC PRINCIPLES	SCALE POWER LAWS (Geoffrey West) OBJECTIVES	Universal laws of scaling LEADING INDICATORS
1. SIZE	The bigger the better	Inflection point of S-curve	Economies of Scale	Steady but exponential growth	Linear growth of metabolism and maintenance
2. DEBT	D:E, better than industrial avg.	Increasing D:E ratio	Maintenance	Linear development	Superlinear trend
3. INNOVATION	High R&D investments	< Top 50 of industry	Innovation Cycles	High rhythm with age	Slowing rhythm
4. INDUSTRY TREND	Growing industry	Inflection points	Growth	Higher than market	Relative decline of growth
5. ECONOMY TREND	Growing Economy	Inflection points	Growth	Higher than economy	Relative decline of growth
6. ACQUISITIONS	Programmatic M&A	Opportunistic M&A	Size	Sustained exponential growth	Phase transitions by size changes
7. RESOURCE ALLOCATION	Re-Allocation > 50% p. 10 yrs	Incremental vs. big moves	Growth	See above	Inflections points
8. CAPITAL INVESTMENT	Top of industry	Incremental vs. big moves	Growth	See above	Inflections points
9. PRODUCTIVITY	Δ Top of industry	Increase > Top30 industry	Metabolism	Higher than maintenance	Inflections points
10. Differentiation	Margin Growth	> Top30 growth rate	Metabolism	Higher than maintenance	Inflections points

Figure 3.16: Leading indicators for Scale and Economic Profit power laws.

	Leading Indicators	Narratives	Metrics
Principle	Critical issues shaping the evolutionary path	Changing the focus from the past to the future	OKR (Objectives and key results)
Objective	Signaling deviations from an optimal curve	Getting familiar with evolutionary processes	Navigate towards the optimal curve
Example "Innovation"	Slowing innovation rhythm with age	Optimal scale rather than return on investment	Speed of iterations of experiments

Figure 3.17: Characterizing leading indicators, narratives, and measurement.

Methodology and tools

In their sequence, the steps from leading indicators to metrics are shown in Figure 3.18, again illustrated by the process of innovation.

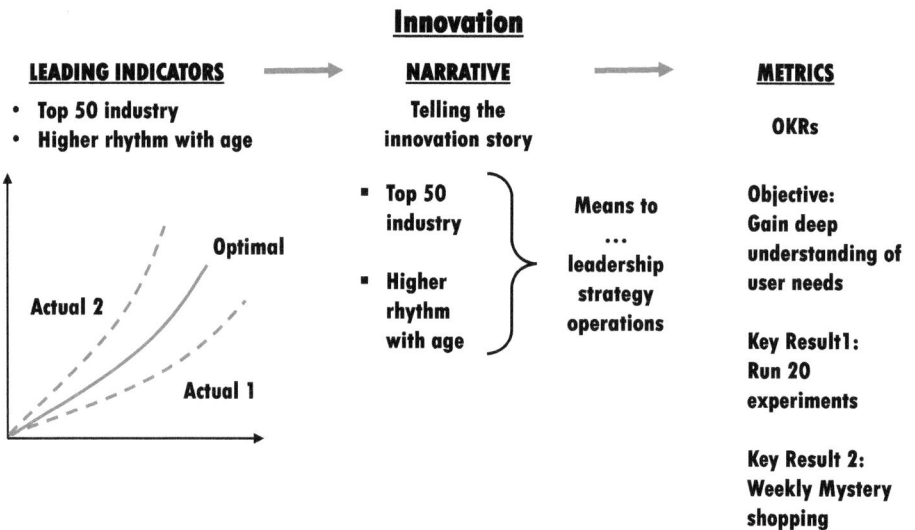

Figure 3.18: Innovation – From leading indicators to OKRs.

Rita McGrath (2019, 81) illustrates the way **leading indicators** are positioned on a growth curve by using the concept of "inflection points." She refers to Jeff Bezos, founder of Amazon, who characterizes inflection points as "gradually, then suddenly": "It isn't usually all that difficult to identify key trends. The hard part is knowing when to move and bringing the organization with you when you decide to act." She advises to proceed as follows:

> The best path forward, therefore, is to deploy a discovery-driven approach in which you plan to convert assumptions into knowledge, rather than simply try to prove that you were right. Your goal at this stage should be to generate as many possibilities as you can and to see if you can invalidate them quickly . . . Habitual entrepreneurs use a set of practices . . ., such as building varied, nonredundant networks of connections for advice, resources, and insights . . . Discovery-driven planning asks you to set some parameters for a future state – and then to work backward to figure out what must be true to make a future state real . . . The idea is to make . . . 'little bets' . . . before making a large commitment. (McGrath 2019, 125, 102)

The field of Higher Education serves McGrath (2019, 57) as an example to identify inflection points. Despite their popularity, MOOCs (Massive Open Online Courses) with millions of learners have not brought an inflection point that could disrupt higher education. Rita McGrath identifies university degrees as the biggest obstacles to disruption. With the present state of four-year college degrees, 50% of potential employees are lost. The main question remains which activities could be initiated to remove this barrier and to reach a new inflection point where the number of graduates from programs with less than four-year college degrees are on the rise.

Once leading indicators are positioned, they must be translated into the language and basic understanding of the people in charge. **Narratives** tell the story behind bare numbers and statistics; they motivate leaders and employees to steer a course in line with a future-oriented orientation. In his book "How to Future," Scott Smith (2020) presents his approach to storytelling under the heading "creating ways for others to engage with your future stories" (2020, 143). He moves from well-crafted scenarios to artefacts with the goal of bringing situations to life with objects. In one of his projects, he was asked to explore the impact of big data on culture (2020, 150). As the artefacts were initially launched in the cities of Manchester and Barcelona, they chose a representative common interest for both cities – football.

Scott Smith developed a "scenario-to-artefact canvas" which can also serve as a guide to translate leading indicators into narratives:
- What forces and issues are converging?
- What might happen as a result?
- Which slice of the future gets into focus when the forces come together?
- Which persons are affected by this development?
- What are their needs and concerns?
- How can this need, and concerns, be met?

(Scott Smith 2020, 155)

Building a futuring culture
Scott Smith provides a list of ways to shape longer-term, futures-focused organizational behavior.
- Framing provocation: "Any time you raise a future-focused question, have some implications, impacts and alternative approaches at hand."

- Driving conversations: "Find situations where you can represent the voice of the future in present-focused or near-future projects."
- Expanding speculation: "Provide tools and opportunities . . . to play with speculative ideas, prototypes, and situations."
- Seeding agility: "Expose yourself and others to small practices of futuring on an ongoing basis – at work, at home, on your commute."
- Impacting future policy discussions: "Set aside space to spell out future implications of present decisions. Consider in advance what new measurements you might use to estimate impact."
- Projecting vision: "Encourage others to clarify how vision relates to strategy and organization."
- Public engagement: "Share your own knowledge about the future with people and groups outside your organization and learn about theirs."

Smith (2020, 179)

Narratives play a central role in the process of bringing the idea of leading indicators to life in everyday working environments. But they must be complemented by measuring the performance resulting from such a new orientation: how successful are we in discovering new opportunities and critical threats at the earliest possible time? Here, the concept of OKR comes into play.

OKR (Objectives and Key Results) is anything but new, but still fresh. The idea to combine qualitative objectives with quantitatively measurable key results dates back to the early 1970s, when Andrew Grove introduced the concept at Intel (Grove, 1995). He was inspired by Peter Drucker's approach of management by objectives (Drucker, 1954) which is based on the belief that leaders define an objective (the what) and let their colleagues define the solution (the how) of a given situation. This philosophy is still part of many agile practices to ensure the optimal split of responsibilities and to get the best out of a cross-functional team (Denning 2018).

OKRs are characterized by the following factors (Doerr 2018):

- Focus on outcome, not output, by expressing the benefit and reason of the why of an activity. This means to be crystal clear about the true nature of a goal. Simple example: a software should be rather evaluated by the usefulness of implemented features for the users (outcome) and not the number of lines of code (output).
- They are ambitious and in the best case they ignite high performance in a team. They provide, in this regard, almost the quality of a narrative, that is why they complement each other and should be treated as two sides of the same coin: an aspiring idea can be expressed in numbers!
- OKRs operate in cycles (typically three to six months) and include a continuous inspect and adapt logic. From an initial planning to regular check-ins of the key results and a closing retrospective, the OKR cycle provides relative stability in uncertain times. Lastly, the cycles can be easily synchronized with the iterative logic of agile ways of working, e.g., sprints in the famous Scrum framework.
- They create transparency in an organization, because they reveal how different teams contribute towards a bigger goal – which implies that dependencies between teams or departments become tangible and better manageable. Additionally, they

help to reduce the efforts for useless alignments, because in the OKR world one has technological solutions in place that make it easy for other colleagues to understand the priorities of a team (or individual). It is possible to anticipate up front to what extent you can expect support from another team (or person).

The general syntax of OKRs can be explained with the example of a person that uses the framework for a personal development plan. Imagine you want to live a healthier life. You start by envisioning how you would feel when you lose some kilograms of weight and how you are able to hike a mountain trail in high speed. This is the narrative part which is also known as the compelling story in many change management theories. Then one continues with stating qualitative goals that contribute to the vision like "I have changed my eating behavior because that gives me energy" or "I do regular sport so I improve my fitness."

Then one defines for every objective a corresponding key result, which helps to make sure to stay on course towards the desired path. To pick up the example, one could define the following key results and think about metrics that make it possible to measure (or count) its progress:

Objective 1: "I have changed my eating behavior because that gives me energy"
Key Result 1: I eat only one piece of meat per week.
Start Metric: 0
Target Metric (for three months): 12

This key result is interesting because it works towards a threshold (maximum value). But you could turn it around and create a second key result for the same objective:
Key Result 2: Three times per week, I have cooked at home only with fresh ingredients (no canned or processed food).
Start Metric: 0
Target Metric (for three months): 36

A bad example for a key result would be the sheer measurement of the body weight and aiming towards a certain kilogram value because the body weight is a lagging indicator. For sure, the goal in this example is to lose weight but it is only the result of certain actions; and that is what OKRs are made for: you want to actively steer towards an ambitious goal and measure the actions that bring you forward.

Coming from this chain of thoughts, the OKR framework fits perfectly into the concept of weak signals and the creation of leading indicators, as presented in Figure 3.17. After the detection of a weak signal, the shape of the power law curve is determined and leading indicators are positioned on its plotted path, including the span of deviation that is acceptable (confidence interval). For the definition of the X-value (which represents t, time), one can use the length of their OKR cycle to divide it into smaller temporal pieces (see Figure 3.15). Next, one takes the end of the upcoming cycle on the X-axis, to find the Y-value according to the power law they are riding. That is the strategic number the individual wants to achieve to ride the curve towards the needed result.

Now OKRs enter the scene to initiate the desired action to reach the expected Y-value. The following question arises: "What must be the qualitative outcome of an activity to reach the expected value on the Y-axis till the end of the cycle?" The answer will be one or more objectives that pay into the leading indicator of the power law curve. One wants to try out different objectives because it will increase the variety and thus enhances the chance to reach it (Ashby's law). The truly hard part starts when thinking about feasible key results which pay into the chosen objective. OKR practitioners know that the key results are the decisive levers to create impact.

Good key results can be identified by the following attributes:

- The measurement is easy and can be automatized. In managerial practice, nothing is more troublesome than collecting metrics manually. One of the reasons why people often skip OKRs is the feeling that the effort is too high. But you can build a dashboard that aggregates the numbers for you. Pro tip: be nice to the people who know how to access and use data.
- They give you clear guidance in day-to-day work and help people to prioritize and focus on value-generating actions. This aspect is closely connected with the next point.
- The used metrics are not hidden counters of actions that just add the number of steps or actions you take. A typical example for a bad key result: imagine your objective is to increase customer satisfaction – and you would define that a number of customer interviews shall be conducted to understand the customers' satisfaction. That would lead to a system's optimization towards achieving the number of interviews – and not increasing the customer satisfaction. Alternatively, you could choose a key result like the number of experiments, to gain a data-driven understanding of your customers' preferences – and speeding up the learning process of what is important to the customers.

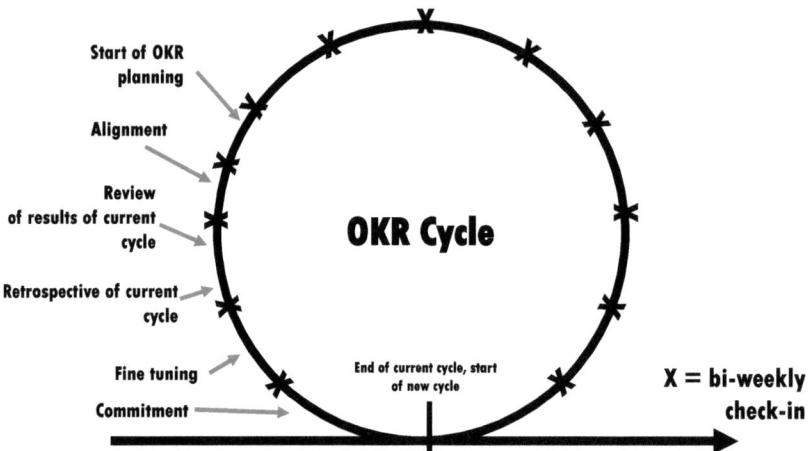

Figure 3.19: A prototypical OKR cycle and its events.

In a nutshell: well-designed key results are action-oriented drivers of the dynamics of power laws. The OKR framework illustrated in Figure 3.19 creates the pulse of the organization.

Managerial practice

Case study: "Mobile App development in the wholesale industry"

To take up again the **wholesale industry case**, some insights are shared about defining OKRs in the app context. First, remember that only the following parts of the application can be directly controlled by the product team (see also Figure 3.11).

-   The user experience design and corresponding customer journeys (which means the integration of underlying processes, which equals the pure "interfacing" of functionalities).
-   The technical stability and ability to deal with exceptions (resilience) – of course only within given constraints, due to the dependencies to other services. Example: core features like the digital customer card are available, even if a user has no internet connection available.
-   The creation of features that are device specific, like automatically opening the app when a customer enters the store.

At the same time, it is inevitable to emphasize that corporate interests must complement the technological efforts. This implies the creation and implementation of global standards within the group. Here for illustrative purposes are some examples of how the corporate governance policies can accelerate the impact of measures in the countries. It all starts with creating a new reality around the strategic lever of the customer card:

-   Create incentives when employees in the stores and call centers promote the digital card, e.g., when an existing customer has lost the physical card. Instead of providing the physical version, the employee could explain the benefits of using the digital card = the app
-   New customers get per default the digital version. Only if a customer asks actively for a physical card will it be issued
-   Promote the app wherever possible on all channels to all customer segments

Even though it has been stated before, the difficulties of changing an autopoietic system when being a player (participant) shall not be underestimated. Therefore, keep the system perspectives always in mind. They are entangled in a very tricky way. While technological aspects have rather the quality of an input-output system (from a business perspective), and the business-related aspects seem to be of autopoietic nature, the exact opposite is "true" for tech folks. For them their field of expertise is an autopoietic jungle, while the business part of the app seems to be just a simple input-output-system. This way of thinking is characterized by the following statements: "The business guys just have to decide . . ." versus "the developers should stop complaining and just build a functioning app . . . ."

This makes the cooperation of business and tech quite delicate, and a specific function in the organization is needed to bridge the gap. People are needed to translate the different "realities" in the system into a language that business and tech can understand. This is more than a normal translation process and could be called "transduction" (leading over something). These "transducers" play an important role in the next step of our methodology, which deals with the viability of an organization.

What would be the message – the **narrative** – to be spread? The next paragraph summarizes the story in the form of an "elevator pitch":

> After roughly three years of existence, the app is well established and generates already a lot of business value (ca. 1/8th of the food delivery order volume, a nine-digit number in Euros!). The set of core functionalities is (almost) explored – now we want to *exploit* the potential. Clearly, the number of active users is still way too small, compared to the total customer base on a global scale. In an ideal world we could reach 30x more users for the app. For B2B customers this touchpoint has the power to change the game – because this type of customers expects highly personalized and time-saving features. The imperative: scale the top 3 features into all countries and solve at the same time the top 3 problems of our customers who are interacting with us. We have enormous opportunities to grow and to make the app a trustworthy, reliable companion in the pocket of our customers.

This narrative must be told on all levels and on all occasions to spread the word. Additionally, the aspect of "BizDevOps" needs to be added, because Business (Biz), Development (Dev), and Operations (Ops) must work together as one team to make it happen. This insight is another example of the relevance of Ashby's Law of Requisite Variety introduced above: the increase of possible system states to absorb the environments' states is only achievable if a diverse team with different skills acts as a whole – to absorb the variety and to gain control.

Coming from this narrative, the OKRs are phrased in the following way – due to internal complexities the readers will find here a rather simplified version, but it is still relatively close to the original statement:

Objective (to initiate non-linear growth by entering the exponential part of the curve): "The app contributes to a significant growth of sales for the stationery and eCommerce business, which is driven by the number of active users."

Key Result 1: we increase the amount of ROPO customers from X to Y (ROPO = research online, purchase offline – relevant only for the stationery business).

Key Result 2: we increase the traffic towards the eCommerce touchpoint, because that allows customers to shop with us without leaving the online context.

This example illustrates the deciding factor of OKRs: to achieve focus, one should be bold enough to reduce the number of objectives and key results as much as possible. One objective and two key results are enough to ignite measures that drive the leading indicator of monthly active users. As with every other strategic activity, saying "no" to all the seductive options is a crucial part of the process to lay out the path into a promising future.

Case study: "Living composition in the machinery industry"

In the previous step, the curve of perturbation recovery time was chosen to develop scenarios about the evolution of Bucher Industries' Russia business in times of war and beyond. The step ended with the following statement: "New types of weak signals have to be defined to detect impending expropriations and substitutions of executives as early as possible." At the same time, weak signals for the future course of war must be identified to anticipate potential downturns in sales.

Bucher Industries also had to answer the question if the experiences gained in the context of the financial crisis in 2008 still applied to the context in Russia if the curve had to be adapted or if such an adaptation was no longer possible. The management decided to adapt the curve to the new restrictions of Russian authorities and to the impending lack of spare parts. To "ride the curve," leading indicators were positioned to detect critical deviations early enough. Leading indicators were supplemented with narratives to shift the focus of management and employees on the dynamics of the business rather than following traditional measures of success. Finally, goals and metrics enabling the pursuit of the evolutionary path were established.

- **Leading indicators** were positioned at the following issues: speed of sales recovery, effect of low company profile, development of sanctions, impending investments, positive attitude towards local authorities.
- **Narratives** were formulated concerning workforce ("no layoffs"), management ("priority for locals"), role of the Group ("remote").
- **Metrics** are operationalized leading indicators and narratives to monitor their impact.

4 Navigating for impact: Weak signals in action

4.1 Starting the exploration

The first phase of Leading by Weak Signals focused on the **perception** of driving forces and evolutionary paths of complex systems. Although these systems are – due mainly to their autopoietic nature and/or their dynamic evolution – not easily accessible, ways and means must be found to cope proactively with complexity. After having gained the best possible insights, Leading by Weak Signals enters the second phase of **intervention for impact**, as shown in Figure 4.1.

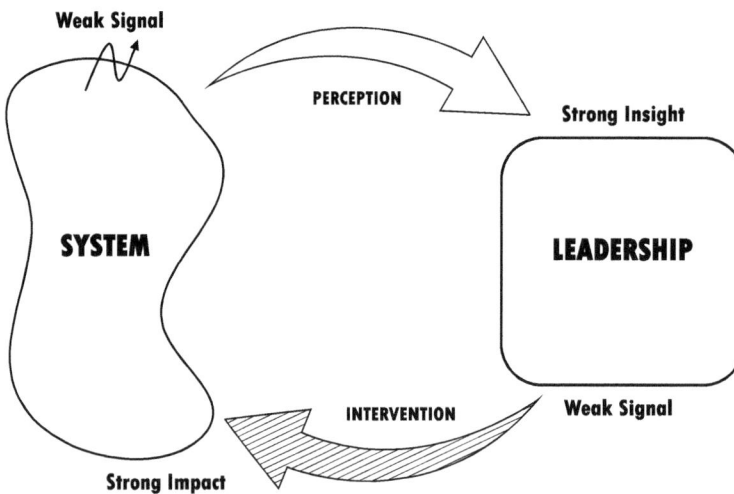

Figure 4.1: Leading by Weak Signals – the intervention phase.

In Figure 4.1, the term "weak signal" turns up twice, but each with a different connotation. Weak signals of systemic change on the left-hand side of the chart indicate small deviations in a system that initiate a process of discovery to find regularities or patterns "behind the scenes." This process leads to strong insights about the evolutionary path of the system and to monitoring devices enabling successful leadership of the system in focus, as shown in steps 1 to 5 of the methodology.

Weak signals of leadership on the right-hand side of the chart characterize proactive moves which act in line with the principle of achieving strong impact by least invasive intervention. These signals are derived from knowledge about the functioning mode of viable systems and their self-organizing properties, as depicted by the Viable System Model (Beer 1972) and to be presented in the following.

In Figure 4.2, the intervention phase is positioned in the scientific and the management model. In the scientific model, the focus now changes to **variety prolifera-**

https://doi.org/10.1515/9783110797886-004

tion by generating options to get access to the system and to navigate by using its self-organizing forces. Here again, the distinction between input-output systems and auto-poietic systems plays a crucial role. In the management model, the insights gained are transformed into interventions to get the desired **impact**. Here again, Leading by Weak Signals defines the rules: achieve your goals with minimal invasive intervention.

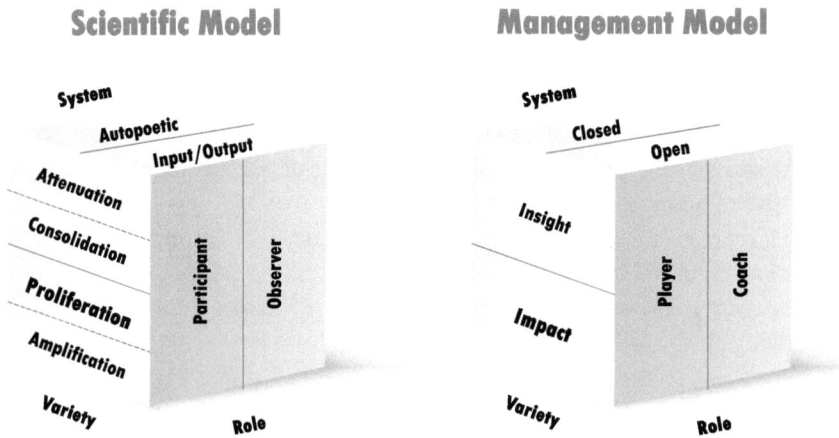

Figure 4.2: Intervention with weak signals, located in the scientific and managerial framework.

The intervention in a complex system proves to be very demanding, as the following example of the rising Covid-19 pandemic illustrates.

COVID-19 – From insight to impact
Under the title "The Virus," Gal Beckermann (2022, 211) recounts the fight of the US epidemiologist Eva Lee at the outbreak of COVID-19. Lee had the ability to plot the path of contagion and then design systems for disseminating cures. When news emerged in January 2020 that a new coronavirus was spreading through the Chinese City of Wuhan, she began to collect the sparse data that was already available. They were a weak signal at most, maybe an indication of a "bad flu year." Researchers wondered if this would be more like H1N1 of a few years earlier, or would it be like the 1918 pandemic? With the time, she was beginning to see the virus's stealthiness, and she gathered a group of other researchers to "start interventions and now." Other researchers complained that they needed more data to understand what they should be doing. For Lee, this was way too slow an approach, so she decided to communicate with new narratives, proposing a hurricane analogy or treating it as a stroke with acute coronary syndromes. She wanted to persuade political leaders and the public to act, before the storm arrived. In the beginning, her group pictured themselves as an early warning system, but now they shifted to making recommendations, even if no one was drawing on their knowledge – they acted "as if." The main questions were: what do we know about the virus, how do we know it, and what does it mean for actual communities? The biggest challenge they confronted was misinformation. In the first three months, sites with fake news were shared at about the same rate as credible ones, and over 60 percent of retweeters were bots. What had started as an ad hoc emergency response now became a long-term project against disinformation. For every new helpful intervention imposed, there was another setback, like the president declaring that the pandemic would be over by Easter, or that

to ingest or inject bleach would be the proper solution to fight the pandemic. With no success on the national level, they decided to get in contact with local leaders in states like California and Maryland – and for the first time they were successful in putting their insight into practice.

In terms of our methodology, Eva Lee had explored the curve of the COVID-19 pandemic relying on the sparse data available. She aimed at exploiting the curve by identifying leading indicators and by developing narratives to convince government and the public of the virus' dangers. But she was blocked by disinformation and forced to change the perspective by moving to another curve – depicting the dynamics of fake news – to proactively take influence.

When, in step 5 of the methodology "leading indicators" signal change (a surprise or a deviation from the power curve), proactive measures must be initiated, taken from a set of options to master complexity. Following the logic of our methodology, there are two categories of options:
- How to react to deviations from the selected curve, assuming that the basic power law is still valid?
- How to react if deviations from the selected curve indicate a false choice of the underlying power law?

Our focus will be on the first category. If the second category turns up, the methodology must be run through again starting with step 3.

To start the search for options to intervene by weak signals, the following two questions must be answered:
- Which **generic framework** can provide guidance in the process of developing options for mastering complex systems?
- How can the **self-organizing forces** of the system be identified and enhanced to enable an optimal navigation in the sense of Weak Signal Leadership?

The process of finding a suitable **framework** focuses on the fundamental understanding of the preconditions for viability. Only when these preconditions are met and viability is sustained and ensured one can speak of "mastering" complexity. Here, the Viable System Model (VSM) created by Stafford Beer (1972, 1974, 1985) comes into play. This model enables the design of input-output systems to meet the structural requirements of viability. With respect to autopoietic systems, it identifies access points for structural coupling to enhance their viability.

Before diving into the theory behind systemic viability, a disclaimer must be made. The VSM provides a gigantic framework for understanding complex organizations. Therefore, a simple but not trivial explanation of the basic functions of the model will be presented first. At the same time, the readers are encouraged to spend more time with this model, because it allows to diagnose and design organizations in a profoundly unique way. The next paragraphs are just an *amuse bouche*, they cannot replace the original works of Stafford Beer, who created the model, starting in the 1970s (Beer 1972).

In a first modelling step, the environment is explored, where the system in focus is embedded. This approach is totally different from the typical organizational diagrams (top-down or matrix) which are common in today's enterprises. This type of perspective provides a powerful new orientation: one starts with the decision about the most important stakeholder in the environment. The VSM is deeply customer-centered – and even more empathizing the importance of customers, who need a specific value-in-use, unlike other frameworks which promise to provide scaled business agility. In a nutshell: no system can exist without its environment, and there would be no environment in the absence of an embedded system. Both aspects are structurally coupled. That means in practice, that every time someone uses the term "system," the question should be answered: "What is the environment of the system in focus?"

After having clarified the system (and its boundaries), one models upwards through the subsystems of the model. They are numbered to indicate the rising responsibility for the whole – the higher the number the higher the responsibility. Simply spoken, this logic expresses the insights that value generating units can be only responsible for their "local" actions, while management functions are accountable for overarching synergies in the enterprise and the functioning as a "whole." It cannot be overstated that the accountability logic of the VSM is agnostic to persons or roles. In the first place it is about the function and only second comes finding out how a certain subsystem is brought into an operational mode, e.g., by people, roles, meetings, tools, or other structural aspects. Usually, a mix of these aspects make it work.

This comprehensive overview characterizes the subsystems, which constitute the viable system embedded into its environment, as illustrated in Figure 4.3.

System 1: this subsystem is responsible to produce and deliver value to its customers. It is called the operation of the system and works in (relative) autonomy. If several System 1s jointly produce value, the interdependence is shown by a "zig zag line" which symbolizes the transport of "matter," be it a physical artifact like wood or a programming code.

System 2: balances the activities of System 1s. It is responsible to harmonize the production flow and thus fulfill a regulatory function. It dampens fluctuations and keeps the system in a golden corridor of efficiency.

System 3: has a privileged position in the model since it oversees the activities of all System 1s. It is responsible for synergies between all the System 1s, by providing a fair distribution of resources and rules. It is accountable for the mid-term results of the organization.

System 3*: this subsystem takes care of detecting "blind spots." Originally, Stafford Beer called it the audit channel. In the context of knowledge work we prefer to use the term retrospective system.

System 4: this subsystem is in charge of exploring the environment and developing strategies and scenarios for the organization. Essentially, it is responsible for the capability to adapt and, therefore, it is the place for innovation and the long-term development of the whole.

System 5: the ultimate authority of the organization since it defines its identity. Even though it is far away from operations (System 1) it is responsible for all activities of the system. It balances the interests of the "inside and now" (System 3) and the "outside and then" (System 4).

The Viable System Model will be the "north star" in the process of generating impact in the face of complexity. It provides the overall framework to be complemented by additional approaches to allow a more in-depth exploration from a specific perspective, namely the **enhancement of self-organization**.

Acquiring knowledge about the organizational structure presented in Figure 4.3 prepares the ground for minimally invasive interventions in complex systems by using and enhancing their self-organizing forces.

The approaches presented in Figure 4.4 are not that distinct in nature. In managerial practice they are combined to get the best out on every level. Furthermore, the enterprise and team (or team-of-teams) level are influencing each other. A brief introduction to these approaches will provide a better idea how they differ, even though they can and should be used to complement each other:

Market-driven ecosystems on enterprise level: Network Organizations
- Providing the overarching idea of a flexible structure that allows its members to deliver value to others in the network.
- The linkages are constituted by value streams resulting in a constant exchange of material, energy, or information.
- The degree of autonomy of the members is by nature very high, but in principle they need to finance themselves (profit and loss responsibility).

Market-driven ecosystems on team level: Agile Practices
- Implementing adaptive workflows within a network organization (fostering autonomy).
- Creating value in a complex environment by enhancing an incremental approach and by learning cycles focused on what the customer really needs.
- Interpretation of roles and leadership in a distributed way; the most competent person is in the position to make decisions, or to activate the team if decisions are too complex for a single person.

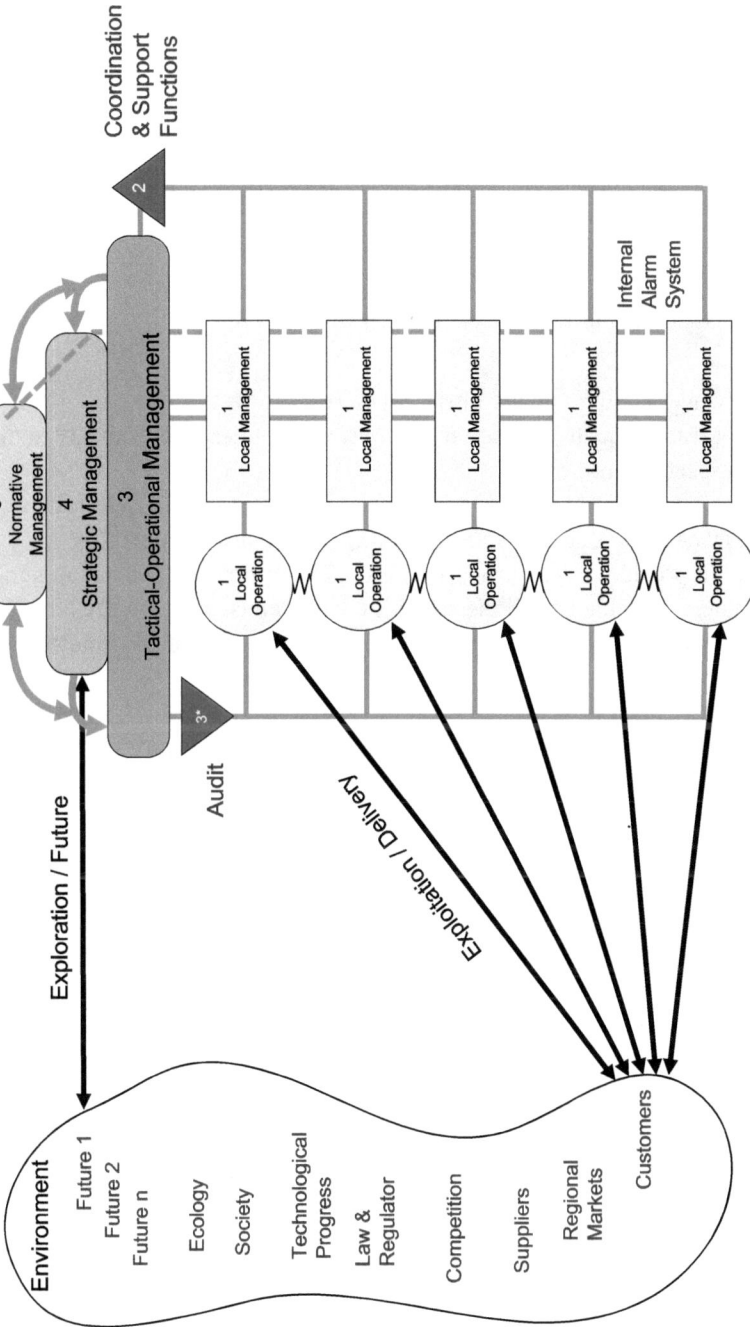

Figure 4.3: A simplified version of the Viable System Model visualizing its parts and its environment.

	Market-driven ecosystem	Technology-driven ecosystems
Enterprise level	**Network Organizations**	**Enterprise Tech Stack**
Team or team-of-teams level	**Agile Practices**	**Microservice Architecture**

Figure 4.4: Self-organizing structures for corporate and team levels.

Technology-driven ecosystems on enterprise level: Tech Stack
- Tech stack arranges the technological solutions in the enterprise from a customer or user perspective (frontend).
- From the user interface down to underlying services, the boundaries of the technical landscape are defined to reduce the jungle of corporate systems.
- The aim is to provide a clear frame which implements on the one hand enough freedom to create value within the corporate constraints, while on the other letting the teams decided how to exploit the given tech stack and contribute in the best possible way.

Technology-driven ecosystems on team level: Microservice Architecture
- Microservices are small technical solutions that ideally are related to one business problem and therefore fulfill exactly one task.
- Comparable to micro-apps that have a dedicated purpose, they should be as autonomous as possible, within the given tech stack.
- By decoupling the user interface (frontend) from underlying solutions (backend) it becomes easier to prevent huge monolithic applications (see also power law "Loose Coupling, High cohesion"). Unfortunately, over time, all systems have the tendency to turn into monoliths. It seems as if this is the price which must be paid for tackling the universal forces of entropy.

Once the basic options for intervention are explored, the best combination of approaches must be selected in line with the methodology of Leadership by Weak Signals. This selection follows the rule of "intervention with minimal invasion," based on Malcolm Gladwell's (2000) construct of **"tipping points"**: how can the self-organizing forces of the system be put at the service of triggering change processes? In **input-output systems** the process is rather straightforward, as the tipping points can be easily deducted from the structure of the Viable System Model and the complementary approaches of Figure 4.4. **Autopoietic systems** require a fundamentally different approach. First, the sensors at the system's boundary must be detected and be used to infiltrate change initiatives. In Figure 4.14 of step 7, the tools to achieve this goal are presented and then illustrated by examples from business practice.

Finally, the **concept of nudging** (Thaler and Sunstein 2012) must be addressed, as it meets with widespread acceptance in the context of tipping points. It proposes the use of fine control to move a system in a certain direction justified by in-depth knowledge about the future. But as we learned in our introductory part, complex systems cannot be predicted exactly, neither as to their dynamics and nor as to their evolutionary path. The only way to initiate change in complex systems is by structured experimentation, in our case derived from anticipated power laws, and not by lulling people into a false sense of security by extrapolations of past and present data. These kinds of predictions ignore the range of potential outcomes of forecasts (Tetlock, 2015). It is **not** about "random experiments" for the sake of experimenting, but about testing reality based on weak signals and the anticipated likelihood of being relevant to understand and drive relevant futures.

4.2 Step 6: "Framing": Creating self-organizing viable systems

Conceptual foundations

Given the logic of the Viable System Model (VSM), how can it be enriched by the approaches presented in Figure 4.4? It is essential to dive deeper into the theory of viable systems, especially to enhance the understanding of the market-driven logic. An essential feature of viable systems is their **fractal or recursive nature**: they contain in turn viable systems nested in the overall system. A common picture to visualize this idea are the famous Russian dolls, also known as Matryoshka dolls. Each doll fits into its "upper" or "lower" mate, because they share the same shape and physical proportions. This logic might sound quite abstract, but it correlates with our daily experience in organizations.

Deep dive into the Viable System Model and its recursive structure
Figure 4.5 shows the production process of an enterprise (System 1) as an input-output-system (a value stream), while the management functions (System 2-5) take care of all the other tasks, which are not directly related to generate value for a customer, but still are prerequisite to create viability (autopoiesis).

In this example, the operation is a team of software developers who code an application. The management function is maintained by a mix of developers from the operation itself and some people who take care of tactical, strategic, and normative issues. Together, they shape the "complete management system" up to System 5 which finally represents the basic beliefs which enable decision making and creating togetherness for the whole.

Instinctively, it is evident that such a rather simple setup contains another recursion level within the operation – here three individual human beings which shape System 1, as shown in Figure 4.6.

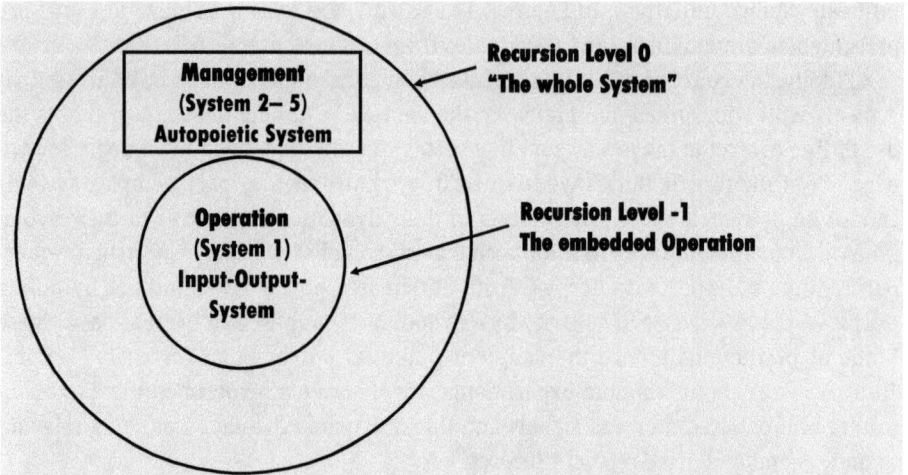

Figure 4.5: Basic illustration of recursion levels in the Viable System Model.

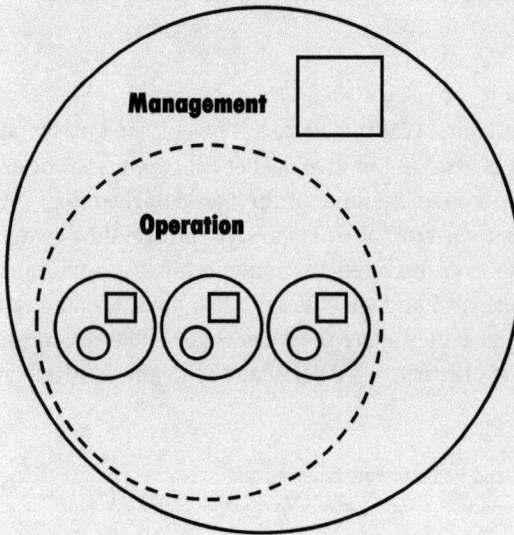

Figure 4.6: The operation contains again viable systems (three people).

Figure 4.7 shows three recursion levels at a glance. In addition, some "neighbors," B and C, come into play. Lastly, an overarching management function complements the "upper" recursion level.

All in all, two messages should be clear: a viable system consists always out of other viable systems. It is a self-similar structure, which can be compared to a fractal – on every level the systems 1s to 5 can be found. Secondly, any viable system, that is a human-made construct, ends up with the single human being the last "node." That is important to state since it shows that the VSM is ultimately in its deepest core about human beings.

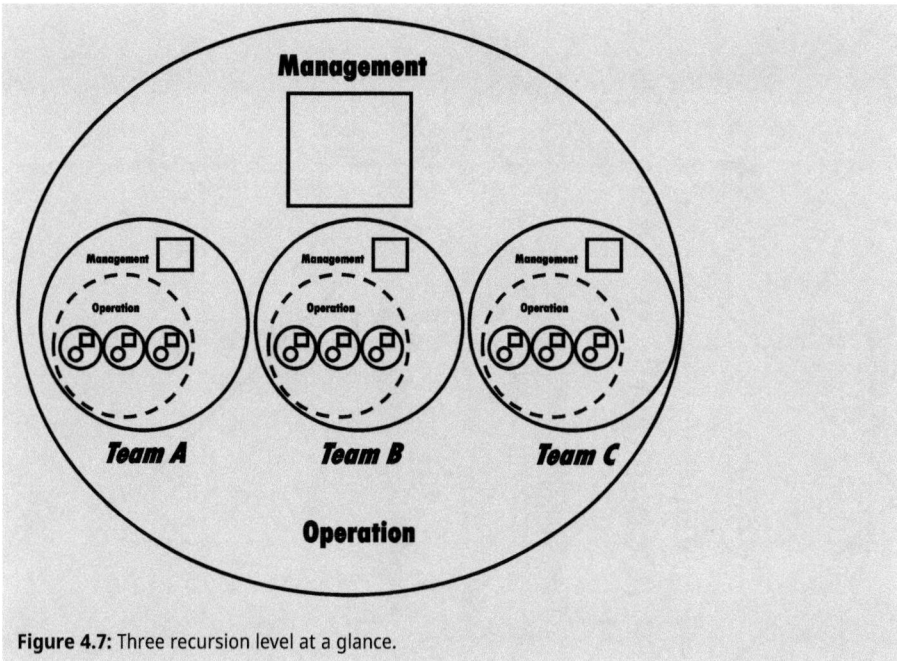

Figure 4.7: Three recursion level at a glance.

The fractal feature is crucial to understanding how self-organization (autonomy) and centrality (cohesion) are balanced in the Viable System Model. This insight refers to the first essential balance in organizations introduced by Ivo Velitchkov (2020), and it makes clear that an optimal state between these two polarities is not static, but it is a dynamic process that depends on external and internal perturbances.

This phenomenon is explained in Figure 4.8 by extending Figure 4.3 with the concept of variety on the horizontal and vertical levels in the Viable System Model. While the horizontal channels (connecting the operation with the environment) shall be as self-organized as possible, to ensure the best time-to-market delivery of value, the vertical channels shall expose cohesive forces to keep the system together as a whole.

The balancing act is quite delicate, because two extreme scenarios need to be prevented:

- Stasis: if the vertical variety is too high, e.g., driven by an enormous bureaucracy and a high number of polices and rules, the system will become hyperstatic and will not be able to deliver value-in-use on the long run.
- Chaos: if the horizontal variety is too high, e.g., because an exaggerated level of autonomy is provided, the organizational cohesion is endangered, since no one takes care of the whole.

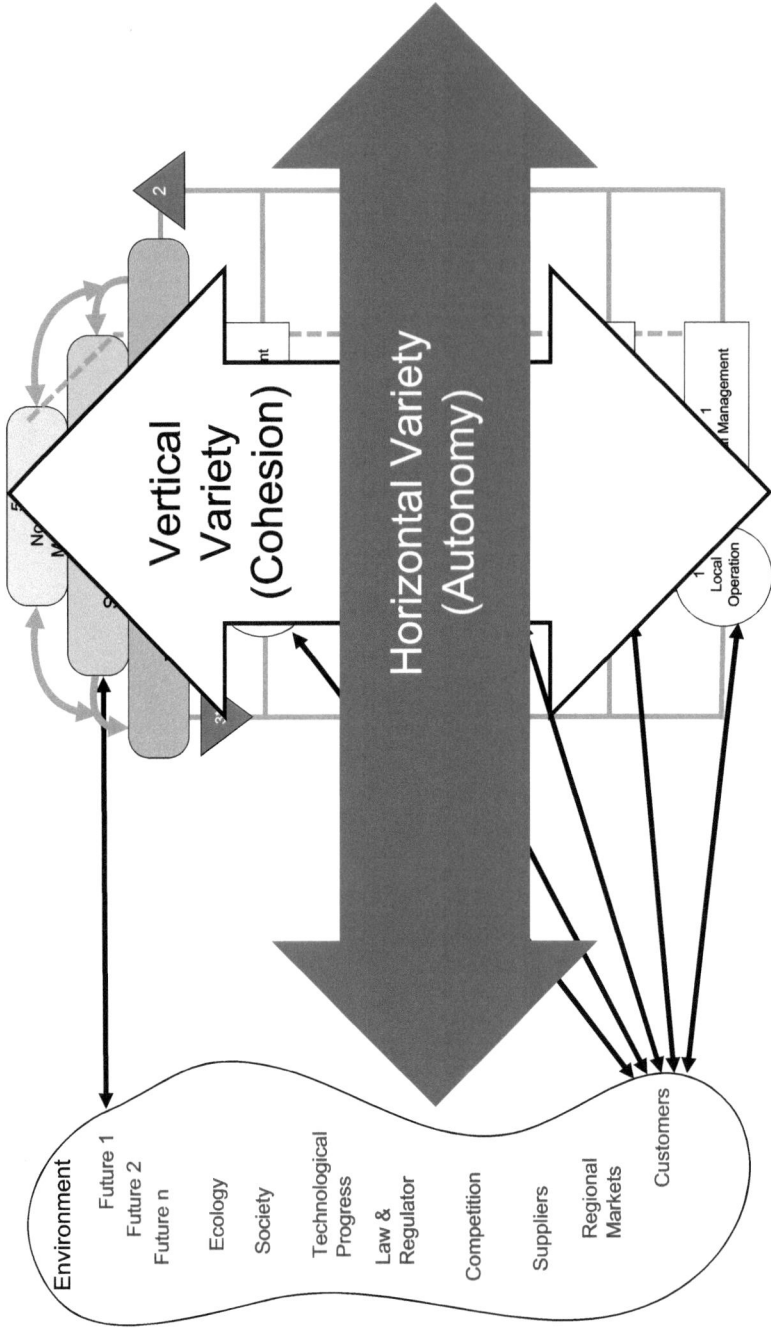

Figure 4.8: The essential balance of autonomy and cohesion in action.

Fractality and autonomy/cohesion are two fundamental aspects that can be learned from the VSM for the understanding of viable self-organization. Fractality is needed, because the dynamics of the environment are too high to be controlled by central governance and management would be completely overwhelmed by operational activities. In nature, one finds the same principle to reduce the complexity, namely the division of cells. But slicing an organization into smaller units come with a price. The costs for splitting an organization into divisions are high, because small autonomous units still need some sort of overarching coordination to stay together as a whole. It will always be a matter of the best trade-off between coordination costs and profits from supporting customers to achieve their goals in a very timely manner. That is what customers are essentially paying an organization for, being able to solve problems in a relatively short period of time.

In the last paragraph, the topic changed from fractality to a second aspect: the balance between relative autonomy and cohesive forces (or: attractors) to glue the whole together, especially in a turbulent environment. This organizational aspect explains how viable self-organization behaves like a **mobile** in motion. It is a continuous balancing act on many recursion levels at the same time. That is why viable systems utilize internal and external sensors to discover early warning signs and weak signals – to be the deciding step ahead of the "devil."

In the context of Leadership by Weak Signals, the VSM is also helpful to operationalize the topics shown in Figure 4.4. Market-oriented ecosystems provide the overarching frame for agile practices like Scrum. Their artifacts, roles, and events are the same on every recursion/network node level, also known as "Scrum of Scrums," with its several offsprings. In the technology-driven context, the usage of the VSM on the enterprise level is somehow different. The idea of technology driven systems originates from System 5, as this kind of decision is part of the identity of a system. From there it emanates to System 4, which is responsible for the discovery of new opportunities and innovation. The usage of technology is of strategic importance, and its advantages must be spread to all subsystems of the VSM – especially for successful standardization and for close alignment with the people taking care of tactical questions. Basically, we are talking here about another essential balance (Velitchkov, 2020) which deals with the question of exploiting the existing business model and of exploring the next generation. The level of the team or team of teams is reflected in the VSM by its fractality. That implies that the technological specification needs to reappear in the same way: the "tech stack" (the technological structure used to build product) on the enterprise level needs to be supported on lower recursion levels in a similar way. The team level is important to bring the abstraction of a tech stack to life. This is often realized by a so-called "microservice architecture" which ensures that different parts of the tech stack can be built by relatively autonomous teams. That refers to the power law of "Loose coupling and high cohesion."

Methodology and tools

The four approaches of self-organization presented in Figure 4.4 are at the same time implementations as well as refinements of the viable system model. They are on the one hand categorized by the organizational levels of the enterprise and team (or teams of teams). On the other hand, a distinction between market- or technology-driven approaches is drawn. In the following, their implementation in managerial practice will be illustrated.

Market-driven ecosystems for the enterprise level: Network organizations

Under the theme "Everyone an entrepreneur," Gary Hamel and Michele Zanini introduce in their book *Humanocracy* (2020) an approach to enhance self-organization on enterprise level. They illustrate the basic logic by referring to the Chinese company Haier which competes worldwide with household names such as Whirlpool, LG and Electrolux, generating some $40 billion annually with 50,000 employees. Their approach departs from bureaucratic norms in seven critical ways:

– From monolithic businesses to micro enterprises: the organizational model mimics the architecture of the internet. While incredibly diverse, the web is held together by common technical standards that make cyberspace navigable and allow sites to swap data and other resources.
– From incremental goals to leading targets: instead of taking last year's performance as a starting point, growth objectives are set "outside in." Every unit is expected to become an ecosystem business and to continually reexamine its core assumptions.
– From internal monopolies to internal contracting: in traditional forms of organization, employees are often insulated from market forces, and their structural relations are predetermined. Here, the units are free to contract with any other units, also with corporate functions.
– From top-down coordination to voluntary coordination: in most companies, coordination means centralization. But trade-offs are best made by those closest to the customer. Therefore, any unit is not only free to hire and fire corporate services but can also go outside if it believes external providers can better meet its needs.
– From not-invented-here to open innovation: every new product or service is developed in the open. New technological inventions are shared in a "patent pool," and they are rewarded when used in a final product. By moving product development online, the time from concept to market is dramatically reduced.
– From innovation phobia to internal venturing: internal entrepreneurs post ideas online and invite others to co-develop the business model. They set up internal incubators with nodes for development, distribution, and administrative support.
– From employees to owners: units have the freedom to decide which opportunities to pursue, to set priorities, and to form both internal and external partnerships. They make hiring decisions and decide about pay rights and distribute bonuses.

Hamel and Zanini (2020, 120)

In *Reinventing the Organization*, Arthur Yeung and Dave Ulrich (2019, 93) present the organizational logic of autonomous units with shared resources in enterprises like sport associations, shopping malls or private equity firms. Its building blocks are platforms, cells and allies, whose interaction generates four specific capabilities: external sensing, customer obsession, innovation throughout, and agility everywhere. Figure 4.9 gives an impression of the structural form of such market-oriented ecosystems.

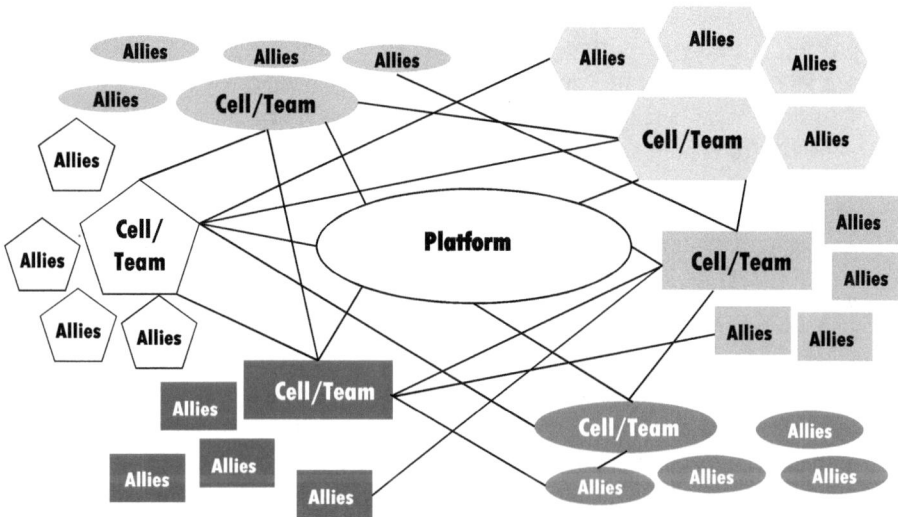

Figure 4.9: Structure of a market-oriented ecosystem (Yeung and Ulrich 2019, 96).

Cells (sports teams, firms in private equity partnerships, shops in malls) are customer-oriented entrepreneurial units; platforms (cloud computing, supply chains, user traffic) provide the cells with valuable common activities and resources to succeed in their respective markets, and allies (contractors, experts) supplement platforms or cells. This structure looks familiar, but its strength lies in the ability to build unique capabilities:

- External sensing: the platform can analyze big data, compile customer profiles or (in the spirit of this book) observe and interpret weak signals.
- Customer obsession: by combining platform expertise with business knowledge from the cells, customers can be approached as to their latent needs for targeted recommendations.
- Innovation throughout: again, supporting the entrepreneurial spirit of the cells with the findings of external sensing (using network effects) will produce and dissipate innovative ideas.
- Agility everywhere: less impeded by resource constraints and armed with knowledge and access to key technologies and data, new ideas can be brought faster to the customer.

(Yeung and Ulrich 2019, 96)

Market-driven ecosystems for the team level: Agile practices

The general idea of supply and demand can be brought to life with the vast spectrum of practices that support agility on team level. Also, the scaled variants of agile practices can be useful for team-of-teams constellations. Agile working structures foster not only self-organization, but also self-management and relative autonomy of small entities. The following aspects are crucial to succeed as an agile team (Gomez, Meynhardt, and Lambertz, 2019, 179):

– KYC: know your customer (or consumer) and be able to empathize as much as possible with the most important stakeholder. This aspect is for sure the most essential one when a team wants to act in a market-driven ecosystem.

– Transparency: if a team acts in a market-driven way, a high level of transparency is needed to enable accountability. Transparency is more than sharing information, it means to be collaboratively responsible for a common understanding of contexts, goals, and tasks to be done.

– Cross-functionality: a complex world needs teams which contain different capabilities and skills to build and improve a product. A team should have the necessary skills to act in relative autonomy to satisfy a customer or user.

– Volunteering: it seems obvious that humans like to work on problems that meet their interests and strengths. Insofar as it makes sense to share work in a team according to these criteria, two challenges still remain: on the one hand one team member could have too much work because certain skills are of high demand. On the other hand, there is always work left that is in nobody's interest, but all the same must be done. The goal is to find a fair balance of "wanna do" and "let's get it off the plate."

– Prioritization: in a market-driven environment the team has rarely the situation that they lack ideas on how to deliver value to the customer. The question arises of which task should be done in which order. As a simple guideline ask yourself the following questions: MOSCOW – what must, or should, or could, or would be done to satisfy a customer or user? Never forget: customer value is what the customer values.

Technology-driven ecosystems for the enterprise level: Tech stack

A tech stack on enterprise level consists out of microservices (on team level, as shown in the next section). When planning a tech stack, it is useful to use a "customer journey" and to understand how customers are interacting at various touchpoints. This leads to a generic logic of how different types of customer lifecycle stages need to be incorporated in the conception of a tech stack:

– Customer acquisition: especially for digital businesses, it is important to use a consistent advertising tech stack to identify and target customers. The idea is to be efficient in marketing spending, and at the same time to offer a high level of relevancy and not to bother potential customers.

- Value delivery: the whole business and its value streams need to be integrated into a wholistic, seamless experience. This can be challenging for organizations with an organically grown tech landscape. Interdependencies between different solutions need to be managed to prevent any interruption when customers interact with a value stream.
- Customer Retention: ensuring recurring revenue and a consistent collection of customer data. When the customer data platform is in place, a high level of automation is possible that pays into the efficiency paradigm.

Yueng and Ulrich distinguish three archetypes of market-oriented ecosystems: creativity-driven, product-driven, and efficiency-driven structures. In our eyes, this type better fits with the technology-driven structures of Figure 4.4. In this sense, Figure 4.10 represents the efficiency logic of **Alibaba**, the dominant force in Chinese e-commerce which serves more than 500 million customers in over two hundred countries. Such a frame can ignite efficiency in the self-organization process because it provides clarity of members' roles and contributions in the context of the greater whole.

Technology-driven ecosystems for the team level: Microservice architecture
Self-organization can be enhanced by making use of microservices (self-contained services), which are developed by relatively autonomous teams (bound together by an enterprise tech stack). This type of engineering approach can be characterized by the following attributes:
- Teams provide their solution as a "micro app" which decouples program logic and data storage (back end) from the user interface (front end). This means one team can offer the backend that is consumed by another team that takes care of the front end towards the user or customer.
- A microservice is quite granular and shall take care ideally of only one task, so that in an perfect world one is striving for the optimal simplification of a complex piece of software. This shall mitigate the development of monolithic applications.
- Every team is responsible for their services, which implies that it must be treated like a product. Inherently, a microservice product life cycle has to be implemented to ensure the effective and efficient discovery, development, and delivery of "micro solutions."
- The microservices can be deployed independently from other services and communicate usually via a protocol that is agnostic regarding the underlying technologies.

These points are the foundation to enhance self-organization and self-responsibility on the team level via a technology-driven perspective.

Small front end and large middle platform structure

Front End				
Taobao	Tmall	BoB	Entertainment	

Operations on different devices (PCs, mobile, TV, etc.)

Requirement for transformation: specialization

The boundary between front end and middle platform functions is whether to directly face external customers

Front end: focus on understanding demands and the business logic and creating customer-oriented products and services

Middle End		
Member platform	Merchant platform	Content platform	Merchandise platform	...
Middleware technology		Algorithms: search engines, etc.	...

Business-support platform level: abstraction of shared business logic

Service level: creating an abstract system platform made for higher levels

Requirement for transformation: transparent and easily shared

Alibaba Cloud

Computing level: computing and middleware operating environment, including the Apsaras (cloud) system

Technology back end

Technical support department: data center, network construction, back-end tool development, project management, cloud operations

Technology back end: operations and hardware infrastructure

Function back end (HR, finance, legal, ...)

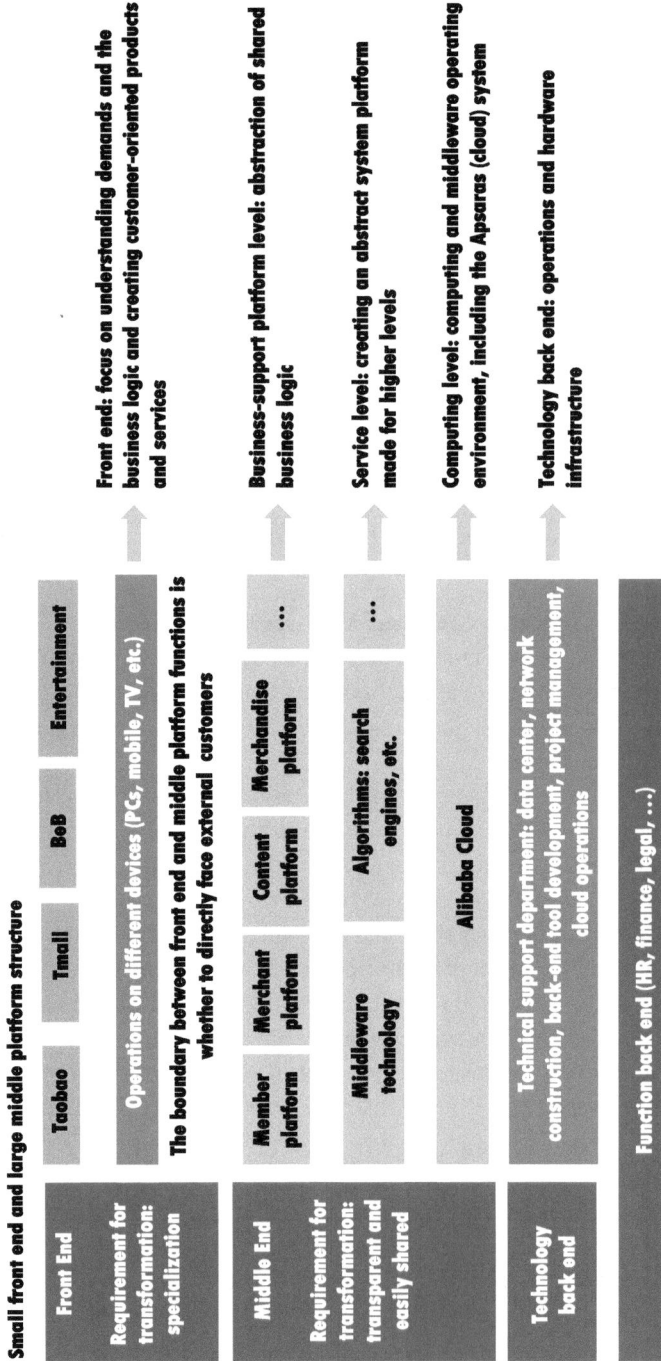

Figure 4.10: Efficiency-driven market-oriented ecosystem at Alibaba, here interpreted as a tech stack (Yeung and Ulrich, 2019, 119).

The big integration: Ecosystems as a network of viable systems
In the following, an integrated view on the issues and concepts of self-organization is offered, with the goal of using the Viable System Model to create a wholistic overview of the organization. At first, a reinterpretation of the Viable System Model will be shown to comfort the market-driven aesthetics. They are represented as a network organization with a central node (platform) and the semi-autonomous operation systems (cells or System 1). To provide an alternative visualization, a circle is sliced into three layers. The following transformations were incorporated to convert the rather technical illustration of the VSM into a more brain-friendly metaphor. The example in Figure 4.11 shows the platform in the center and the surrounding support functions. The operation is found on the outer layer.

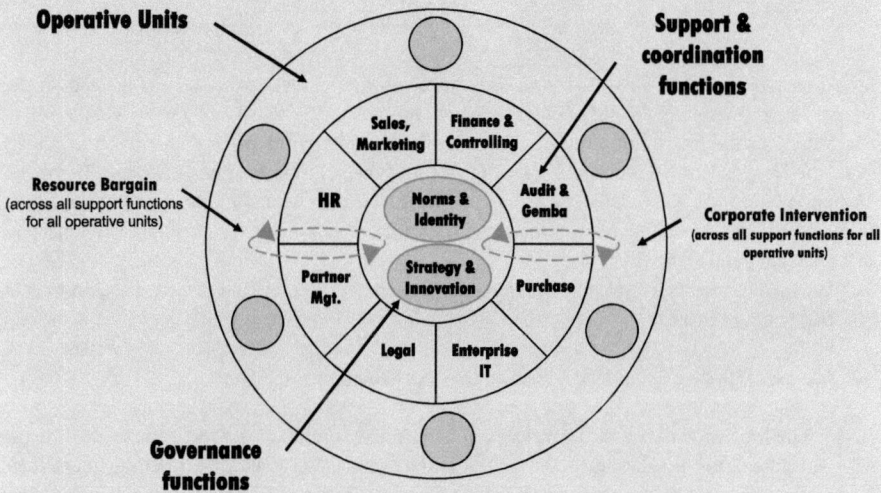

Figure 4.11: Visual re-interpretation of the VSM as a "circle of circles-model.".

A deeper look into the levels in the circle model shows how the Viable System Model (VSM) is woven into an alternative visual narrative:

Operation (Value Delivery): represents the value generating members (or teams in a scaled context). In the language of the VSM, these are the System 1. They are on the outer layer of the circle because they are connected to their environment to deliver value to their beneficiaries. These stakeholders can be twofold:

–   Internal colleagues, which need the result of one entity to transform these results into "something else" which in the next step is valuable for the following beneficiary. Usually, the end of the chain is the:
–   User, customer, or consumer, which is the only reason why value needs to be produced by the transformation of business objects in the process steps before. This entity usually is the one that "pays" for all the transformation steps mentioned earlier. It could be also an exchange of goods and does not need to be money, but for sure it will be a "value for value"-deal.

Support functions (Enabling Value Delivery): Each of the Systems play a crucial role for the maintenance of the "inside and now" of a viable system. These functions are the middle layer in the circle metaphor because they connect their operational units on the outside with the governance functions on the inside. That is why it is crucial to keep in mind that the umbrella term "support" means in detail:

- System 2: Providing the infrastructure for System 1 to ensure the smooth operation of the value producing units. It is about daily enablement.
- System 3: Which is privileged because it can oversee all System 1s and it is therefore able to reveal the potential for synergies in the value creation (which is why System 3 is responsible for the resource bargain and the deployment of overarching operational rules). This element is taking care of mid-term aspects of the organization.
- System 3*: Helps finding missing variety when things go wrong. It is the element which detects anomalies by supporting root cause analysis and similar activities. It will be activated only spontaneously or when needed to "relax" the organization.
- System 4: Any support function needs its own adaptation and innovation plans, e.g., IT strategy, HR strategy, etc.
- System 5: Here the deployment of norms need to be incorporated, e.g., IT policies, HR policies, etc

Governance (Embedding Value Delivery): This meta function is responsible for the viability of the greater whole. Therefore, the business management functions of System 4 and 5 of the VSM are summarized under the term of governance. This classification follows the general idea that the initially mentioned responsibility of viability is mainly the focus of the strategic and normative level. This metafunction is holistically accountable, even though it is usually quite far away from operational realities. To maintain and develop the greater whole, the term Governance is differentiated into two functions, which can be found in the VSM:
- System 4, being responsible for the long-term development by providing scenarios and prototypes that fit future challenges.
- System 5, which delivers the overarching cohesion for the entire system and balances the interests of System 3 (inside and now) and System 4 (outside and then).

To continue the fractal nature of the concept, one must be aware that Figure 4.10 shows only the generic structure of the organization in the context of the central node (platform). Now different cells (or System 1) come into play that connect to the platform (= support and governance functions), simply because it is cheaper to use as central services instead of maintaining them in the cell (see also Power Law Size & Scaling Human Made Systems).

The platform exists because it optimizes the transaction costs for the members of the network (cell), while maintaining a certain degree of autonomy to System 1 (this refers to the power law of Metcalfe). These members could be also called micro entities or micro enterprises. As shown in Figure 4.10, the micro enterprises (MEs) align around communalities in the context of value production. One way to characterize these clusters is an alliance. The driver to form these sub-structures is a result of the everlasting evolutionary pressure to optimize a system towards the lowest effort.

Figure 4.12 shows how the fractal logic can be transformed into a self-similar network structure. The platform and its basic management functions of Operations, Support, and Governance are just "stretched out" into the two-dimensional space, and not zoomed in the same 2D space, which would be the characteristic of a fractal visualization. By stretching the recursion levels into space, the organizational entity of now an alliance represents a node next to the platform which itself is connected to the micro enterprises (MEs). The figure also shows how the micro enterprises are connected to each other by service/value exchange relationships. One ME might be the enabler for value production, while another one is connected to the environment to deliver a good to a customer. But still both systems are operational units in the sense of the Viable System Model, which means they are System 1.

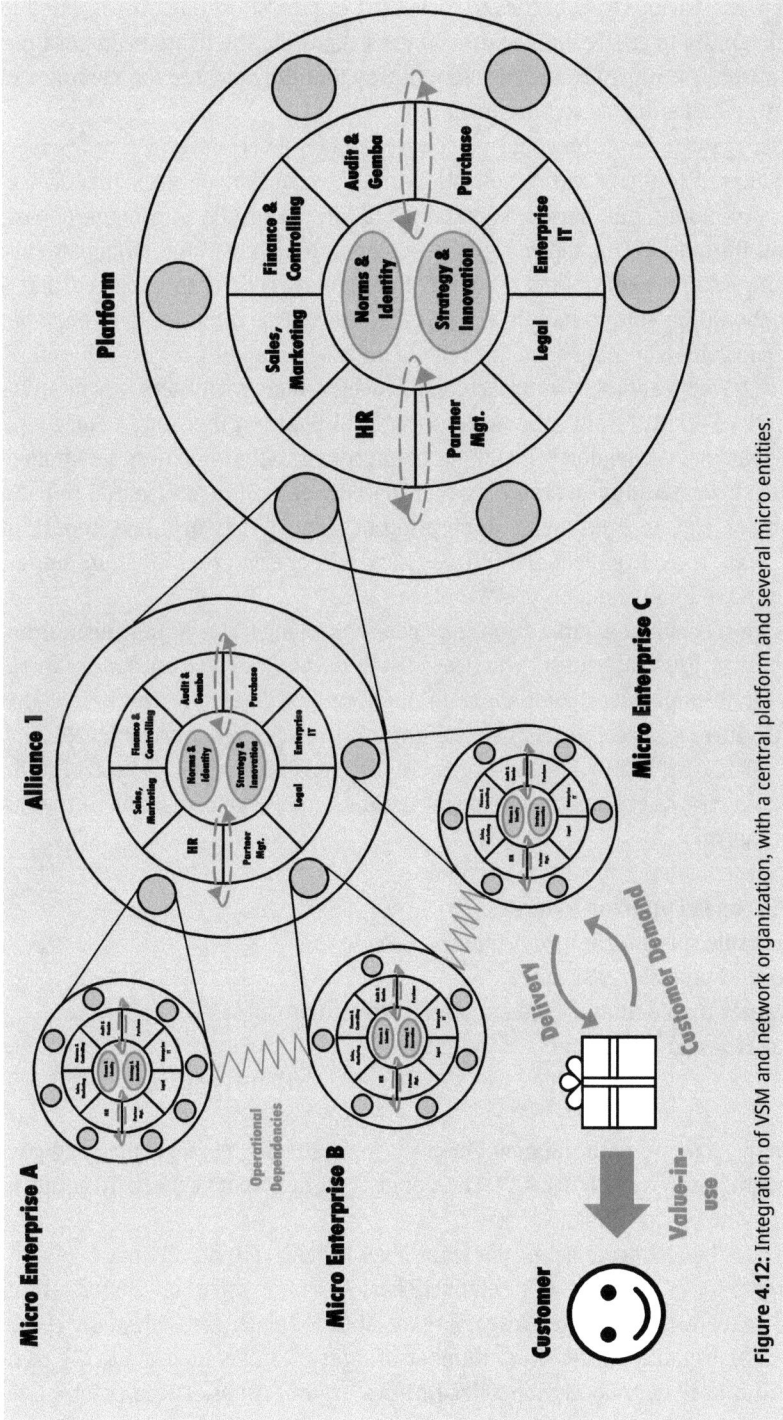

Figure 4.12: Integration of VSM and network organization, with a central platform and several micro entities.

In a next step, the various approaches to foster self-organization must be assessed in terms of their ability to create viable governance structures. The primary imperative: governance structures must be constructed in a way that they include the members of the organization and enhance self-organization.

This process starts with the governance on the team level. Hereby, a new aspect must be considered to foster self-organization and to meet the requirements of Ashby's Law. Traditionally, one person is responsible for the results of a team, department, or unit. But one CEO is never capable to lead and manage huge organizations; the span of topics and expertise is too wide. Even today, it is often expected that a team leader should be able to handle all relevant topics. This often leads to burn-out symptoms, especially when the context of the team is of a complex nature. Therefore, we propose a shared leadership approach on all levels which involves representatives of a micro entity with different capabilities in a "Mini Board of Directors." For a typical software product, the leadership alliance could consist out of business, technological, and design representatives, assuming that these three skills are essential to build a digital product, e.g., an ecommerce application or a social network. It is important to point out that these three leadership roles have a representative function; important decisions have to be taken on the team level.

There is an inspiring example from the French tiremaker and haute-cuisine conveyor Michelin to illustrate these practices: "How do you move from an organizational model that emphasizes compliance to one that energizes contributions?" This question introduces the case in Hamel and Zanini's book *Humanocracy* (2020, 292). The project called MAPPEDIA aims at enhancing responsibility and accountability in teams. The following questions served to test the measures taken to abandon the bureaucratic status quo:

Does it . . .
– anchor in timeless human values?
– provide ample space for improvisation?
– route around points of resistance?
– invite, rather than demand, leaders to reimagine their roles?
– minimize risk and disruption.

(Hamel and Zanini 2020, 310)

Michelin finally came up with the new blueprint for managing performance and governance in teams shown in Figure 4.13. The upper right-hand part especially points to the self-organizing forces of teamwork.

When a suitable governance on the team level is achieved, an alliance or a platform comes into focus. Whereas it is relatively easy to self-organize on the team level (even scaled to team of teams), the larger organizational structures with many recursion levels are tricky, due to the sheer number of internal stakeholders and the communication and decision-making latencies in huge organizations. There seems to be an indisputable fact: the bigger the organization, the greater the challenge to achieve

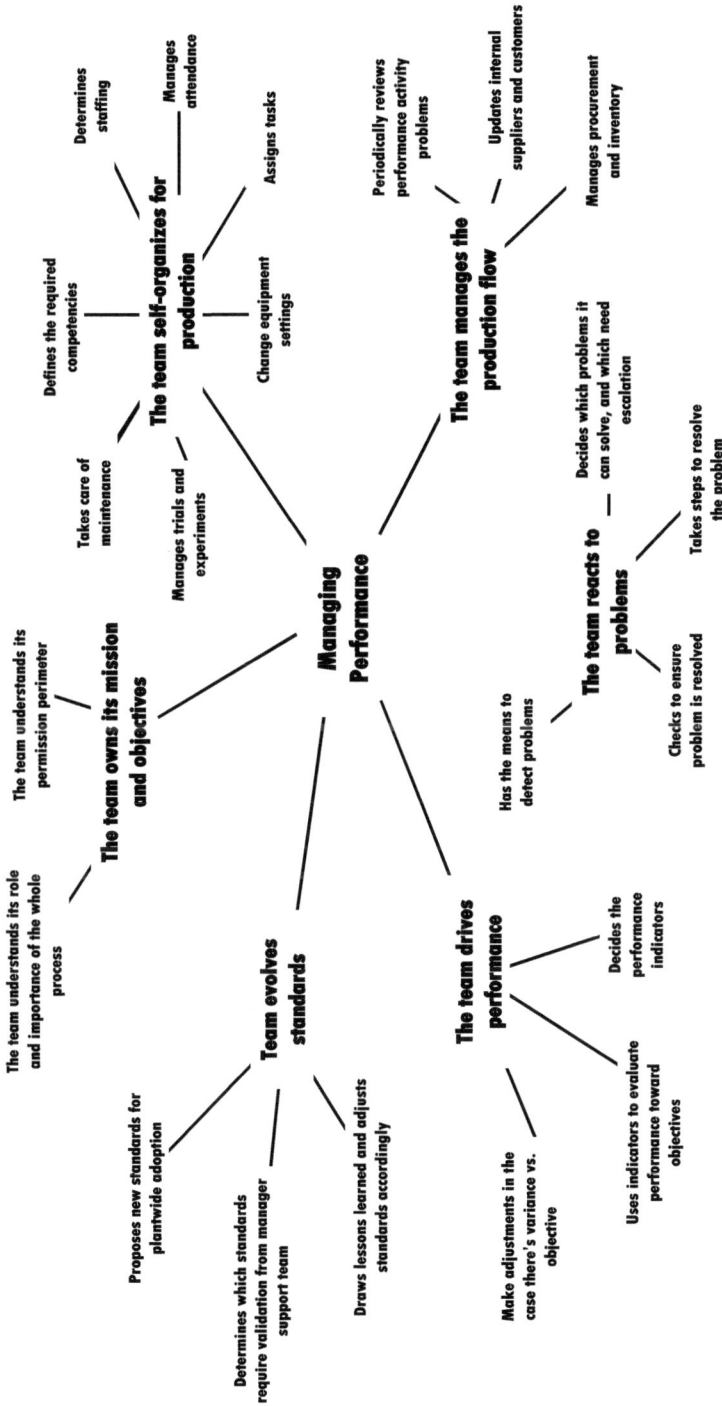

Figure 4.13: Michelin team approach MAPPEDIA to managing performance (Hamel and Zanini 2020, 302).

a system-wide self-organization that is still adaptive and agile – and not a bureau-cratic hydra that kills entrepreneurship and innovation. The usage of the OKR frame-work introduced above is one way to align complex organizations around outcomes and goals. The question still remains of how to align a complex organization on topics which last longer than the typical length of a OKR cycle. A promising approach is com-ing from Elinor Ostrum (1990) which deals with the question of how the commons of a community could be governed. Ostrum researched different types of commons gov-ernance, which span from medieval villages to indigenous tribes in the Amazonas. Fi-nally, she came up with the following principles to design a functioning governance system:

–   Define clear group boundaries.
–   Match rules governing use of common goods to local needs and conditions.
–   Ensure that those affected by the rules participate in modifying the rules.
–   Make sure the rule-making rights of community members are respected by out-side authorities.
–   Develop a system, carried out by community members, for monitoring members' behavior.
–   Use graduated sanctions for rule violators.
–   Provide accessible, low-cost means for dispute resolution.
–   Build responsibility for governing the common resource in nested tiers from the lowest level up to the entire interconnected system.

(Ostrum 1990, 90)

Finally, it must be added that maintaining a coordination structure on this level is not only about the why, what, and how, but also about the who. This is a very ambivalent statement, since it is hard to neglect that "personalities" are crucial to create cohesion, as they can break silos with their individual charm and wit. On the other hand, a per-son-based cult could develop, which hinders viable self-organization, because the members of the group are focused on a "leader" while ignoring systemic structures and constraints – especially topics coming from the environment. Nevertheless, the integrative power of a single person should not be underestimated – and one should look out for talents so that their capability can be incorporated in a way that pre-serves human values, while staying open to new ideas and developments.

Managerial practice

First and foremost, it can be extremely difficult to establish a micro enterprise struc-ture in an existing organization, as it was presented above in the paragraph on net-work organizations. It does not matter if either the technological or the social legacy in the system is too high a burden. If the workforce was conditioned for years to com-ply with given rules, and not even daring to challenge the status quo, it cannot be expected that these persons change their behavior overnight. The understandable intent that people should act like entrepreneurs cannot be achieved by commands. Furthermore, a big fraction of the workforce in huge organizations just want to be in operations or services, because they do not like taking risks and prefer to be part of the herd. The following examples illustrate some typical impediments on why it is almost impossible to change the corporate structure:

1) A strong workers council could at least slow down the transition to a market-driven ecosystem – or even veto against fundamental changes.
2) Supporting organizations, who are only indirectly related to value creation, have the challenge to allocate the costs of such an enabling function and to specify the profit. Therefore, the actors cannot be responsible for such a calculation.
3) In business domains, where knowledge work is dominating the value production, it can lead to a high bureaucratic effort to set up and run a "smart contracting" solution, e.g., a private blockchain. It could even kill business agility because of administrative hurdles. The nature of knowledge-work is often not as linear as the processes in manufacturing, where process steps are easier to identify.

In managerial practice, one can aim to let the organization behave like a market-driven network organization, and make use of OKRs, Scaled Agile, and other frameworks to foster an adaptive system.

Case study: "Mobile App development in the wholesale industry"

Our wholesale case featuring the customer app will now illustrate how self-organization is encouraged. The enterprise level as well as the team level will be examined to make the practical implementation as tangible as possible.

On the enterprise level, specific principles are defined to provide a frame and to guide the teams in daily operations. A complete tech stack is not put in place, due to the 60-year history of the organization. The solution landscape is quite heterogenous, from Google Cloud Platform to SAP, Microsoft, Teradata, or Oracle, just to name a few well-known players. In addition, self-developed solutions like the app come into play. Instead of an integrated solution, a set of principles is put in place to provide cohesion for the organization. An ideal state is hard to achieve, especially in organizations which must deal with legacy systems (e.g., customer master data, which are stored in very old systems, just to name a classic topic). These "monolithic" applications are so strongly integrated into the tech landscape so widely used in the organization and highly customized that is seems sometimes impossible to decommission the old systems and replace it with state-of-the-art technology – in fact, it can take a decade to switch them off. There are more aspects which are constitutive for the architecture principles, e.g., being organized around business capabilities, or moving to the cloud.

All in all, they are made to enable technology-driven self-organization, which complements other efforts of the organizational developers, e.g., lean ways of working.

As an example, the architecture principles of METRO digital are presented to illustrate the point.

- We are organized around business capabilities.
- We keep it simple and eliminate accidental complexity.
- We avoid tight coupling.
- We distinguish between autonomous micro services and constraints of the macro architecture.
- Security, compliance, and data privacy is always on our radar.
- We go for cloud first.
- We actively strive for a lifecycle management.

(https://metro.digital/blogs/reaching-thegalaxy-handbook-part-1, accessed September 21, 2022)

Other measures complement the overarching architecture principles. It is about socalled circles, which have the authority to define standards in the organization. There is for instance a circle for the topics of data management, which tackles technological and business aspects of this subject.

As described earlier, the teams are not only empowered, but they are expected to make use of microservices to provide functionalities with the technical landscape. Typical examples would be login features (validation of credentials) or the presentation of articles, which are in promotion. The idea: many services in a complex environment do not have to be constantly reinvented but are developed only once and then treated as a "microproduct." This implies not only the coding part, but everything about maintenance and support for other teams. To manage the microservice zoo (API, application programming interface), a documentation platform is in place where each team can register their microservice and specify the purpose, technical data, and contact information in case some questions arise. It is a lightweight approach which relies on self-organization and self-responsibility – this is especially important when a microservice is reaching the sun set phase and needs to be decommissioned. The usage of microservices is especially relevant for the app team because they often rely on external applications (or functionalities) – they are in the role of a technical consumer. This means they need to be able to access these external functions, and the easiest way is to do it via a microservice. This insight has been already revealed above when using Wardley maps.

Case study: "Living composition in the machinery industry"

Bucher Industries characterizes its organization as follows: "A clear divisional structure with decentralized management and profit responsibility makes Bucher Industries a flexible and adaptable group. With this structure, the divisional management teams have the necessary flexibility to adapt their product and service offering systematically to customer's requirements."

(www.bucherindustries.com)

This statement allows to answer the two basic questions raised above: which generic framework can provide guidance in the process of intervening to initiate change? And how can the self-organizing forces of the system be used to navigate in the sense of leading by weak signals?

The Viable System Model (Beer, 1972) has a perfect match with Bucher Industries' organization, as illustrated in Figure 4.14.

In the following, the five constituent Systems are interpreted from the perspective of Bucher Industries being an autopoietic system.

System 1: The five divisions meet the requirements for autonomous units. They have profit responsibility and the necessary flexibility to adapt the product and service-offering systematically to customers' needs. They are on the next lower level of recursion, again viable systems.

System 2: Balances the activities of Systems 1 and harmonizes the overall production flow. In terms of Bucher's autopoiesis (see Figure 2.11), they fulfill the function of knowledge provision and distribution, supported by Group and Divisional Services.

System 3: Responsible for synergies between all the Systems 1, it provides basic rules and enables a fair distribution of resources. In the "living composition," internal standards and the network of information and communication play an important role. System 3 is responsible for the mid-term results of the organization.

System 3*: Takes care of detecting "blind spots" by implementing an audit channel. This function is prerequisite for a flawless reproduction and conservation of the system's identity.

System 4: Explores the environment to develop scenarios and strategies, using the four boundary elements of "living composition" in Figure 2.11. It is the place for innovation and the long-term success of the system.

System 5: The ultimate authority of the organization shapes the reproduction of systemic identity. It balances the "inside and now" (System 3) and the "outside and then" (System 4).

Viable systems operate in a self-organizing way, with Systems 1–5 interacting in the interest of the whole. This insight enables the detection of "tipping points" which allow to move parts of the system in a specific direction to initiate self-reinforcing processes. This will be the aim of the next step of the methodology.

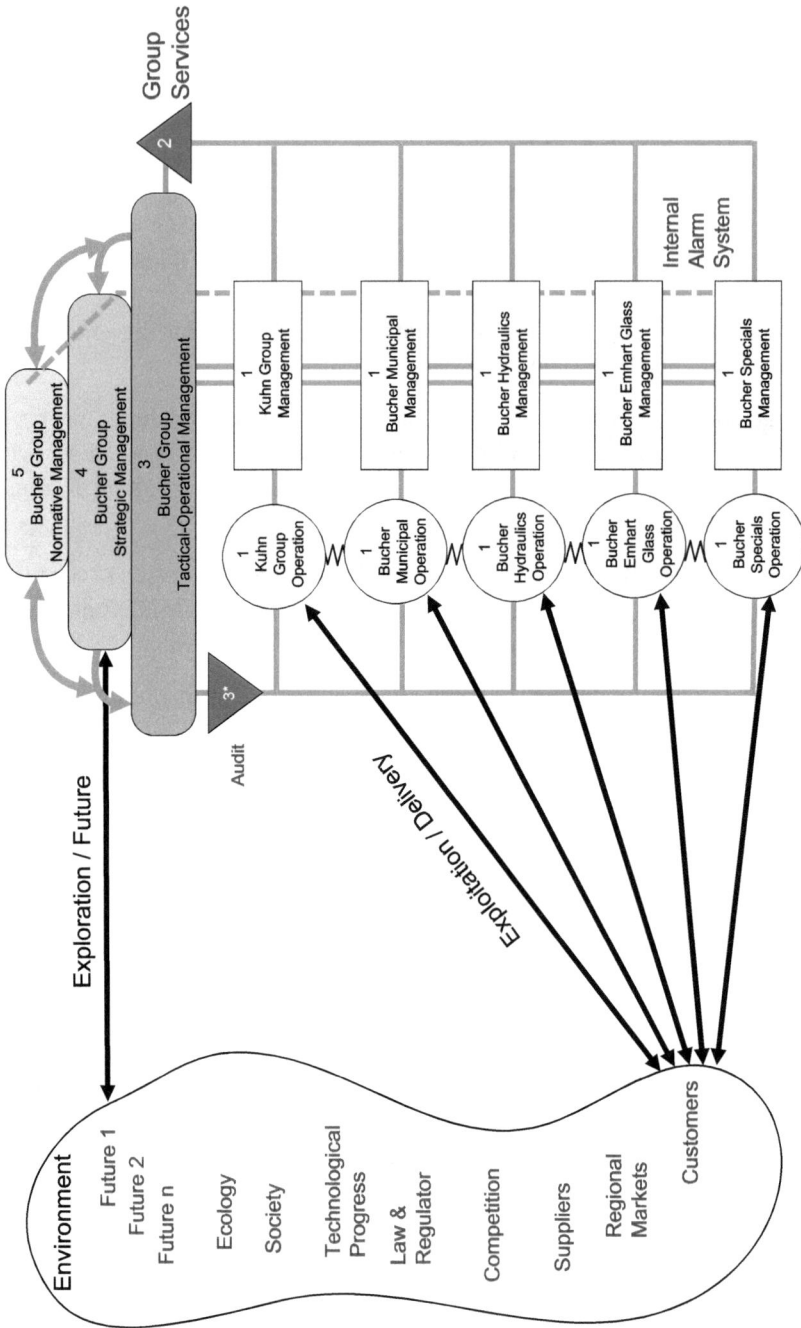

Figure 4.14: Viable System Model of Bucher Industries' organization.

4.3 Step 7: "Tipping Points": Intervening with minimal invasion

Conceptual foundations

Based on insights gained from the above frameworks, proactive actions are now developed in line with the "jiu-jitsu-principle," using minimally invasive interventions to achieve the greatest possible impact. Whereas **input-output systems** can be influenced by design with pinpoint accuracy, **autopoietic systems** cause many difficulties due to the lack of suitable tools and techniques to gain indirect access. But an interesting insight by Sharon Varney (2021, 6 and 9) might open new perspectives: "Constant motion at a micro-level may also re-create familiar patterns at a macro-level . . . Lots of people making lots of small adjustments were able to maintain stability in the face of massive disruption." In a similar way, **swarm intelligence** serves as a metaphor for the use of systemic self-organization by answering the question of how to influence autonomy and cohesion without the presence of a leader. As illustrated in the Infobox "How to manage a swarm" in chapter 2, the "relevant information" becomes essential in this context; everyone who possesses it will be the leader. Tiny impulses can initiate a change process. The relevant information is either local outside information or knowledge of a few scattered participants. Therefore, "intervention" in autopoietic systems means to target the free-floating agents at the system's boundaries according to the rules of swarm intelligence. To be more explicit, in a swarm of 100 people, at least five people with relevant information must be identified to get impact on the course of the system (Fladerer and Kurzmann, 2019, 2077).

Once access is gained to a system, the navigation process is initiated, whereby the **"Essential Balances"** of Ivo Velitchkov (2020) provide valuable insights. He distinguishes between three essential balances of organizations: autonomy-cohesion, stability-diversity, and exploration-exploitation, whereas the first pair applies to our context. Velitchkov discusses (2020, 25) the autopoietic nature of organizations as they reconstruct the meaning of interventions according to their internal logic. Or in his own words: "The difficulty is that you must adapt to somebody who is adapting to your adaptations to their adaptations, and so on" (2020, 248). Therefore, it is essential to experiment at the boundaries of the system to initiate change – but there is no guarantee for success. Cohesion and autonomy are in permanent interchange, they are not predefined by a specific structure. But the basic rule of subsidiarity applies under any circumstances: the autonomy of parts must never be restricted unless the cohesion of the whole is in danger. And good leadership means making a judgment if this is the case – there is no algorithm for such a decision. Cohesion is generally triggered by market pressure, by new technologies or by common enemies, whereas autonomy is mainly achieved by trust. There is a wide field of experiments open for creative leaders. To get started, some practical advice is given to provide an intuitive feeling for accessing and navigating complex systems:

- Develop simple models to understand the basic logic of the system
- Apply different models to experience a change in perspective
- Carry out experiments ("simple bets") to test the systems' reactions
- Identify "pockets of predictability" in otherwise unpredictable situations
- Favor "loose couplings" in a system open to intervention
- Introduce feedbacks to increase a system's structural dynamics
- Operate with deliberate errors
- Don't try to change a system, but to navigate it

Methodology and tools

To support the process of intervening with minimal invasion, Figure 4.15 presents four complementary approaches for getting access and for navigation. Again, the approaches are meant to complement each other because an enterprise consists always of input-output and autopoietic system aspects. This explains the need for a holistic approach which takes both aspects into account.

	Input-output systems	Autopoietic systems
Getting access to the system	Designing for flow, entering via pain points	Coupling for viability, entering via weaknesses
	Value Streams	**Ergodicity**
Navigating the system	Optimizing throughput, managing bottlenecks	Navigating reproduction, initiating autocatalysis
	Theory of Constraints	**Living Composition**

Figure 4.15: Approaches to improve intervention with minimal invasion.

Getting access to input-output systems: Value Streams

As shown in the last step, an essential feature of any viable self-organized system is the existence of operational units (System 1) that can act in relative autonomy. The primary task of these units is the production of value delivered to the customers and their environment. It is in the interest of the operation to ensure a smooth delivery that meets the expectations of customers, so that they are willing to buy and pay. Getting access to an input-output systems starts with **identifying pain points**, detected by weak signals. An effective way to create transparency around operational processes, from an end-to-end perspective, is mapping value streams. It reveals the production steps and important data points. By this it enables self-organization, because the members of the system can finally see the complete picture. It is about breaking operative silos, as Stafford Beer said (paraphrased): the amount of control is proportional to the amount of information the system has – about itself (Beer 1966, 467).

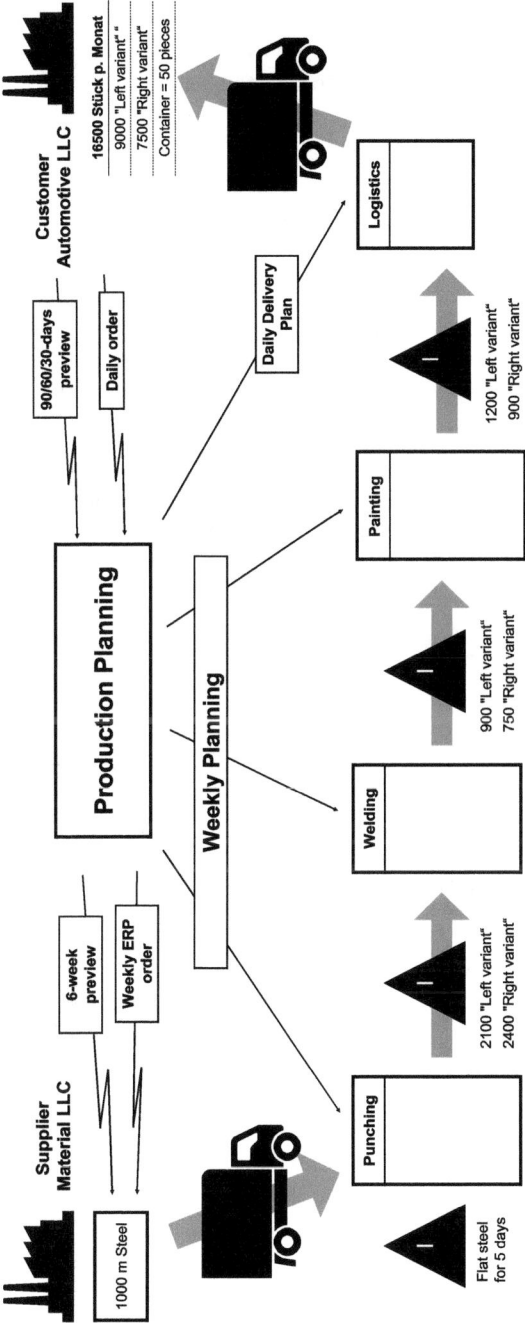

Figure 4.16: A typical value stream in the manufacturing industry (highly simplified to illustrate the input-output-logic).

From an operational perspective, the goal to foster self-organization is to integrate the various aspects of the "machine room" to understand the full value chain – always keeping the customer in focus. This can be illustrated by the framework of Mike Rother and Mike Shook (2003) shown in Figure 4.16 which allows a holistic view of a production sequence. Here, the recording of the value stream begins with the customer, from which one proceeds backwards along the process. Typically, a value stream diagram is divided into five areas: customer, supplier, information flows, material flows including the process steps, and a timeline containing the process and lead time.

The boxes underneath the process steps would contain further information, such as the number of shifts or machine reliability. Between process steps one finds inventories which serve as storage for processed items of the specific step. Bottlenecks and diagnostic points can be identified from the measured lead time.

The value stream perspective can also be applied in the world of knowledge work. The Kanban practice provides an intuitive approach to structure a process and make it tangible for people using this way of work. Figure 4.17 shows a typical Kanban board that contains working steps in the columns and the working packages (Epics) in the swim lanes (Anderson 2010).

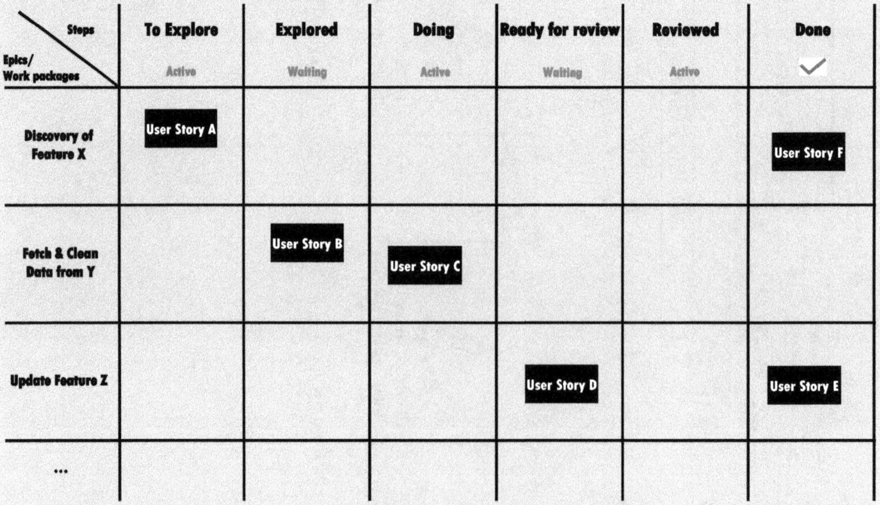

Steps / Epics/ Work packages	To Explore / Active	Explored / Waiting	Doing / Active	Ready for review / Waiting	Reviewed / Active	Done ✓
Discovery of Feature X	User Story A					User Story F
Fetch & Clean Data from Y		User Story B	User Story C			
Update Feature Z				User Story D		User Story E
...						

Figure 4.17: A Kanban board of a software development team.

The columns in the exemplary board alternate between an active state (e.g., to explore) and a passive state (e.g., explored). This is the same pattern as shown in the value stream of a manufacturing process (Figure 4.15), where the inventories, represented by an "I," are like the waiting state. This allows people in the team to understand how "pieces" (or tasks) are flowing from left to right, and where the bottlenecks are.

As is always the case with process-focused tools, a distinction must be made between understanding the actual situation and designing the future picture as the target situation. Typical problems become visible, based on a value stream diagram:

–   The tasks are not clearly defined, i.e., the internal customer and supplier relationship is unclear. Either internal customers do not know what they want, or the internal suppliers cannot deliver the desired quality on time. In any case, the organization creates problems and viability is endangered.
–   Another problem is too many queries and unplanned feedback loops between the work steps, so that many – sometimes informal – feedback processes are necessary to make the system work so that the partner of the next process step can be successful with the results of the actual step.
–   The topic of too many feedback loops and rework due to quality problems points to friction between the process partners because there is obviously no common language and no shared understanding of the nature of the whole process existing: an end-to-end perspective is missing.

The following "access and design metrics" are helpful to understand how the delivery system works – in the truest sense of the word. Most important, two metrics need to be investigated:

–   Throughput, which reflects the number of items/tasks completed in a certain time frame (e.g., 12 tasks per week).
–   Lead time, which reflects the time it takes from the start (e.g., customer order) till the end (e.g., delivery to the customer). It is the sum of the value-adding working time and the waiting times. In praxis, this is not a single number for a working system, but rather a probability distribution, because the size of the tasks and other factors influence the lead time.

Additional metrics could also come into play like the number of errors or the need to correct already produced items. Also, the number of blocked tasks can be helpful to get access to the working system and reveal it to itself.

Realistic capacity planning
In managerial practice, another topic is often forgotten or ignored in the context of knowledge work: realistic capacity planning. A person contracted for 40 hours per week is supposed to work with 100% mental capacity during this timeframe – an illusory assumption. Depending on the country, the number of working days per year varies from 250 (Germany) to 260 (United States), so the average is taken: 255, subtracting 55 for vacation, sick leave, regular meetings, and mandatory trainings, followed by deductions for little breaks, mental costs for context switching (= the plague called multitasking), having a coffee, informal communication, and time to switch meeting rooms. Furthermore, the effects of bad prioritization, pressure from stakeholders, missing knowledge/capabilities, malfunctioning technologies, and other factors are included. At the end of such a calculation, only 40% to 50% capacity is left available to value-adding work (around 120 days per year).

The importance of realistic capacity planning cannot the overstated, be it merely to get a feeling of what is available for value-adding work. This knowledge is a good starting point to optimize lead time and throughput, because over-commitment can be mitigated (another plague).

Navigating input-output systems: Theory of Constraints

According to the Theory of Constraints (Goldratt 1990), the root cause for problems in a delivery system are bottlenecks which determine the overall throughput of a system, as illustrated by Figure 4.18.

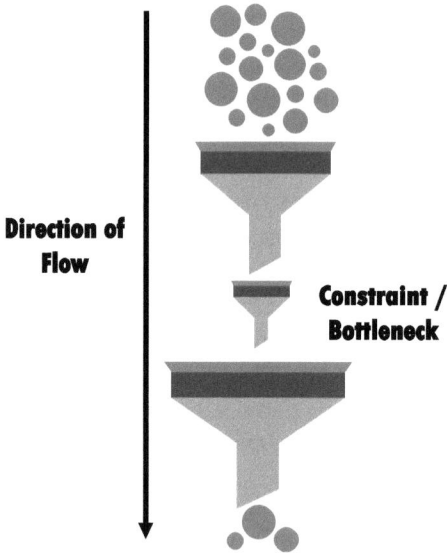

Direction of Flow

Constraint / Bottleneck

Figure 4.18: The funnel model of the theory of constraints – one constraint limits the throughput (flow) of the system.

According to Goldratt, good flow management is based on a sequence of steps:
1. Identify the system's constraints.
2. Decide how to exploit the system's constraints.
3. Subordinate everything else to the above decision.
4. Elevate the system's constraints.
5. If in the previous step a constraint is broken, go back to step 1, but do not allow inertia to cause a system constraint.

(Goldratt 1990, 76)

As shown in Figure 4.18, the Kanban board consists of active and passive columns (working and waiting). This helps to understand where your bottleneck is located. A good starting point is to measure the cycle time per column (process step). One can also measure the average age of work in progress as it influences the lead time. But the simplest way to find the bottleneck is to look at the Kanban board and spot the column with the highest number of cards. If for instance the "Ready for Review" column is full of tasks, it indicates that the following step "In Review" does not have sufficient capacity to work on all the tasks, which means that the previous step is producing too much output for the process neighbor. A solution must be found on how to get additional capacity from other members of the team to help review tasks/results. One can also relieve them from administrative or bureaucratic tasks to gain more capacity. The most important intervention, which is as simple and powerful, implements "work in progress limits (WIP)." They help the workforce to understand their overarching capacity and let the system organize around the problem to dissolve it, with the effect of providing better flow of value towards the customer.

Finally, another counter-intuitive decision needs to be taken to leverage the bottleneck and make it a real feature. A state of under-load is introduced by setting the capacity only up to 70%. This buffer creates resilience because it allows coping with high dynamics of a turbulent environment. You can also make use of this "unproductive" time by investing it in personal learning and developing the system. That is why the following three **performance metrics** are crucial for self-organization in input-output contexts:

- Throughput controlling, by managing bottlenecks (which is close to the empirical process control theory, as practiced in the agile framework Scrum).
- Lead time, which represents the total speed of flow in the system (that is very close to Kanban systems).
- Buffer usage versus progress, a basic measure to understand the delivery reliability of the working system and the likelihood to keep promised deadlines.

The way to organize a working system with the goal to increase the throughput is fundamentally different from the usual cost-efficiency paradigm (and the typical cost controlling fantasies). It requires an organizational culture that can consciously (re-)learn the patterns of viability and unlearn toxic behavior. That is why the topic is closely connected to the autopoietic dimension, which will be explored in the next section.

Herman Haken, a German physicist, introduced the first complete laser theory in 1962, and by accident he discovered fundamental properties of self-organization. His insights are not only applicable in physics, but also in biological, psychological, and sociological systems – and they are also relevant for input-output systems. The theory of Synergetics (Haken 1983) aims at understanding how parts of a system act together to create a greater whole (order) – and how the greater whole controls the parts to create a greater whole. Obviously, it is a circular logic, like the chicken and egg problem. From a systems perspective, the two parameters of "order and control" are coupled. It does not matter where one starts to foster self-organization, the one parameter will always lead to the other: control leads to order and order leads to control. This type of self-referential loop is the main cause for self-organization.

Wolfram Müller (2016, 139) combined Haken's ideas with Goldratt's Theory of Constraints, and he came up with the logic of Figure 19 to enable productive input-output systems that can control themselves in a viable way.

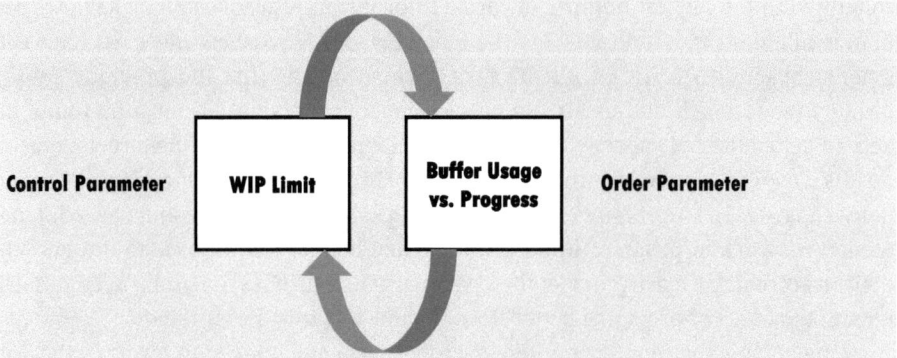

Figure 4.19: Synergetic loop of self-organization for input-output systems.

As controlling parameter, which defines the "boundaries of the system," the WIP limit introduced above was chosen. The order parameter is a plot that compares buffer usage versus progress. This metric is used as a feedback signal to help the team to organize itself and make functionally informed decisions, to prevent the excessive consumption of the buffer. In Figure 4.20, light grey, medium grey and dark grey areas are shown. Obviously, the red area means the inability to deliver in time. The illustration shows a "fever curve" of a project over the course of time; in this case it is a successful project because it was able to deliver – while still having some capacity (buffer) left.

Especially in multi project environments, this type of plot can be very useful to get an overview of the project portfolio as to which projects need help, and which projects can afford to shift people to the place where they can release pressure from a constraint (see Figure 4.21).

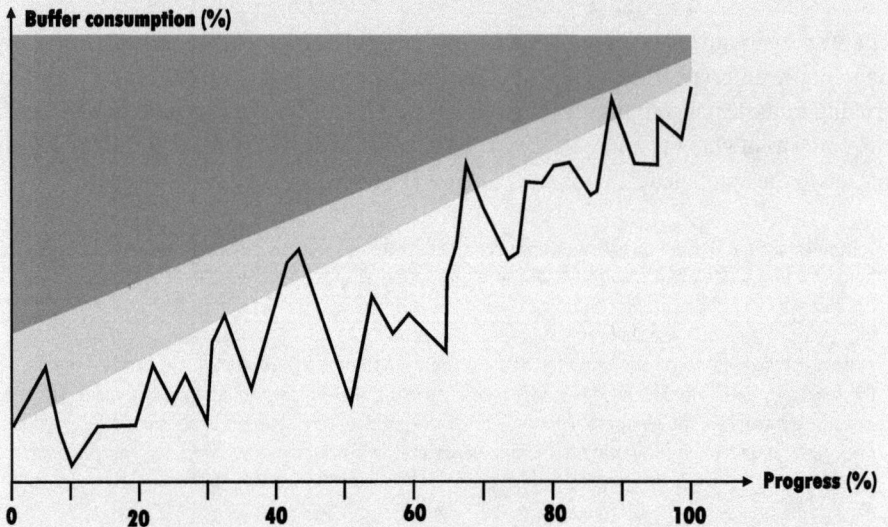

Figure 4.20: The "fever curve" of a healthy system, never being in the "red area".

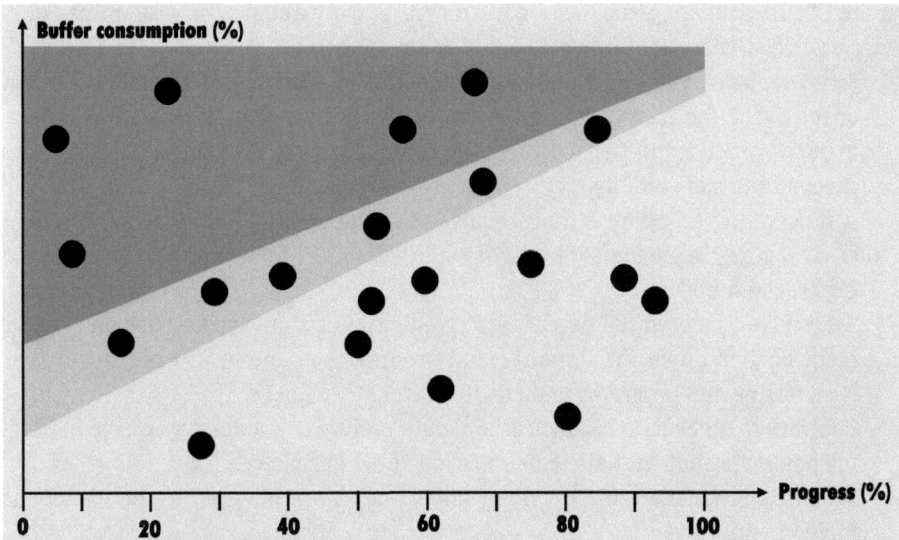

Figure 4.21: Overview of a project portfolio, with stressed projects in the "red area".

These kinds of charts need to be provided on a daily base to enable a control loop with low latency, which means the team can perform as an adaptive system and correct deviations in a self-organized way.

Getting access to autopoietic systems: Ergodicity

Ergodicity specifies organizational rules which shape the growth path towards systemic viability (Dellana 2020). This framework aims at detecting access points to autopoietic systems by focusing on their **potential weaknesses**. Although direct intervention from the outside is not possible, change can be initiated by structural coupling or by active participation. The following rules serve to identify weaknesses in the interplay of the center of a system with its periphery with the goal to intervene with minimal invasion:

- Avoid all activities which damage or destroy the preconditions of viability.
- Prioritize growth that serves the conservation of viability.
- Limit down-side risk near the center of a system, encourage small upside-risk experiments at its periphery.
- Don't measure performance by averages, as they favor the "running of the business" at the center rather than the 'changing of the business' at the periphery.
- Pay attention to the periphery: A system can work well and fail locally.
- Enhance "skin in the game" – walk the talk.

(Dellana 2020)

In the COVID pandemic, the Swiss government (a truly autopoietic system) has been steering a relatively open course along these principles:

- Swiss democracy has its foundation in federalism, with largest possible autonomy of the parts (the "cantons"). There was no direct intervention by central government, as practiced in Germany, e.g., by compulsory vaccination, as it destroys the preconditions of viability.
- A functioning economy is a prerequisite to cope with COVID, which called for a crisis regime, implemented by (Swiss-tailored) "short-time work" and by supporting crucial industries.
- Switzerland favored the decentralized redistribution of vaccines. Central government pushed down the initiative and ordered the cantons to experiment with local testing and programs to motivate citizens.
- Contrary to other nations, Switzerland didn't rely on national averages to monitor the pandemic, but left data to be collected at the periphery.
- When cantons failed to meet their duties, they were pilloried in the media and forced to improve.
- "Skin in the game" was achieved by a popular vote on the course of the government – and the Swiss population agreed with a wide margin.

The epidemic was tamed better than in other European countries, but it was only partly successful, because almost a third of the population refused to get vaccinated.

The COVID example provides valuable insights about how messages spread in autopoietic systems. But how to use them for targeted intervention? The most common way to get access to an autopoietic system is by **imitating** its given rituals, by copying language or by signalizing togetherness: "I belong to your group, as we share the same topics and use the same codes." This procedure is also quite common in managerial practice when people are "onboarded" to an organization (typically as new hirings). The new colleagues learn everything about the paralanguage and other signs or symbols which indicate that you are a member of the enterprise. They also learn about topics which are **not** mentioned. Just imagine a Harley Davidson Club, that shares the topics of "rocker/rebel lifestyle," and whose code of belonging is defined by fashion, music, and, naturally, driving a Harley Davidson. Now visualize a scene, where a long-time member suddenly shows up with a Honda bike; undoubtedly, this would create some discussions in the club which touches matters regarding identity and what it means to be a "true member" of the club.

Another example of accessing autopoietic systems illustrates the tandem of "topic and codes" by referring it to **real impostors**. They scan and imitate topics and codes of social (sub)groups and focus on the weak spots. They spread false compliments and give others the feeling of being special. By this, they gain trust and play the role of a "fake pilot." Luckily, this type of fake behavior is often decoded – it is just a matter of time, the latest when it causes heavy damage. Another subtle way to enter an autopoietic system is to copy the topics and codes, then change the behavior to become a respected member of the group.

How can the success of accessing and coupling with an autopoietic system be **measured**? The metric must focus on the speed of the distributing "coupling messages" that could be seen as "cultural memes." Hereby, power laws come into play again, namely the Contagion Theory and Kucharski's formula:

$$R = D \times O \times T \times S$$

$$(Duration \times Opportunities \times Transmissibility \times Susceptibility).$$

From the perspective of a new member, intending to get access to the group, it depends on:

D: For how long have I been interacting with members of the group?

O: How many people were available to be "infected" with coupling messages?

T: To which extent were the coupling messages embedded in an environment that gives these messages a special credibility?

S: To which extent are the members open for new coupling messages?

For sure, it is hard to quantify the exact R value, but that lies the nature of autopoietic systems – it is all about experimenting to get access.

Navigating reproduction in autopoietic systems: Living Composition
The concept of Living Composition was introduced above in the context of identifying weak signals in autopoietic systems. The process of improving an organization's living composition, as outlined by Marjatta Maula, can be summarized as follows:
- Create awareness and communicate the need for change, by referring to the continuous evolution of the shared understanding for corporate identity.
- Enhance the strategic pillars of systemic identity: Co-evolution with the environment, free-floating boundary elements, identity-generating leadership processes, adapted triggers from and experimentation with the outside world.
- Improve the knowledge flow in the areas of sensing the environment and memorizing basic change in the living composition.

(Maula 2006, 199)

In managerial practice, the identification of tipping points to initiate autocatalysis focuses on the above strategic pillars of systemic identity:
- Co-evolution with the environment: autopoietic systems must co-evolve with their environment, otherwise they become pathological and degenerate. Nokia and Eastman Kodak are examples of such an evolution, as they were convinced of their superior technology and their appeal to customers and forgot to challenge their purpose. Although the identity of autopoietic systems results from internal reproduction, sensors must maintain a link to the outside. These sensors are tipping points for intervention from outside. When the patterns of observation are identified, the system can be provided with information to influence the internal

decision-making processes. Both Nokia and Eastman Kodak still exist but are far from being market-leaders in their realm.

- Free-floating boundary elements: as illustrated in former paragraphs, autopoietic systems are often characterized by swarms of agents at their periphery. They are responsible for innovation, and they trigger changes of corporate identity. By observing or influencing these agents, access to the internal organization can be gained with minimal invasion.
- Identity-generating leadership processes: this approach can only be taken by "players" within autopoietic systems. Here, the state-of-the-art leadership approaches focusing on purpose, corporate values, and servant leadership come into play.
- Adapted triggers and experimentation with the outside world: Autopoietic systems experience a multitude of external inputs to which they react only after having transformed them into their "language." Experimentation means to exploit such triggers in various ways to identify the optimal impact, be it inside out or outside in.

Again, the question arises of how the impact of such interventions could be **measured**? The Viable System Model serves to find a proper metric because the maintenance of autopoietic reproduction is the task of System 5. This system is responsible for the leadership climate and the overarching well-being in the organization. Therefore, all sorts of activities are relevant to help improve the "cultural condition," e.g., employee surveys that measure the understanding for vision, mission, or corporate values. Often the quantitative NPS (Net Promotor Score, Reichheld 2003) logic is applied to figure out which factors are attractors or detractors, but open questions are also admitted to acquire qualitative data. Digital platforms allow an efficient use to distribute those "pulse checks" and derive insights in a fast manner. The typical yearly questionnaire should be replaced by regular surveys (e.g., bi-weekly) which can be answered easily because they are very focused. This gives the management an almost real-time impression of how the employees think and feel about the company, which is a marker of the ability to be a living composition.

Managerial practice

Case study: "Mobile app development in the wholesale industry"

In practice, intervening with minimal invasion can be a delicate matter, especially by simplistic nudging in the autopoietic realm. As the **wholesale case** illustrates, the product manager of the app is kind of a "circus director" who can solely orchestrate the team of developers and user experience designers and must be clever enough to know that execution speed and quality cannot be commanded. In knowledge work, there is a fine line between being a motivator and explainer of overarching business contexts or being a user of the carrot and stick method to keep the herd moving. Take for example a product manager who is joking about starting to program together with his team, if certain tasks will not be finished soon. Of course, they do not risk having him in the developer team, because the manager might create a lot of mess in the code. This demonstrates how tasks and priorities, wrapped into a good portion of humor, serve as a minimal intervention. This type of signaling needs to be carefully used because when it is practiced too often it will no longer show any impact.

On the enterprise level, it pays out to send out every two weeks a short but concise employee survey. It takes not more than ten minutes to answer questions which deal with the overall commitment to corporate core values, vision, mission, or the corporate strategy. Also, there are open questions in each survey, e.g.: "What would you do if you have a magic wand? What would you change?" This survey is a great source for weak signals, and helpful to understand the organizational climate and to be able to solve problems at an early stage – with minimal interventions.

Next to these autopoietic aspects, the app team is well equipped to self-organize around metrics of an input-output system. Most important is that the team has a high-level view of their "types of work" and how working time is allocated, as Figure 4.22 illustrates:

Share	Type of work	Description
40%	Product operation	Maintenance of a highly integrated solution, iOS and Android updates, third level support, data analytics
20%	Initiative support	Involvement in strategic activities like multichannel sales, decommissioning of old applications, cloud migration
23%	Organizational overhead	Time booking, corporate events, team meetings, planning, review, retrospectives
17%	**OKR**	**Capacity to contribute to goals**

Figure 4.22: The amount of free capacity for Objectives and Key results (OKR) is relatively small, because operational topics consume a lot of the available working time.

This simple calculation is not only useful for the team and for resource allocation, but it also helps in discussions with stakeholders to manage expectations.

Next, WIP limits (Work in Progress limits) are used in specific Kanban boards to ensure a steady flow of incremental product improvements and new features. Another way to detect bottleneck is achieved by daily stand-up meetings and by bi-weekly team retrospectives. Finally, when dealing with constraints, the logic of the (technical) product organization becomes a challenge, because every product team wants to keep developers for themselves. There are cultural and legal reasons why it is hard to move people across teams and to support them in times of trouble. This is of course a topic for top management which needs to find solutions for these over-arching governance issues.

Case study: "Living composition in the machinery industry"

To identify the "tipping points" to intervene by minimally invading the reproduction of the system, the focus lies on the logic of the Viable System Model, applied to Bucher Industries in Figure 4.14. Reference must also be made to the elements of "living composition" introduced above. System 5 will be started with, as it takes overall responsibility for the viability of Bucher Industries.

Tipping points to influence the identity and its reproduction (System 5)

- In managerial practice, the specification of a systems' **purpose**, based on normative assumptions, receives great attention. As argued above, the POSIWID approach ("Purpose Of a System Is What It Does") fits better with the process of reproducing the identity, determined by complex interactions of different business and cultural backgrounds. Tipping points positioned near the center of this interaction serve to achieve a smooth and continuous running of this process.
- The targeted use of **narratives** enables a mutual understanding of different business and cultural backgrounds in the interest of structured decision-making.
- **Surveys** on corporate climate and decision-makers' readiness to engage in change provide a sound basis to strengthen the identity of the system.

Tipping points for enhancing the strategy process (System 4) are found at the boundary elements of the system:

- How to place the **sensors** to successfully lead the process of co-evolution with the environment
- Where to position **scouts** for detecting and initiating innovation
- How to increase speed and variety to cope with **triggers** and to professionalize **experimentation**

Tipping points for operational excellence (System 3) focus on efficiency of internal processes:

- Internal **standard processes** and state-of- the art **information networks** are continuously monitored with respect to their efficiency as well as to their fit with the best industrial solutions. Tipping points are identified in the process of structural coupling discussed above.

Tipping points to strengthen the detection of blind spots (System 3*) are identified in the auditing function:

- The information flow from the bottom to the top is often interrupted by self-imposed filters on different systemic levels, be it by accident, intent, or negligence. For the higher levels of the system to get authentic information, they need direct access to lower-level functions. Tipping points focus on the design and the monitoring of the audit system.

Tipping points to enhance the flow of knowledge (System 2) aim at the interaction of the operational units (System 1):
- How can synergies between the operational units be achieved without restricting their autonomy? As these synergies often arise in the context of informal information flows, it is challenging to position tipping points as an outsider.

Tipping points to enhance the autonomy of operational units (System 1) and to increase the value for customers deserve special treatment:
- The operational units (System 1) must be viable systems themselves to live up to the demands of autonomy. Therefore, tipping points have a variety of options to take influence, as all Systems 1–5 are at their disposition on this lower level of recursion. Interventions could be on the levels of identity, effectiveness, efficiency, synergy or value creation.

5 Anchoring the weak signal spirit

5.1 Starting the exploration

Initiating proactive change in response to the rising complexity in managerial practice and sustainably ensuring systemic viability in uncertain times – with this mission, Leading by Weak Signals was launched. The first seven steps provide guidance to cope with a variety of problems in a systematic way. But one step is still to be designed – the anchoring of Leading by Weak Signals as the basic framework to deal with complexity and uncertainty. This framework must be institutionalized as a corporate function of the same importance as human resources, controlling, marketing or sales. It is about building a "corporate look out or radar system" that continuously collects information about the environment and internal issues. This function commonly bears the name of **"Corporate Intelligence" (CI)**, which differs from the traditional market and competitor analyses, as it goes beyond desk research and the creation of data dashboards (even though these aspects are also of high importance for CI). It is also different from "Business Intelligence" which denotes an internal visualization and analysis unit which is focused mainly on quantitative data (Michaeli, 2012, 18). In our approach, we address all types of weak signals which allow a holistic understanding of the "outside and then" and the "inside and now," to paraphrase the Viable System Model. The maturity of this function can be evaluated (as shown in Figure 5.1) by plotting the value of CI on the y-axis, and the evolutionary phases (time) on the x-axis. Here again we see power laws in action: S-curves in combination with Wright's law (here marginal cost/benefit balance).

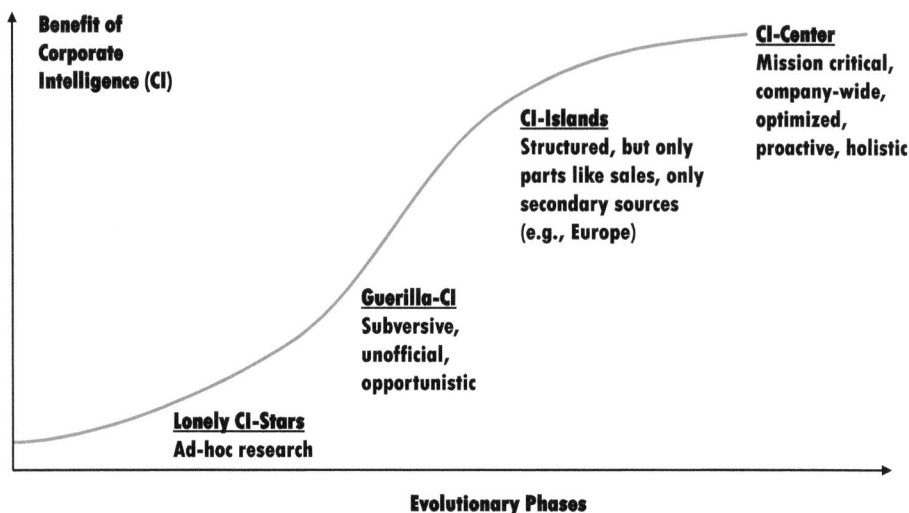

Figure 5.1: Evolutionary phases, or maturity levels of corporate intelligence (Michaeli, 2012, 6).

https://doi.org/10.1515/9783110797886-005

The investment in professional Corporate Intelligence pays off, as more than 70% of enterprises using a formalized CI function appreciate the effort because it supports strategic management and helps to make well informed decisions (Altensen, Glasbrenner, and Pfaff 2003). This function is also a central part of the "Strategy & Innovation" function (System 4) of the Viable System Model. Due to the fractal nature of the VSM, it is not only present in an overarching corporate entity but spread out across all recursion levels. Corporate Intelligence is everybody's job! By this it is part of the core set of functions that sustain viability! It is no longer a commodity with an exotic touch, but an integral part of the whole system. It is embedded in decision-making processes and not only serves R&D, sales, and marketing, but also all processes that make the organization work, like procurement, sourcing, or legal. Only then it is possible to acquire a relative complete picture of "what is happening around us," and what this means for future trajectories of evolution. This implies that the tactical parts of the system must be connected to the intelligence function, to operationalize the insights and test new ideas directly in the market.

In terms of our scientific and management models shown in Figure 5.2, the development of the Corporate Intelligence function aims at amplifying the variety of future interventions and at securing the impact achieved through Leading by Weak Signals.

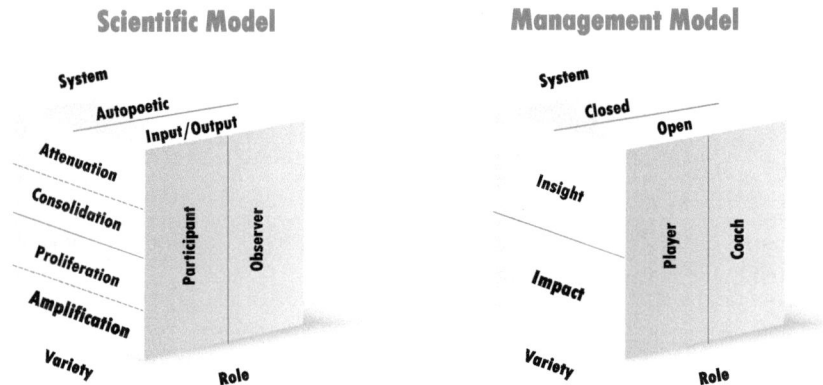

Figure 5.2: Scientific and managerial framework of Leading by Weak Signals.

Anchoring the weak signal spirit in managerial practice therefore has two directions of thrust: Establishing – on a permanent basis – a framework which enables profound insights on relevant futures and setting up monitoring devices to sustainably secure impact. This will be dealt with in the eighth and last step of our methodology.

5.2 Step 8: "Alertness": Organizing for future surprise

Conceptual foundations

The institutionalization of Leading by Weak Signals requires a different approach for input-output systems and autopoietic systems, as shown in Figure 5.3. To gain insights on critical changes in input-output systems, perception must be perfected by establishing and calibrating state-of-the-art early warning systems. To secure lasting impact of interventions and to enable sustainable evolution, the principle of subsidiarity must be consistently organized. In autopoietic systems, the focus on change is at their boundaries, as this allows access by using peripheral sensing to detect weak signals. The monitoring of impact is achieved by permanent experimentation and optimization of interventional activities.

	Input-output systems	Autopoietic systems
Preparing for surprise: **Intelligence**	**Calibrating early warning**	**Sensing peripheral change**
Securing Impact: **Evolution**	**Organizing Subsidiarity**	**Optimizing Experiments**

Figure 5.3: Frameworks dealing with surprise and to enable evolution.

Methodology and tools

The frameworks of the four quadrants presented in Figure 5.3 are now elaborated and illustrated in the managerial context.

Preparing for surprise for input-output systems: Calibrating early warning

High Resilience Organizations (see above) have acquired an enormous set of practices to deal with unexpected turns of life (Weick and Sutcliffe 2015). They are improving their skills as often as possible in complex and chaotic environments to prevent a disaster and to control a critical situation. This might sound trivial, as policemen, firefighters, soldiers, or pilots train daily or weekly, testing and developing their reflexes to move fast through the OODA loop introduced above. Unfortunately, in managerial practice, trainings are often understood as a costly interruption of work which diminishes the generation of value.

Preparing for surprise is achieved by models enabling a shared view on the world. The **Wardley maps** previously introduced illustrate the evolutionary drift of components to get a deeper understanding for potential weaknesses. As shown in Figure 5.4, one could even model hurdles to slow down a competitor to keep their own momentum – and so avoid being surprised by unexpected moves.

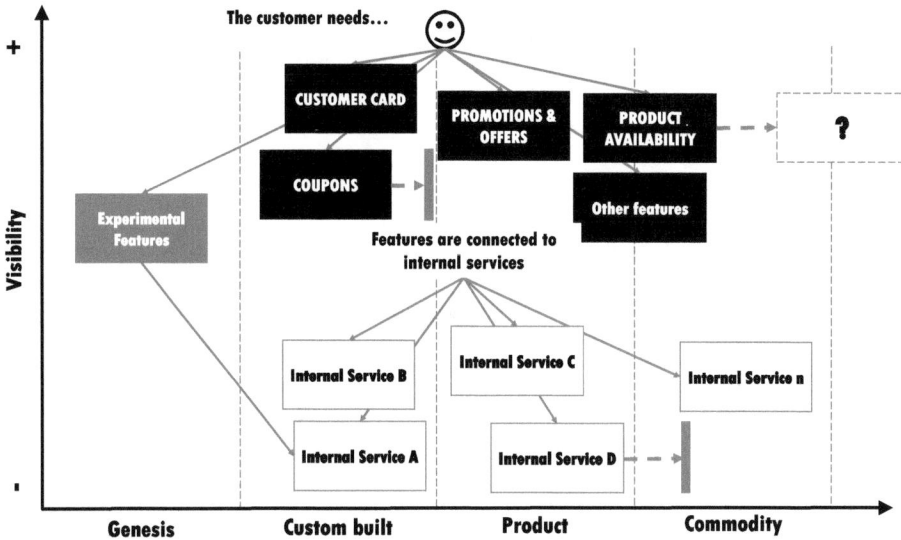

Figure 5.4: Wardley map to design hurdles or traps for the competition (Image Credit Simon Wardely, CC BY 4.0).

Quantitative models take a different approach, they operate with data and thresholds. If a certain value gets either too high or too low, an internal or external warning signal gives advice to take a closer look at the specific context. Like smoke detection in an apartment, the leadership team wants to discover unusual patterns very early. Quantitative warning systems are especially useful, as the measurement of data can be automated. This allows surveillance of a high number of metrics by machines. The data can be visualized in the form of dashboards, which are accessible from any device (laptops, tablets, or mobile phones). The flexibility of the presentation layer allows the creation of virtual control rooms, where leaders can check the data for suspicious behavior.

Finally, the **Viable System Model** comes into play because it offers, as shown in Figure 5.5, two internal communication channels to detect early warning signals.

On the one hand, the model contains System 3* which is the "audit channel" that should be regularly contacted to make sure that the internally planned activities are on course, and this without being interfered by the operational units (System 1). The Viable System Model also contains a superior alarm channel, called the Algedonic Loop. It connects the operational management units with the normative management functions in case of a catastrophic or godsent event. This loop is designed to circumvent the regular meeting and committee structures of an organization to make sure that time-critical events can be managed in the most effective and efficient way. A simple example from practice are whistleblower platforms which provide a secure communication channel for the person revealing sensitive information.

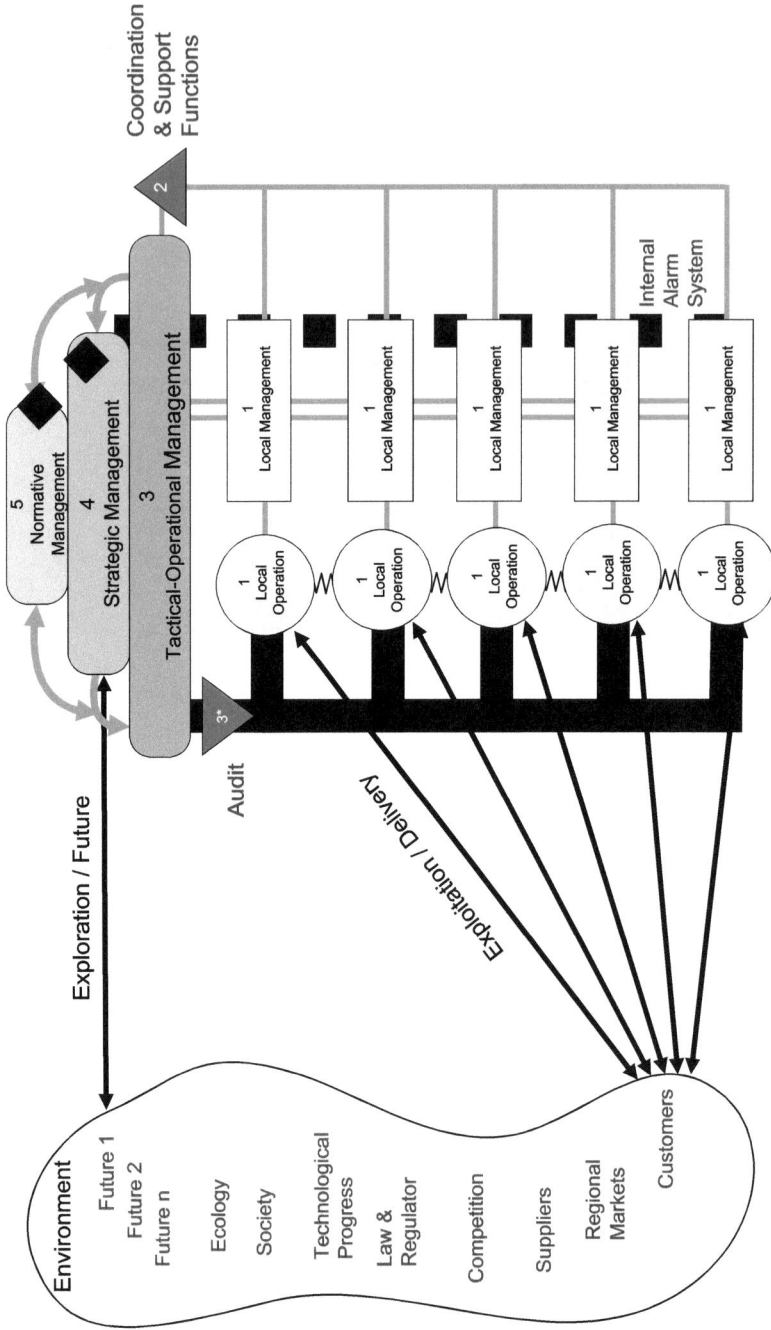

Figure 5.5: Anomaly detection channels (audit System 3* and the internal alarm (algedonic) system, shown as exaggerated thick lines in black).

All these measures need to be considered in a holistic way – it is not about an "either–or" but an "as-well–as" integration to get the widest and deepest scan of internal and external affairs.

Preparing for surprise for autopoietic systems: Sensing peripheral change
The design of an intelligence framework for autopoietic systems starts with the identification of its boundary elements focused on innovation and infrastructure. To establish sensors capable of receiving weak signals at the optimal place, the concepts of "living composition" (Maula, 2006) and "swarms of agents" (xxx) were introduced above. These "agents" are cells of innovative activity which might trigger change in the reproductive processes of the autopoietic system. These triggers allow detecting critical developments early enough, and this from the outside in, as well from the inside out, as shown in Figure 5.6.

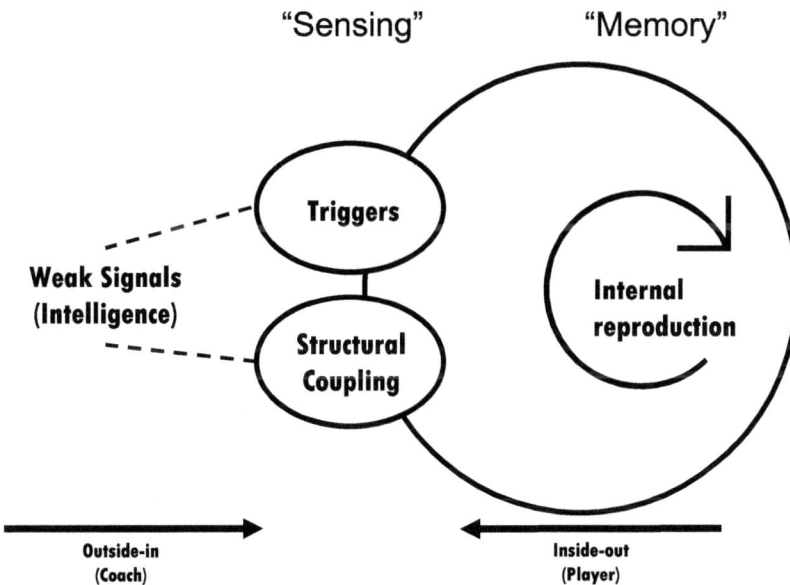

Figure 5.6: Designing intelligence for autopoietic systems (based on Maula, 2006).

To detect boundary elements related to infrastructure, the concept of structural coupling comes into play again. Autopoietic systems are open to people, material, and information which opens a door for influencing these issues in the internal reproduction process.

To develop an intelligence framework for autopoietic systems, the following questions must be answered:

– Which **elements** constitute the boundary of the system? They are non-physical parts of the system that connect the system to its environment through reciprocal interaction with the environment.

- Which boundary elements are dedicated to innovation and infrastructure? For **innovation**, swarms of loosely coupled agents are dedicated to exploring the future with the goal to co-evolve with the environment. For **infrastructure**, the openness of the system as to information, material, and people is the basis for structural coupling and for getting access to the internal structure – but not the internal organization – of the system.
- Which **instruments** are available to access to an otherwise closed system? For an autopoietic system, **triggers** from the outside are not perceived as inputs, but as disturbances which are translated into their own internal logic. But they serve the system to establish contact with the outside world to co-evolve. **Structural coupling** uses vital infrastructure issues of the autopoietic system to establish at least informal contacts with the outside.
- How can these insights be used from the **outside** (in our logic by a "coach") to develop an intelligence infrastructure? Weak signals must be positioned to cover the main leadership tasks of exploiting the present and exploring the future. **Exploiting** aims at developing and securing the infrastructure. Weak signals are an integral part of building up a structural coupling relationship with the autopoietic system. **Exploring** aims at innovative activities, and weak signals are an integral part of systematically developing options for triggering.
- How can these insights be used from the **inside** (by a "player") to co-evolve with its environment? The structural coupling aims at getting information about state-of-the-art infrastructure in the environment. Weak signals are placed to gain such knowledge at the earliest possible moment. The interpretation of triggers from the outside should become more diverse, to avoid tunnel vision.

Securing impact for input-output systems: Organizing subsidiarity

Functional redundancy is mandatory to increase organizational resilience by structural buffers. This enables the system to deal with internal and external perturbations. It is recommended to think in **cost of ownership** and to interpret buffers as investments in the capability of the system to deal with surprises. It will pay off when circumstances unfold, which everyone had judged as "it can't happen here." An elegant way to organize such structures can also be found in Viable System Model (VSM). As illustrated above, any operational unit is again a viable system, due to the recursive logic of the model. It implies that interventions from "above" are only allowed if the greater whole is in danger. This way of thinking is closely connected to the Theory of Constraints introduced above. As this theory states, there is always at least one bottleneck that determines the throughput of the total system. Therefore, structural buffers in the system are needed to overcome the constraint and ensure a functioning overarching flow of value towards the customers. In this context it is not important whether constraints appear in operational or managerial units, what counts are limitations of operational autonomy. In a bureaucratic world, corporate decision-making is separated from operational units. This leads to a congestion in the system because all decisions must be taken by the management, which in the end leads to a high information and decision latency in the organization. The company loses speed to deliver value in the best independent way. In the end, subsidiarity – and therefore the viability of the enterprise – is endangered if bottlenecks on operational and managerial levels are not properly handled.

As shown in Figure 5.7, the sequence of questions by Martin Pfiffner are useful to determine whether a function should be centralized or decentralized:

1	Can we afford to delegate this task to an operational unit, do we have the resources?	If yes, continue with the second question. If no, this task/function will be taken care of at the central level.
2	Has the task a relevant influence on customer decisions?	If yes, the task will be allocated to the operational unit, as it is critical for success – and we can afford it. If no, continue with the third question.
3	Can we achieve relevant synergies with this task?	If yes, the task will be allocated centrally. Although it would be possible to leave it up to the operational unit, integrative cooperation is more promising, without constraining operational autonomy. If no, it is of no importance where to locate it. The task is not critical for success, nor can any specific synergies be achieved. Due to the principle of subsidiarity, we allocate it to the operational unit.

Figure 5.7: Centralize or decentralize – relevant questions (Pfiffner 2020, 219).

The organization of subsidiarity is not only a matter of the input-output nature of a system, but it is also related to autopoietic matters, especially regarding questions about leadership and the conception of human beings. Give autonomy always a chance, even in turbulent times – withstand the desire to control the system via top-down logic, as long as the whole is not endangered.

Securing impact for autopoietic systems: Optimizing experimentation

Leading by Weak Signals is characterized by detecting external and internal change at the earliest possible moment to initiate proactive intervention. With the intelligence framework, the detection side is institutionalized. But how to ensure that proactive measures sustainably take effect? Faced with autopoietic systems, the only way to be successful is the optimization of experimentation, as shown in Figure 5.8.

As in "sensing the periphery," the focus of experimentation is directed on the boundary elements of innovation and infrastructure. The background knowledge about the functioning mode of autopoietic systems allows the enhancing of the experi-

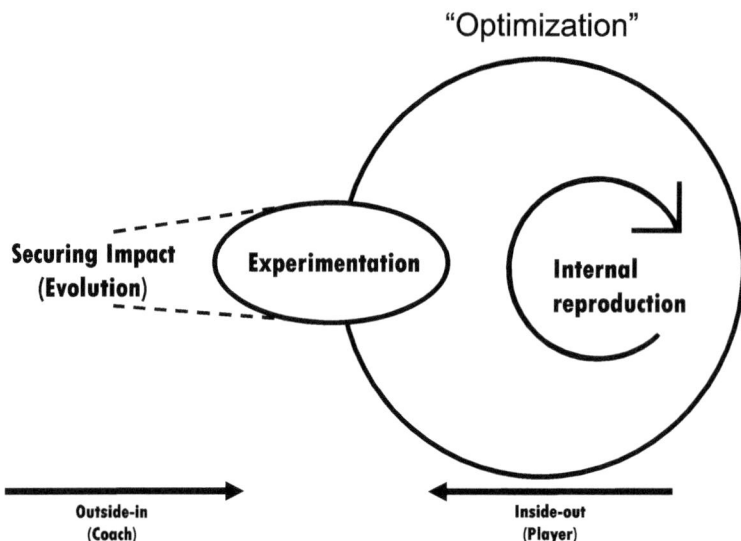

Figure 5.8: Experimentation is key to ensure impact at autopoietic systems.

mentation process: how can triggering and structural coupling be perfected in such a way that interventions can be steadily monitored, and their success be ensured? Here some general advice about the "art of experimentation" is due.

The validation of hypotheses in autopoietic contexts is quite difficult. Due to the subjectivity of this type of system, one can never be sure if a hypothesis can be accepted or rejected. Heuristics and applied critical thinking are the only option to put the pieces of a puzzle together. This practice requires mental skills and a social environment ready to continuously perturbate the system – without stressing it! The confidence level of perceived weak signals is always of relative value, it needs ongoing re-evaluation to either increase or decrease the quality of the signal. One starts with lightweight experiments to gain fast feedback about the quality of triggers and structural couplings. This monitoring costs energy, time, and money, so a validation budget is essential for success.

The internal reproduction of processed weak signals can be amplified by using open documentation formats, because they accelerate the socialization of results. This is an easy yet powerful way to make them accessible in the organization, which inherently fosters productive self-organization.

Managerial practice

Case study: "Mobile App development in the wholesale industry"

Due to the novelty of the framework and the methodology of this book, a perfect match of practical examples cannot (yet) be provided. Furthermore, it is inevitable to leave the context of **the wholesale case** because the app example is, according to the logic of Figure 5.1, only an ad hoc activity of corporate intelligence, a "lonely CI star." It is not an institutionalized entity which must be continuously scanned for weak signals. But it is possible to find "historical" examples which might inspire managerial practice in the process of discovering of weak signals. The global food player Unilever discovered, via text mining (automated indexing and analysis of documents), the strategy of a competitor a year in advance (Zanasi, 1998) – just imagine to what extent today's artificial technology can process data and extract meaning out of it.

Another example for institutionalizing the discovery of weak signals can be found at ZF Trading, which is the sales organization of the third largest automotive supplier in Germany. The trading organization traditionally focused on the home market and European neighbors, but it missed opportunities in the Americas or in Asia. This was not a problem in 2002 (Neubold 2006, 209ff), when competitors only acted locally. But globalization led to a situation where even smaller local players started to enter the global stage. The conclusion became clear: an integrated intelligence structure was needed to share relevant information – and to give the sales force deciding insights to stay one step ahead of the competition. Clearly, the ambition of this initiative was to create a network that connected the colleagues in all countries with the headquarter in Germany, and which enabled a smooth information flow between the countries.

In a first step, a project team was set up with full commitment of the top management. Furthermore, an autopoietic "trick" was necessary, as the term "Competitive Intelligence" of this endeavor would have provoked confusion in the organization: "Internationalization of Market Research" was introduced to get everyone onboard. Right from the start, a participative approach was chosen to get the buy of colleagues in all locations. It began with a survey to define the boundary logic of regional and local structures. By involving colleagues in overarching matters, the project team increased the acceptance in the organization – which was crucial to anchor such a new organizational function in an existing company. According to Neubold (2006, 212), the human factor was put in the center of attention, by providing high-level of freedom to the local people to define their local network. Local and global learnings were shared across regions and locations to find a proper balance. The ambition was to overcome an over-centralized reporting system and to bring the principle of subsidiarity into practice, as shown in Figure 5.9.

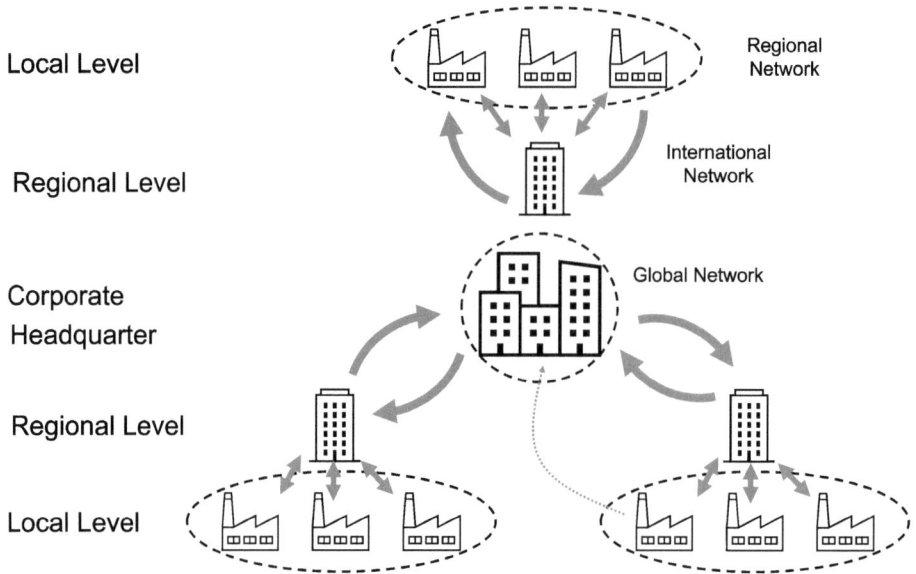

Figure 5.9: The CI network structure ZF Trading (adapted from Neubold, 2006, 213).

This structure looks similar to recursion levels in the Viable System Model – which supports the idea that this it reflects the best geographic slicing to ensure success for the sales function all over the globe. The operationalization of this network was strongly supported by technology, e.g., providing online platforms that supported the storage and exchange of relevant information.

One last piece of advice when anchoring Leading by Weak Signals: look out for those who want to contribute to build this function to get the critical mass throughout the enterprise. Be bold enough to start small, but keep on iterating to let it grow in an step by step fashion. Be aware that this function, by mainly supporting the value generating units, will always be a cost center. But keep also in mind, it is an investment in organizational viability – the main goal of Leading by Weak Signals.

Case study: "Living composition in the machinery industry"

The design of an intelligence framework for Bucher Industries starts with the reinterpretation of Figure 4.14. The basic structure of a viable system remains invariant, but the functions are relabeled in Figure 5.10 to gain deeper insight into autopoietic reproduction in managerial practice.

The role of each function in the process of **generating weak signals** and **monitoring impact** of interventions will now be outlined:

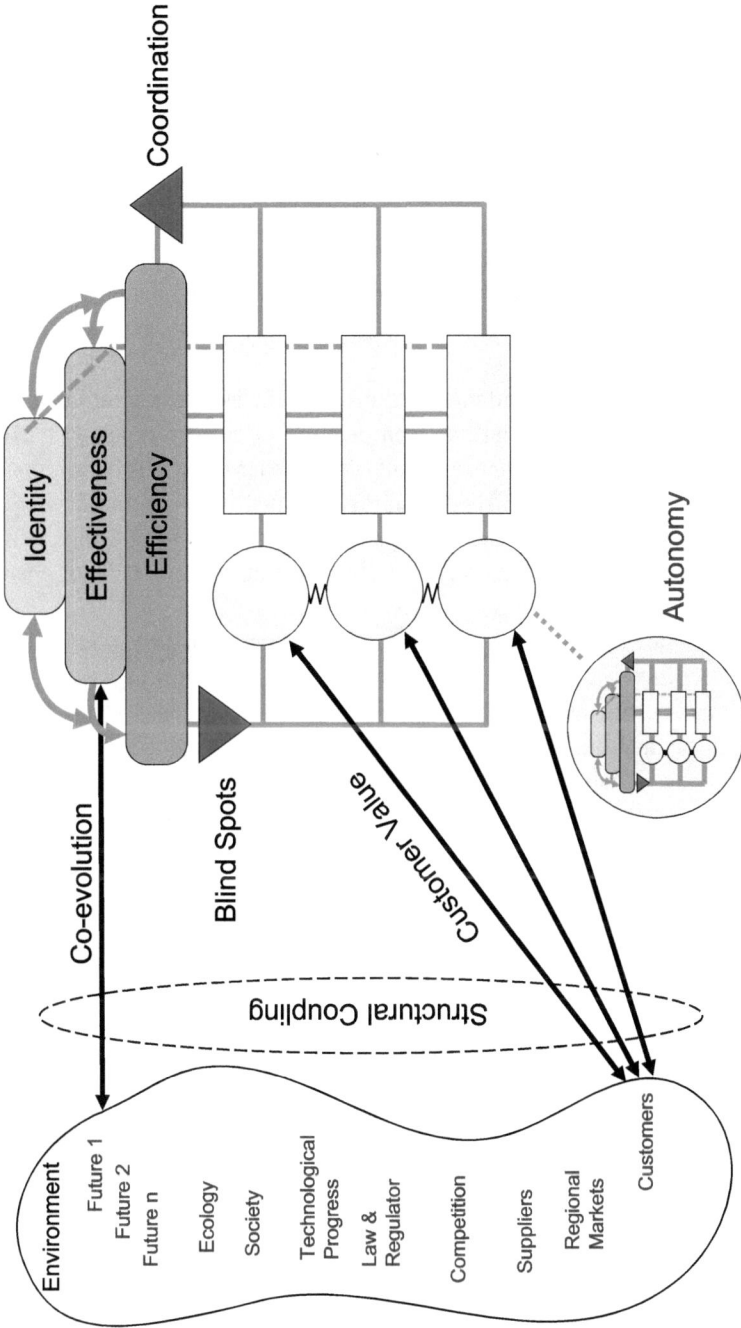

Figure 5.10: Bucher Industries as a viable system of autopoietic reproduction.

- **Identity:** weak signals for a (positive or negative) change of identity are positioned to observe the following issues: level of trust, supportive narratives, embodiment of purpose, mutual respect in decision-making, communication flow beyond hierarchies, diversity in management. Internal and external surveys on a regular basis serve to monitor impact.
- **Effectiveness**: weak signals must prevent being hit by unexpected external events, but also enable the detection of unique opportunities. They initiate activities based on the concepts of co-evolution, reacting to triggers, experimentation and structural coupling, as illustrated in Step 1 above. The impact is judged by high resilience and reaction speed, supported by flat hierarchies and by delegation of authority to lower levels.
- **Efficiency**: weak signals are positioned at critical instances of the internal standard processes: are critical deviations from leading indicators reported early enough for proactive intervention. Are the divisions on par with their operational task, by being close to the customers, by market-oriented research and development, and by creating customer value? Is the "machine room" of the Group well-balanced? The impact of intervention is assessed by the mid-term quality of operational results.
- **Coordination**: weak signals monitor the mutual adjustment of divisional activities. They detect flaws in the knowledge flow between divisions, as well as between divisions and higher order leadership functions. Impact is reached when the whole is more than the sum of its parts.
- **Blind spots**: weak signals are positioned to detect critical incidents, major accidents or even catastrophes which escape the attention of the responsible managers in the operational domain – because of bad luck, carelessness, or even by intentional manipulation
- **Autonomy:** As shown in Figure 5.10, the divisional units are highly autonomous. They are viable systems themselves and depict (recursively) the same organization as the whole Group. This means that all of the above functions are present in the microcosmos. The divisions must again determine weak signals for their specific context and establish specific measures to monitor the impact of interventions.

Epilogue

At the beginning of our adventurous journey to explore the concept of weak signals and to provide leaders with a framework to master the emerging shift to small data, we illustrated the main pillars of our approach by famous quotes. With the eighth step, our methodology has been completed – it is now time to look back and to validate these insights.

The first quote by Peter Drucker (1980, 2) illuminates the process of mastering complexity: "Turbulence, by definition, is irregular, non-linear, erratic. But its underlying causes can be analyzed, predicted, managed."

There is no doubt that turbulence, resulting from complexity, exhibits these properties, but are its underlying causes really accessible? While developing our methodology, this assumption has been increasingly confirmed. Starting with the discovery of patterns behind weak signals, the evolutionary path of a system can be followed by "riding the power law curve." This enables prediction, not in a mechanistic way, but as an educated guess or heuristic: a curve is selected and tested to serve managerial intervention. If it does not fit, the curve is dropped, and a new one comes into play. Finally, using the self-organizing forces of the system enables leaders to cope with the inherent complexity.

The second quote by John Kay and Mervyn King (2020, 670) illustrates the distinction between risk and uncertainty: "To identify a probability of inventing the wheel is to invent the wheel. To ask, either before or after the event, 'What is the probability of such an event?' is not an intelligible question."

As illustrated above, the authors of the quote suggest the terms "puzzle" for risk and "mystery" for uncertainty. Puzzles have well-defined rules and a single solution, mysteries offer no clear definition and have no "correct" answer; they ought to be approached by asking "What is going on here?" As probabilities cannot meaningfully be attached to alternative futures, our methodology introduces power law curves as the basis for developing scenarios, again focusing on Small Data. They fit better with uncertainty, by forcing executives to reflect on the full picture. Big Data is mainly about correlation, not causation – a potential source of erroneous decisions. Finally, the use of self-organizational forces to intervene in complex systems is superior to the approach of "nudging." The latter bases on the unjustified claim to know an uncertain world.

The third quote by Stafford Beer (1972, 69) deals with exploration and exploitation: "Instead of trying to organize a system in full detail, you organize it only somewhat; you then ride on the dynamics of the system in the direction you want to go."

Our methodology perfectly matches this quote. Instead of developing detailed models of the present situation, it starts the exploration phase with a "small-world model": What is going on behind the weak signal? Can a pattern be identified? Which power law could be the origin of this pattern? Can pattern dynamics be characterized

https://doi.org/10.1515/9783110797886-006

by a curve? The result of this process is a first insight into a potential evolutionary path of the system – without singular features, objectives, or metrics. The exploitation phase starts with "riding the curve" (to use Beer's term). Leading indicators are specified to identify deviations from the curve, narratives are developed to motivate the workforce, goals are activated to judge success or failure. Finally, proactive measures of intervention to correct or reinforce the chosen course are specified. This detailed model depends largely on the right choice of a curve, otherwise a new one must be selected, and the process starts anew.

The fourth quote by Herbert A. Simon (1971, 40) illustrates the law of requisite variety: "A wealth of information creates poverty of attention."

To master the complexity of a system (measured by its variety), equivalent variety must be provided by leadership. To achieve a balance, systemic variety must be attenuated on the leader's perceiving side, and it must be amplified on his or her reacting side. In managerial practice, the two sides are often mixed up, with leaders preferring to amplify variety on the perceiving side by demanding evermore data to increase the quality of their decisions. But this wealth of information leads to disorientation and poverty of attention for crucial issues. On the reacting side, the development of proactive measures to intervene properly is neglected. To avoid this poverty of attention, the perceiving side should focus on pattern recognition, as proposed by our methodology in the form of detecting power laws acting "behind the scenes." It is crucial to carefully select the data points and the "objects" marked for continuous scanning. On the reacting side, a "inventory" of proactive measures must be developed to intervene early enough. This is achieved by a circular process, as shown in Figure 1.2.

The fifth quote by Gregory Bateson (1979, 101) differentiates autopoietic systems from input-output systems: "When I kick a stone, I give energy to the stone, and it moves with that energy; when I kick a dog, . . . it responds with energy got from metabolism."

The distinction between autopoietic systems and input-output systems is the most important feature to understand the basic logic of our methodology. In every step, it plays an essential role, shaping the process of discovery and the selection of methods and tools. In complex settings, autopoietic systems are predominant. They are closed to the outside with respect to the continuous reproduction of their identity, beliefs, decisions, knowledge, and communication. The governance and the strategic organization of companies, political parties, churches, or NGOs are typical for such systems. Their closure demands a special kind of leadership, be it by participation or by structural coupling. In complicated settings, input-output systems are the normal case. They can be designed, as the elements and their relationships are known and relatively stable over time. The introduction of this basic distinction in the development of our methodology was an experiment, but it has paid off. In each step, the differentiation makes sense and improves the understanding for important challenges of managerial practice.

The sixth quote by Stephen Elop (2011) distinguishes participants from observers of a system: "We are standing on a 'burning platform', and we must decide how we are going to change our behaviour."

This statement illustrates that the internal reproduction of a company's identity can differ fundamentally from the perception of the outside world. Why did Nokia fail although it had the best strategic management and the best products of their industry? The key to the decline probably lies in their underestimating basic rules of autopoiesis. They didn't do anything wrong but missed the technological progress and the rise of new competitors. They fell into a state of pathological autopoiesis by focusing mainly on their identity, their beliefs, and their superior organization. They cut their interaction with the technological ecosystem and finally lost their customers. But who knows, we are only observers of an autopoietic system!

References

Altensen, A., C. Glasbrenner, and D. Pfaff. *Kick-Off-Study Competitive Intelligence*. Fachhochschule Giessen-Friedberg, 2003.

Anderson, D.J. *Kanban - Successful Evolutionary Change for Your Technology Business*. Blue Hole Press, 2010.

Ansoff, H. I. "Managing strategic surprise by response to weak signals." *California management review* 18, no. 2 (1975): 21–33.

Ansoff, H. I. *Implanting Strategic Management*. Prentice/Hall International, 1984.

Ashby, R. *An Introduction to Cybernetics*. Chapman & Hall, 1956.

Baghai, M., S. Coley, and D. White. *Alchemy of Growth: Practical Insights for Building the Enduring Enterprise*. Basic Books (Illustrated edition), 2000.

Bateson, G. *Mind and Nature*. Dutton, 1979.

Bazermann, M., and M. Watkins. *Predictable Surprises*. Harvard Business Press, 2004.

Beckerman, G. *The Quiet Before: On the Unexpected Origins of Radical Ideas*. Crown, 2022.

Beer, S. *Decision and Control*. Wiley, 1966.

Beer, S. *Brain of the Firm*. Allen Lane Penguin, 1972.

Beer, S. *Designing Freedom*. CBC Publications, 1974.

Beer, S. *Diagnosing the System for Organizations*. Wiley, 1985.

Boyd, J. *Essence of winning and losing*. 1995. Accessed January 23, 2023. https://ooda.de/media/john_boyd_-_the_essence_of_winning_and_losing.pdf.

Bradley, C., M. Hirt, and S. Smit. *Strategy Beyond the Hockey Stick*. Wiley, 2018.

Cameron, W. B. *Informal Sociology, a casual introduction to sociological thinking*. Random House, 1963.

Chaisson, E. *World Futures*. Gordon and Breach Science Publishers, 1996.

Checkland, P., and S. Howell. *Introducing information management: The business approach*. Elsevier, 2006.

Choo C. W. *The Knowing Organization – How Organizations Use Information to Construct Meaning, Create Knowledge, and Make Decisions*. Oxford University Press, 2006.

Christensen C. *Innovators Dilemma*. Harvard Business School Press, 1997.

Cleveland, J., et al. *Welcome to the Edge of Chaos 2.0*, Island Press, 2020.

Cobham, A. "Priority Assignment in Waiting Line Problems." *Journal of the Operations Research Society of America* 2, no. 1 (1954): 70–76.

Coffman, B. *Weak Signal Research, Part III, Sampling, Uncertainty, and Phase Shift in Weak Signal Evolution*. 1997. Accessed January 28, 2023. https://legacy.mgtaylor.com/mgtaylor/jotm/winter97/wsrmatur.htm.

Conan Doyle, A. *The Hounds of Baskerville*. Grapevine, 2019.

Day, G., and P. Shoemaker. *Peripheral Vision*. Harvard Business Press, 2006.

Day, G., and P. Shoemaker. *See Sooner, Act Faster*. MIT Press, 2019.

Dellana, L. *Ergodicity*. 2020. http://Luca-dellana.com.

Denning, S. *The Age of Agile – How Smart Companies Are Transforming the Way Work Gets Done*. AMACOM, 2018.

Doerr, J. *Measure What Matters: The Simple Idea that Drives 10x Growth*. Portfolio Penguin, 2018.

Drucker, P. *The Practice of Management*. Harper & Row, 1954.

Drucker, P. *Managing in Turbulent Times*. Harper and Row, 1980.

Elop, S. *Memo to Nokia employees*. February 11, 2011.

Fenn, J., and M. Raskino. *Mastering the Hype Cycle*. Harvard Business Review Press, 2008.

Fladerer, J., and E. Kurzmann. *The Wisdom of the Many*. Books on Demand, 2019.

Gapminder.org. July 10, 22. Accessed January 28, 2023. https://www.gapminder.org/factfulness-book/mistakes/.

Gladwell, M. *Tipping Point*. Little Brown, 2000.

Goldratt, E. *What is this thing called Theory of Constraints and how show it be implemented?* North River Press, 1990.

https://doi.org/10.1515/9783110797886-007

Gould, J. *Punctuated Equilibrium*. Harvard University Press, 2007.

Gomez, P., and G. Probst. "Organizational closure in management: a complementary view to contingency approaches." *Cybernetics and Systems* 20, no. 4 (1989): 311–320.

Gomez, P., M. Lambertz, and T. Meynhardt. *Verantwortungsvoll führen in einer komplexen Welt*. Haupt, 2019.

Google. *Ngram Viewer*. n.d. Accessed January 24, 2023. https://books.google.com/ngrams/graph?content= alignment&year_start=1800&year_end=2019&corpus=de-2019&smoothing=3.

Grove, A. *Only the Paranoid Survive*. Profile Books, 1995.

Haken, H. *Synergetics*. Springer, 1983.

Hamel, G., and M. Zanini. *Humanocracy*. Harvard Business Review Press, 2020.

Helms, M., and J. Nixon. "Exploring SWOT analysis–where are we now? A review of academic research from the last decade." *Journal of strategy and management* 3, no. 3 (2010): 215.

Johnson, N. *Simply Complexity*. Oneworld Publications, 2011.

Jurney, R. *Agile Data Science – Building data analytics applications with Hadoop*. O'Reilly, 2017.

Karnow, St. *A Verdict on Vietnam*. Washington Post, October 28, 1984.

Kay, J., and M. King. *Radical Uncertainty*. The Bridge Street Press, 2020.

Keck, D. "A future of light." *IEEE Journal of Selected Topics in Quantum Electronics* 6, no. 6 (2000): 1254–1258.

Koch, R. *Beyond the 80/20 Principle*. Nicholas Brealey Publishers, 2020.

Kucharski, A. *The Rules of Contagion: Why Things Spread – and Why They Stop*. Wellcome Collection, 2020.

Kondratieff, N. D., and W. F. Stolper. *The Review of Economics and Statistics* 17, no. 6 (1935): 105–115.

Koomey J., S. Berard, M. Sanchez, and H. Wong. "Implications of Historical Trends in the Electrical Efficiency of Computing." *IEEE Annals of the History of Computing* 33, no. 3 (2011): 46–54.

Koskinen, K. *Knowledge Production in Organizations*. Springer, 2013.

Lawrence, P., and J. Lorsch. *Developing Organizations: Diagnosis and Action*. Addison-Wesley, 1969.

Maturana, H., and F. Varela. *De Maquinas y Seres Vivos*. Editorial Universitaria, 1972.

Maula, M. *Organizations as learning systems: 'Living composition' as an enabling infrastructure*. Emerald Group Publishing, 2006.

McGrath, R. *Seeing Around Corners*. Mariner Books, 2019.

Metcalfe, R. *There Oughta Be a Law*. The New York Times, July 15, 1996.

Meynhardt, T. "Public Value Inside." *International Journal of Public Administration* 32, no. 3–4 (2009): 192.

Michaeli, R. *Competitive Intelligence, Strategische Wettbewerbsvorteile erzielen durch systematische Konkurrenz-, Markt- und Technologieanalysen*. Springer, 2006.

Moore, G. "Crossing the Chasm." *Harper Business Essentials* 10 (1991).

Moore, G. Cramming more components onto integrated circuits, *Electronics* 38, no. 8 (1965).

Müller, W. *Management 4.0 – Handbook for Agile Practices*. BoD, 2016.

Nassehi, A. *Unbehagen*. C.H. Beck, 2021.

Neubold, K., Creation of a worldwide CI network in *Competitive Intelligence, Strategische Wettbewerbsvorteile erzielen durch systematische Konkurrenz-, Markt- und Technologieanalysen*, by R. Michaeli. Springer, 2006.

Ostrum, E. *Governing the Commons – The evolution of institutions for collective action*. Cambridge University Press, 1990.

Pearl, J., and D. Mackenzie. *The Book of Why: The New Science of Cause and Effect*. Basic Books, 2016.

Perrow, C. *Normal Accidents*. Basic Books, 1985.

Pfiffner, M. *Die dritte Dimension des Organisierens*. Springer, 2020.

Ramirez, R., and A. Wilkinson. *Strategic Reframing*. Oxford University Press, 2018.

Reichelt, Frederick F. "One Number You Need to Grow." *Harvard Business Review* 81, no. 12 (2003): 46–54.

Rodrigue, J.-R. *The Geography of Transport Systems*. Routledge, 2006.

Rother, M., and J. Shook. *Learning to see*. Lean Enterprise Institute, 2003.

Rumsfeld, D. *Press Conference by US Secretary of Defence*. 2002. Accessed April 23, 2020. https://www.nato.int/docu/speech/2002/s020606g.htm.

Scheffer, M. "Early-warning signals for critical transitions." *Nature* 461, no. 3 (2009).

Schwaninger, M. "Cybersystemic Education: Enabling Society for a Better Future." *Kybernetes* 48, no. 7 (2019): 1376–1397.

Shannon, C. E. "A Mathematical Theory of Communication (PDF)." *Bell System Technical Journal* 27, no. 3 (1948): 379–423.

Shiller, R. J. *Narrative Economics*. Princeton University Press, 2020.

Simon, H. "Designing Organizations for an Information-Rich World." In *Computers, Communications, and the Public Interest*, edited by M. Greenberger. Johns Hopkins Press, 1971.

Smith, S. *How to Future*. Kogan Page, 2020.

Stevens, W. P., G. J. Myers, and L. L. Constantine. "Structured Design." *IBM Systems Journal*, no. 2 (1974): 115–139.

Tetlock, P., and D. Gardner. *Superforecasting: The Art and Science of Prediction*. Crown, 2015.

Thaler, R., and C. Sunstein. *Nudge*. Penguin, 2012.

Tradoc G2. *Applied critical thinking handbook (Formerly the red team handbook)*. University of Foreign and Military and Cultural Studies, 2015.

Vargo, S., and R. Lusch. *Service Dominant Logic – Premises, Perspectives, Possibilities*. Cambridge University Press, 2014.

Varney, S. *Leadership in Complexity and Change*. Walter de Gruyter, 2021.

Varela, F. "Two Principles of Self-Organization." In *Self-Organization and Management of Social Systems*, edited by H. Ulrich and G. Probst. Springer, 1984.

Velitchkov, I. *Essential Balances*. WorthEditing, 2020.

Von Krogh, G., and J. Roos. *Organizational epistemology*. St. Martin's Press, 1995.

Wardley, S. *Wardley Maps*. 2020. Accessed January 28, 2023. https://learnwardleymapping.com/book/.

Wardleypedia. *Weak Signal Analysis*. n.d. Accessed July 22, 2022. https://wardleypedia.org/mediawiki/index.php/Weak_signal_analysis.

Watson, T. *A Business and its Beliefs*. McGraw-Hill, 1963.

Webb, A. *The Signals Are Talking*. Public Affairs, 2016.

Weick, K., and K. Sutcliffe. *Managing the Unexpected*. Wiley, 2015.

Weinberg, G. *An Introduction to General Systems Thinking*. John Wiley, 1975.

West, G. *Scale*. Weidenfeld & Nicolson, 2017.

Wright T.P. "Factors Affecting the Cost of Airplanes." *Journal of the Aeronautical Sciences* 3, no. 4 (1936): 122.

Yeung, A., and D. Ulrich. *Reinventing the Organization*. Harvard Business Review Press, 2019.

Zanasi, A. "Competitive intelligence through data mining public sources." *Competitive Analysis Review* 9, no. 1 (1998): 44–54.

Zipf, G. K. *Human behavior and the principle of least effort*. Addison-Wesley, 1949.

List of figures

https://doi.org/10.1515/9783110797886-008

About the authors

Peter Gomez is Professor Emeritus for Strategy and Organization at the University of St. Gallen, Switzerland. He was the Rector of his University and President of the Swiss Stock Exchange SIX. He has published widely on Leadership in a Complex World, Systems Thinking in Corporate Practice, and Managing for Public Value.

Mark Lambertz is a Digital Native of the first hour since he learned to program with his first Apple computer at the age of 12. In 1995, he founded one of the first digital agencies in Germany and sold it after 20 years. Today he applies his technological and organizational knowledge in an international company as a transformation manager in the mobility sector headquarters of Robert Bosch GmbH. His focus lies on the Viable System Model, which enables a holistic view of organizations' culture, processes, roles, and value creation.

https://doi.org/10.1515/9783110797886-009

About the series editor

Bernd Vogel is a Professor in Leadership and Founding Director of the Henley Centre for Leadership at Henley Business School, UK.

Bernd has more than 20 years of global experience in research, educating, speaking, and consulting with outstanding companies, business schools and universities. He supports organisations and people in life-long learning journeys that transform lives, organisations, and society. He bridges academia with practice and is an executive coach.

His expertise is in leadership and leadership development; future of work and leadership; strategic leadership to mobilise and sustain healthy energy and performance; developing leadership and followership capability; healthy and performing senior management teams; change, transformation and culture; leadership development architectures.

Bernd features regularly in media. He publishes in top-tier global academic journals and has written and edited several books, case studies and industry reports.

Throughout his career Bernd has had academic roles at the Leibniz University Hannover, Germany, and University of St. Gallen, Switzerland. He has held global visiting positions at Claremont Graduate University, USA; IESE Business School, Spain; and Marshall School of Business, USC, USA.

https://doi.org/10.1515/9783110797886-010

Index

https://doi.org/10.1515/9783110797886-011